# Write What You Don't Know

# WRITE WHAT YOU DON'T KNOW

## An Accessible Manual for Screenwriters

**Julian Hoxter**

continuum

Published by the Continuum International Publishing Group
80 Maiden Lane, Suite 704, New York, NY 10038
The Tower Building, 11 York Road, London SE1 7NX

www.continuumbooks.com

Library of Congress Cataloging-in-Publication Data
Hoxter, Julian.
    Write what you don't know : an accessible manual for screenwriters / by Julian
    Hoxter. p. cm.
    ISBN-13: 978-1-4411-0210-2 (pbk. : alk. paper)
    ISBN-10: 1-4411-0210-8 (pbk. : alk. paper) 1. Motion picture authorship. I. Title.
    PN1996.H735 2011
    808.2'3--dc22
                            2011003732
ISBN: 978-1-4411-0210-2 (Paperback)

Typeset by Fakenham Prepress Solutions, Fakenham, Norfolk NR21 8NN
Printed and bound in the United States of America

All excerpts from 'Knocked Up' are courtesy of Universal Studios Licensing LLLP

# Contents

# Acknowledgments

There's a long list, and it starts with my parents Hans and Shirley, who supported me in everything, even though they didn't always understand exactly what they were supporting!

I want to give special mention to a few people who have directly or indirectly helped, influenced and generally supported me in developing my ideas and in writing this book. Let's start with my students of the last 16 years, many now friends and some even collaborators. I'm first and foremost a teacher and this book has been written to help students like them. It couldn't have been written without the inspiration I have always taken from their energy, enthusiasm, creativity and critical engagement. It couldn't have been written without them teaching me that sometimes, as a teacher, you have to start from unexpected places to make the journey easier. The idiosyncratic style and structure of this book is testament to that.

The best friends are the ones who challenge you and make you defend your opinions. I have been most fortunate in sharing a love of films with a bunch of writers and artists who never let me get away with easy answers, always call me on my sloppiest thinking and don't complain when I call them on theirs. Of these, Roy Brown, Jo Bushnell, Franc Donohoe, Billy Smith and Martin Stollery have been the staunchest supporters and guides.

I am grateful to the many colleagues in England who helped me develop as a teacher. Amongst them I want to single out my old friend Tony Moon, a terrific educator whose influence I can feel throughout the pages to come. Our many years working together, team teaching, hearing student pitches and doing story development 'on the fly' have been the most valuable preparation I could imagine for trying to write about the way ideas develop and how to guide students along a constructive path.

In California I have been lucky to have had the help and support of another group of talented and generous friends and colleagues. Amongst them my particular thanks go out to my old UCLA buddy Scott Sublett, Screenwriting Professor at San Jose State University who encouraged me to come to San Francisco and who I promise to visit more when I finally get around to buying a car. I am grateful to Steve Ujlaki, former Chair of the Cinema Department, whose kindness and support made the transition to teaching in the American university system relatively painless; to Aaron Kerner for his friendship and unfailing help and advice (often in Fly Bar on Divis.); to Pat Jackson, an inspirational teaching partner and the best corrective to long meetings you could find. Thanks also to Steve Kovacs for his support and encouragement—and not least for a place to crash after my arrival in California. To Scott Boswell, Alanna Young and Katherine Kwid for many things, including putting up with my stupid noobish questions and for not mentioning that, even though I am no longer a noob, the stupid noobish questions keep coming. Finally to Joe McBride, friend, colleague and mentor, I cannot adequately express my gratitude to you and your family for all your kindness, patience, advice and support.

Thanks also to Alex Fu, Amanda Avanzino and Mike Sparks, friends and talented ex-students who collaborated with me on a competition winning short and a TV pilot script this past year. They gave great input and encouragement as I was writing the book. A talented writer, Alex has taken over the duties of calling me on my dumbassness this side of the pond—even though, in turn, he needs to get over his rather unhealthy Christopher Nolan obsession.

Mike did the excellent frame grabs for Chapter 3, and Amanda was the first willing victim who offered to read through the whole draft as it emerged and gave it her most valuable critique. She also did a great job putting the diagrams into shape for the book. That's what you get for adopting the new guy.

Last, but by no means least, many thanks to my editors at Continuum Books in New York. I am grateful to David Barker who somehow found my little blog and saw in it and in my course syllabi the potential for this book. It just goes to prove that if you get stuff out there good things can happen. Very many thanks also to Katie Gallof for her patience and sterling support throughout the publishing process.

# Introduction

## Oh Joy, Another Screenwriting Book

This is a book about screenwriting.
There are many like it, but this one is mine ...

### 'Kneel before Book!'

I'm guessing you want to know up front whether my book is worth reading. To be honest, I was hoping I'd have you at 'Kneel before Book!' Well, perhaps that was too much to expect given that I'm not actually Terence Stamp.

As I write these words we are already a long way into the story. It is November of 2010 and I have finished my draft. You discover me in the middle of proof reading and general fiddling. In revisiting this introduction, I'm trying to point it more directly at explaining my intentions for the book. That should help you make up your mind. I'm junking some bits and re-writing other bits and moving yet others around and I think I see the light at the end of the tunnel. It's an enjoyable process that will end arbitrarily when I run up against my submission deadline in a few weeks time.

Oh—there's a first point in my favor, I can write to a deadline. That's a very important skill for a screenwriter and not to be dismissed. Nevertheless, it doesn't really answer your perfectly reasonable question. Maybe we should flash back to the beginning. It's an overused cinematic cliché, but that's because it often works. Are you sitting comfortably? Then I'll begin ...

DISSOLVE TO:

The idea for this book came after I moved to San Francisco in 2008. I was honored to be hired as the first screenwriting faculty in the famously alternative and independent minded Cinema Department at San Francisco State University. Before coming to SF State I taught

1

screenwriting and production in England for almost fifteen years. It felt like the right time for a change and I was excited to have the chance to develop my ideas with new colleagues and students in a new department. You probably don't care about this part very much, but a little backstory brings us all up to speed fast—besides it was kind of a big deal for me and it led directly to writing the book.

Soon after arriving I decided it would be a good idea to have a place to put my class materials online. I also relished the chance to indulge my inner critic with the occasional rant about movies. You'll come across evidence of both those impulses as you read on. There will be sober-minded helpfulness and lighthearted rantiness, all bound up in kind of an unusual style, for reasons I'll explain in a moment or two.

Not being a computer techie kind of guy I went out and bought Apple's MobileMe because it looked like an idiot-proof way of making a website. Yes, my computer skills suck that badly. My first question was: What should I call my blog? Names and titles are really important and I wanted to find something that would sum up my approach to teaching screenwriting for my students and anyone else who happened upon it. Sadly I never thought of calling it: 'Kneel before Blog!' Rather, as often happens in moments like this, the first thing that came to mind was a terrible platitude. Well, I thought, I'm certainly *not* calling it 'Write What You Know'. That's the very worst title imaginable. In fact it's the exact opposite of what I believe—oh wait a minute …

And so the 'Write What You Don't Know' blog was born. We'll talk about what I mean by my title at some length later on. Let's start by saying it's about breaking out of our comfort zones as writers and using our creativity to the fullest. Anyway, I went ahead and posted some initial lightheartedly ranty stuff as well as my first syllabi. Very soon afterwards I was approached by Continuum Books, who liked the style and the concept of 'Write What You Don't Know'. They asked me if I could turn it into a screenwriting book. Thus my baby blog was doomed to being little more than an online class notice board as I channeled my energies into writing this book.

Now I had always planned to pitch a screenwriting book once I got my feet under the table at SF State. Continuum's offer just moved the whole process forward and helped to clarify my thinking. Happily, the source material I was adapting already had its target audience and an opinionated and (I flattered myself) dryly humorous tone. That encouraged me to focus this book on the specific experience of the student just starting out. It also gave me license to write in a much more personal style than is the norm for books like these.

Being a writer myself and having taught screenwriting for so many years, I had a clear sense of what young aspiring writers should know about their craft. That's all very well in the abstract but, much more importantly, I had a wealth of evidence about how they *actually* approach the challenges of writing and where they often go wrong. This book tries to put those insights to good use. We are going to work our way around to talking about all the obvious stuff. However, we'll do so in an unusual order, born from working with students.

Let's be honest, in some ways this book is similar to all the other screenwriting manuals you'll find out there in bookland. Of course we are going to talk about characters and scenes and structure and plot and dialogue and format and all the other important stuff you need to know about as you start developing your first scripts. On the other hand, this book is also about ideas and creativity and how to kick your synapses into action as much as it is about how to format a slug line.

I also want to have a bit of fun as we go.

I'm a teacher who writes rather than a writer who teaches. I started teaching at a university right after leaving film school and fell in love with it immediately. Happily I have also been able to pursue a wide range of creative projects along the way. I have written and been brought in to re-write feature films. Some of them have been optioned, developed and even made. I have produced and directed documentaries on subjects as diverse as democratic education, the treatment of heroin addicted criminals and the people who make life-sized Daleks in their garden sheds. I also collaborate with an artist friend of mine on installations and gallery shows. It seems to be common in books of this kind to puff yourself a little to prove you know what you are talking about, so, yes, I have won awards both as an educator and as a filmmaker—yay me! I am also British, so I think that's quite enough self-promotion.

Here's another thing I want to make clear up front—and this is really important. I am not trying to sell you snake oil. This book isn't the One True God of screenwriting, and I don't pretend it is. I believe it can be helpful and I offer it as a friendly companion, not an all-powerful overlord. In other words, I'm not really asking you to 'Kneel before Book!' I have also read more than enough screenwriting books to know where I want to place my own on a scale from One to Watching Paint Dry. That means there will be jokes and some of them might not suck.

Fortunately for all of us, writing feature films can be a relatively simple game. It has well-established rules and systems of precedent. These have been developed over many years and are designed to make your life as a writer easier. This is great because every other aspect of your life as a writer is likely to be fraught and complicated. It will not always feel easy as you write, but that's the trouble with good games: the rules are how you learn to play, not how you go on to excel. You also need experience of various kinds, creative inspiration—oh, and that pesky little thing called talent.

Sadly, I can't give you talent, but I can help you to get the most from the talent you have.

To this end we will focus on your creativity and think about how to marshal it to the task of writing. We will go on to work through many of the key challenges you will face as a screenwriter. This will paint a picture of how films work and how the screenwriter fits into the process of their creation and production. Certainly this is a book about what you do when faced with a blank sheet of paper or computer screen, but it is also about how your work fits in with that of the many other professionals who are collectively responsible for the creation of a feature film and who look to your screenplay for information and guidance in so many ways.

I left something out of that little discussion, by the way, because I wanted to give it special attention. For a screenwriter it's more important in the end than experience, inspiration and talent combined. In order to succeed you need to dig down deep inside yourself and find a reservoir of determination and persistence. Of course you need talent, but that won't get you very far without the ability to finish your scripts. You need to be able to keep plowing ahead no matter what, and that is non-negotiable. Everything else depends on it.

Right, now we can get started.

## Breaking the ice

I'm going to begin by making a few assumptions about you, my implied reader. Fortunately, a high school football coach in a bad teen movie is not currently yelling at me, so, when I assume, it makes an ASS neither of U, nor of ME.

We have to start somewhere and, like in any new relationship, assumptions, needs and first impressions are mostly what we have to go on.

*I assume* that you are interested in the process of screenwriting. I also assume that you want to write. You may be new to it all and looking for help starting out, or you may have written for many years and be searching for a way to tone up your writerly muscles. This book is intended to be helpful in either case, but it is geared *much* more to the beginner than to the expert.

This book is about developing your knowledge and skill as a writer, not about telling you how to get an agent. There are many books on the market promising to tell you that, and their answer is usually a variation on the theme of: write something great, get a potential sale and (guess what) agents will appear! Agents are mostly all about negotiating deals, not finding you work. You don't need to worry about all of that now. If your writing sucks, no agent will look at you. Job one is avoiding the suck. I *assume* that you bring to this book your deep and abiding love of film. This is important, because if you don't love your medium why spend your time and emotional energy on something about which you don't really care? This may seem obvious, but you would be amazed how many students end up in a writing class only because it seemed marginally less boring than The Techniques and Aesthetics of Slip Glazing in Contemporary Latvian Pottery.

Of course some of them go on to fall head over heels and find, to their surprise, that maybe they want to be writers.

I often think of screenwriting as the hardest easy thing you will ever try to do. We'll come back to this in a chapter called, conveniently, *Screenwriting, the hardest easy thing you will ever do*. It will certainly take up a big chunk of your life, if you do it properly. The humorist Leo Rosten reminds us that 'the only reason for being a professional writer is that you just can't help it,' so if love isn't somewhere in the mix it's probably not what you should be doing.

*I assume* that you come to this book with a whole range of questions. Some may be pretty elementary, such as: What does a screenplay look like and why does it look like that? Some may be more informed, such as: What is the difference between a scene breakdown and a beat sheet? Some may be pretty much universal, such as: Why does my 'second act' always turn around and beat me with sticks? (Trust me, those of you who haven't written a screenplay yet, this is pretty universal. Just ask those of you who have.) Some may be more advanced and deal with the intricacies of character development, scene structure, story world creation or dialogue.

Finally—and this is a big one, because if I am wrong I have just spent a long time writing this book to no purpose—*I assume* that you would like to read a screenwriting book that tries to be friendly and accessible. We will go on to deal with lots of important issues and to give you a wide range of helpful examples, suggestions and advice. There will be serious content here, but it will be couched in a chatty version of my writerly personality.

If you are, indeed, my implied reader, then I have already made a good first impression with the tone and intent of these pages. There are lots more pages, and some of them have really good stuff in them. Keep reading, because I think we are going to have fun.

If you don't like my tone and intent, then I'm surprised you have made it this far. It seems that you are not my implied reader and that this is not the book for you. I hope we can part ways amicably, after our brief dalliance, wishing each other well on our separate journeys. If you have already spent your money on buying this book I suppose the life lesson would be to try before you buy. That's why bookstores have coffee shops. Perhaps you have a friend who always wanted to try their hand at writing. Pass the book on; you never know where it might take them. If not, you may be able to return it—or there is always Goodwill or eBay.

On the subject of wasting your money, you may very well be asking yourself whether reading a book on screenwriting is worth anything anyway. What if I just launch into writing something and learn on the fly? My answer is: Go for it. The best way to learn anything is to do it. At the very least, you should certainly be preparing to write while you read this book. Indeed there is a whole bunch of other things you should be doing as part of your preparation and support for a career as a screen-writer, and all of them are more important than reading books like this.

Let's take a look at some of them.

## Top ten tasks that are more important than reading this book

### 1. Read actual screenplays

The fastest way to understand how screenwriters write is to read scripts. Don't just watch a bunch of movies, read their screenplays. You will pick up on format and style and you will often notice subtle character or structural choices much more readily than when you are watching the movie and being distracted by explosions exploding and by hot movie stars being hot and starry.

A couple of things to remember: there is a difference between a screenplay published as a book and a working script draft, including mechanical things like page length and the fact that it has almost certainly been cleaned up to represent the finished film rather than the draft(s) used for the shoot itself. A very good series is Newmarket Shooting Scripts. They often include interviews with the writer and indicate any editorial changes to the format or content.

Be wary of reading screenplays you find on the internet. There are some useful sites but many of the 'scripts' you find will be fan transcriptions from the film itself which absolutely are not the same as screenplays. Don't be fooled, and don't use these as your learning examples.

## 2. Read screenplays that are out of your genre comfort zone

We all have favorite genres or styles of filmmaking. Whether you are into romantic comedies, horror movies, action films or improvised micro-budget mumblecore indie features, you will learn more about the craft of screenwriting if you read more widely. Whatever your personal preferences and creative goals, it is inevitable that many of the best scripts were not written with you in mind as a core fan. Remember, being a screenwriter is about telling great stories, so search out the story, not just the genre. I make a point of reading good romantic comedy screenplays, for example, but that's not my preferred genre as a writer. You don't have to write in those genres if you don't want to, just focus on learning about story and you won't go far wrong. This is part of the joy of learning to *write what you don't know*, of which more anon.

## 3. Watch movies out of your genre comfort zone

As with 2 above, this is also part of preparing you to *write what you don't know*. In other words it's part of making sure you become a screenwriter, not just a blinkered My Little Genre doofus. You want to work in a medium, so expose yourself to the breadth of that medium. The genres we just don't like are the genres we have to make a special effort to engage with. They all have something to teach us. This is part of learning to be a professional, not just a fan.

Give yourself little rules and tricks to make you do this. Here's a silly one of my own: I make long haul flights back to the old country every so often. I now have a rule only to watch movies on the flight that I would never otherwise watch—hello *Couples Retreat* (2009: scr. John Favreau, Vince Vaughn & Dana Fox)! Fortunately I have been able to negotiate a deal with all the airlines so that their movie channels are always stuffed full of films I would never otherwise watch.

As a screenwriter, you need to be open to the full history of filmmaking. If you are in film school you will be exposed to a wide range of great movies and have a head start, but if you are not you should make it your mission to seek them out. One thing that unites almost all filmmakers is their love, respect and deep knowledge of the history, traditions and creative scope of their medium. If you want to be one of them, you need to engage as they do.

## 4. Always be culturally inquisitive

We never stop learning, and you never know where the inspiration for your next screenplay will come from. Elia Kazan, infamous House Un-American Activities turncoat and director of *On the Waterfront* (1954), gave a famous speech at Wesleyan University in 1973 in which he outlined the skills a film director needs. They covered the bases from literature to military tactics by way of the work of the stage acrobat. You can find it on the Directors Guild of America (DGA) website, and much of it applies to screenwriters as well.

My shorthand is: engage with culture, politics and the world, because you are going to tell stories which are directly or indirectly about culture, politics and the world. This is because your stories will be about people and, you've guessed it, people are part of culture, politics and the world. This doesn't mean your stories have to be *about* culture and politics in a direct sense; it means your characters don't live in a vacuum and, if you want to make them come alive, neither should you.

### 5. Find some writer friends

Even if none of you have written a screenplay before and you are all struggling to find your first ideas and learn what script format is and how to beat it into submission, it helps to have friendly faces around you to share your struggles. You may not want to collaborate with someone else directly from the start; indeed, I would strongly advise against this until you have written at least one full screenplay. Try and find the beginnings of your own voice before you work with someone who will (quite naturally) be trying to impose their voice on you. You need confidence to push back, and what's the point of being a writer if you can't find yourself in what you have written?

A writing group, assuming its members are actually dedicated to writing (in my experience this is by no means certain), will give you the moral support to keep going, and constructive criticism on your work—the most important thing for a new writer. The idea is to find people who get you but are not clones of you. You don't want to write an action movie and have your friends read it and be all 'awesome explosions, bro.' This kind of feedback is no use to you at all, and besides it has too many 'tribal' tattoos to be taken seriously and smells like an addiction to Axe Body Spray. Try and find someone who isn't (to use that example) just into the action of action movies but knows how to recognize well-developed characters and sound story structures when they read them. That sounds much more useful, no?

Oh, and by the way, if your writing group seems to be more interested in the wrong sort of drama—the interpersonal politics of its members rather than their characters—my advice would be: 'back away slowly.' These kinds of groups can sometimes attract damaged souls who are looking for attention and who get in the way of the true purpose of the group. For best results, keep your personal life personal and your writing life friendly but focused. This is not to say you can't form lifelong friendships in a writing group; just don't join one with that intention.

### 6. Adapt something. Maybe

This can be a very good way of getting started as a writer. In fact that's how I started many years ago. I got into UCLA film school when I was in my mid-twenties and had almost a year before going out to Los Angeles to earn money—international fees are scary—and generally prepare myself. I took my own advice and read a bunch of screenplays, everything from William Goldman to Ingmar Bergman. Then I decided that I should try and write something.

I happened to be reading a novel that had clear cinematic potential, and I resolved to give myself a month and just plough through an adaptation. I did so, learning lessons about format, structure, character, exposition, dialogue, narrative economy and show, don't tell, and lots of other important stuff that we'll go on to talk about in this book. I still have an old copy of that screenplay lurking on my script shelf, and I'll show it to exactly nobody. Ever.

Best idea I ever had, and I recommend it to you, but only if you are able to keep the exercise under control. Don't obsess about it and don't waste time on it, especially if you don't have an option or other permission to develop the source material. Don't pick a 900-page doorstop, or you'll spend all your time working out what to cut. Write a straight down the line adaptation, don't be too fancy, and don't go nuts on rewrites. The point is to learn from doing, so get on with the doing. A month of your writing life is about right for this kind of project, and at the end you will have an actual screenplay. You will know it can be done and it will be easier to focus on all the technical aspects of writing because the basic story is pretty much taking care of itself.

Incidentally, I was chatting with Richard Walter, the long-serving UCLA Screenwriting Chairman the other day. Richard is firmly against students writing adaptations, even though Hollywood recently has been going through an adaptation friendly phase. We might call this movie land executive tendency cover-your-ass-and-screw-originality. In general, I agree with him. It's much better to show that you have an imagination and can do all the writing jobs, than that you want to be a hack and can do half of them. The adaptation exercise I am proposing is time-bound, specific and *not* a precedent for your other projects.

### 7. Take writing classes. Maybe

This is a very personal issue. Let me be blunt: *only take writing classes if you are ready to be taught and you can find a teacher who you feel you can learn from.* Classes can be destructive if you take them from the wrong teacher and are not ready to engage fully with the process.

By the way, I'm not implying that I am the right teacher for you just because you are reading my book. I don't know you and I wouldn't presume. I have taught for many years and I know perfectly well that, no matter what I do or how hard I try, some of my students simply won't 'get' me or will instinctively find me an annoying, arrogant Brit and will resist what I try to teach them. That's fine; there are plenty of annoying, arrogant Yanks to choose from if you don't like me!

Equally as important, deciding to take a writing class means you need to be prepared for real criticism. You must be able to get past your own ego and work with it. You don't have to agree with everything your teacher tells you, but there's no point sitting in class and simply going: 'shan't.' Wrong teacher for you? Get out of the class right now. Not ready to take criticism from a good teacher? Get out of the class right now. You can always take a class later when you are in a different frame of mind.

### 8. Go to film school. Maybe

This is a huge topic and I'm certainly not going to cover all of it here. In some ways it duplicates 7 above. There's no point going to film school if you are not ready to be taught. I mention this because my primary job is teaching at a film school and my colleagues and I sometimes despair at students—usually grad students in my experience—who think they know everything, resist everyone's attempts to help them improve, and end up wasting their time and money running on the creative spot for years. If your ego is fragile or you can't get over the huge chip on your shoulder and be open to constructive engagement with your work, run far and run fast. If you want to be a screenwriter you will *have* to get over those issues some day, but if now is not 'some day,' fair enough.

Also, film school is great if you want to explore all aspects of filmmaking and film studies. If you just want to write, think twice, because, even though a screenwriter needs to know a great deal about what other filmmakers do, if you are not interested in learning all of that right now film school will be a waste of time and an awful lot of money for you. Of course there are writing programs, and maybe one of those would be more your thing (but see 7 above).

This brings us to the general college-versus-job debate, which is also beyond the scope of this current book. My short answer is that you should go with whichever prospect excites you most right now. A college education is a wonderful thing but, despite what your parents may tell you, not everyone is ready to get the most from it straight after high school. This has nothing to do with intelligence and the same applies to grad school.

All I would say is that if you want to be in movies and you don't go to college, have a real alternative plan. People in movie land tend to assume that if you don't have a college degree either you kind of suck or there must be a good reason. Do something constructive; don't sit in your parents' basement *just* playing World of Warcraft, wonderful as it is—apart from the pesky gnomes of course.

### 9. Ignore most of the business aspects of screenwriting for now

If you want to be a writer, write. Until you are any good, the rest of the movie business is irrelevant. You don't need a subscription to *Variety*. You don't need to buy the Hollywood Creative Directory. You don't need to be making up lists of agencies or tracking what deals your favorite writers are making. The only thing you need to focus on is learning to write. Everything else is a distraction. Everything else is just taking time and mental energy away from that primary task.

It doesn't matter that you know who just sold what script to which company. Why? Because, unless your writing is already really good, that world is not your world, and when it is good enough there will be time enough to learn about it. Qualitywise, a new screenwriter is almost certainly several screenplays away from being good enough to show their work to industry types, so spend your time closing that gap. Also the studio will be looking for the *next* thing by the time you are halfway through reacting to and writing the old thing. There are whole sections on this later on.

The exception would be if you plan to try to work in TV writing, especially sitcom. In that case there is more of an accepted way of breaking in by writing sample episodes of existing comedies. If you want to write sitcoms, go buy a book and learn all about it. Personally I recommend Sheldon Bull's excellent *Elephant Bucks: an inside Guide to Writing for TV Sitcoms* (2007) from Michael Wiese Productions. For screenplays, just write.

### 10. Did I mention, just write?

Seriously, do it. However you do it, write scripts, tell stories, learn format. Don't put pressure on yourself; just dig deep into your love of movies and HAVE FUN!

This book is intended to help you. I hope you will also find it entertaining. The tone is intentionally silly in parts—my attempt to keep your read ticking over, because otherwise *manual = yawn*—but the advice comes from long teaching experience. It will not replace the value of working on some, if not all, of numbers 1 to 10 above, however.

Use it if it helps. Junk it if it doesn't. Don't worry about it either way.

# 1

## What's It All About?

### 'I saw Screenwriting Manual with the Devil!'

There tends to be a certain snobbish dismissiveness about books like this amongst some educators. That is understandable in as much as it comes from a resistance to the notion that any one volume can hope to encompass the history and traditions, the business and the art and craft of screenwriting. At least, they would add, not without diminishing it and reducing it to a series of bland diagrams and vacuous generalities. No writer likes to feel their creativity is being constrained by a blueprint, or a template, or even a set of guidelines. And yes, sometimes it can feel like that ... when you take books like this too seriously.

As far as I'm concerned, manuals—now including my own—only become a problem when simple usefulness gets mistaken, by writer and readers alike, for some kind of cargo cult.

```
                IMPLIED YOU
            (coughs)
        Robert McKee!


                FRIENDLY ME
        Oh hello. Nice of you to perk up, but
        in the words of the great Francis
        Urquhart: 'You may very well think
        that; I couldn't possibly comment'.
```

When you read this book you will certainly come across a load of stuff that turns up in most if not all of the other manuals, including that of the estimable Mr. McKee. It's hardly surprising, we are all talking about the same thing; we just imagine your path towards it differently. In the interests of full disclosure, when I get stuck I often refer to John Truby's *The Anatomy of Story* and Dara Marks's *Inside Story*. I recommend them both to you. As a grad student I also learned a lot from Richard Walter's classic book *Screenwriting: The Art, Craft and Business of Film and Television Writing*.

In my classes, when we seek the advice of a simple structural model, we often call upon the late Blake Snyder's *Save the Cat: the Last Book on Screenwriting You'll Ever Need*. Although, as you are now reading my book, you might infer that I regard his title with a certain amount of skepticism. Sometimes it's a great boon to have a piñata to hang up in class and beat with sticks to see what juicy nuggets of help and advice fall out. What's important is not whether, but how you use books like this. Screenwriting manuals don't kill creativity; lazy writers use them as an excuse to kill their own creativity.

For example, *Save the Cat* tends to help and annoy my students all at the same time. I get a mantra from them to the effect of: 'Every time I turn a page I don't know whether to thank him or slap him.' They value his advice but are sometimes frustrated with his unashamedly mainstream tone. Although I never met the man, I imagine he might have smiled happily at this and have found a certain vindication of his project in their responses. It also tells me my students are reading him the right way, with a mixture of open mindedness and healthy skepticism. I suggest you take the same approach to my book.

Trust me, whatever kind of screenplay you are trying to write, a good manual can be a very useful thing to have to hand. That is because there will be times as you write when you can use some checks, correctives and fallback positions. Of course Alejandro Jodorowsky, writer and director of *The Holy Mountain* (1973) and *Santa Sangre* (1989) might not agree. Speaking of his first film, *Fando y Lis* (1968), he says: 'I didn't work with the audience in mind; I just did it instinctively … I am proud of this because it is real.' We will return to Jodorowsky when we talk about creativity but, unless you really are as wildly experimental—ok, as gloriously bat-shit nuts—as he is, a safety net is sometimes a good thing.

Incidentally, I freely acknowledge a great debt to the authors I have just mentioned and the others to whom I will be referring along the way. This book was not written in an attempt to consign them to the dustbin of history, rather to act as a companion piece. I have tried to approach and assess their work from the perspective of a teacher, not a 'script guru'. Indeed, I will be applauding them and directing you towards their ideas rather than trying to pretend they don't matter.

I have done my best to give credit for terms coined by other screen-writing authors as I go. Sometimes it gets a little tricky to determine whether a term or principle in everyday use amongst filmmakers and screenwriters was coined by a particular author or was just picked up by them from the general discourse. I apologize in advance for any such errors and omissions. Anyway, you know which bookshelf Mr. Snyder and his friends hang out on. They will be happy to help you if you ask.

## 'What's in the box?'

My own films and scripts tend to deal with subject matter that involves at least 89% less explosions than your average blockbuster. On the other hand, I am proud to say that I am an enormous geek (what, you hadn't worked that out by now?) and I take great delight in well-made movies that have 89% more explosions than mine. My frame of reference will become clear from the range of examples in this book. Independent movies get some love in what follows but, rest assured, there will be lots of examples from movies which are about more than what that preeminent critic of independent film, Eric Cartman, once called 'gay cowboys eating pudding.'

What you will not find in this book is one single grid designed to solve all of your problems and guarantee you a script sale. 'Oh, if only it were that easy,' blah, moving on … What you will find instead are a range of different models of cinematic storytelling and loads of examples from movies. These are designed to help you look at the structure and purpose of screenplays from different perspectives. This is important, because screenwriters don't just write stories for actors to act out. You will be writing for a diverse set of readers who all need different kinds of information from your script.

Screenwriters bitch all the time about how other people abuse their work. Frustrated at how hack directors would butcher his screenplays during his early days in Hollywood, Billy Wilder once remarked that 'when I was asked whether directors should also be able to write I replied that it was more important that they should be able to read.' Similarly, Dave Eggers and Vendela Vida, writers of *Away We Go* (2009), advise their readers to 'try and find a director disinclined to removing and barbecuing your innards.'

We can only hope this happens in all cases. On the other hand, we should also make a point of understanding exactly how and why other professionals read and use our screenplays. That means directors and actors of course, but also assistant directors and the craft departments, to say nothing of all the casting people and—well, the list goes on. We will talk about your screenplay as a document used by the whole production. When you understand how that works, you will make everyone else's job easier.

Look, stories are still stories. In his admirable book *The Way Hollywood Tells It: Story and Style in Modern Movies*, David Bordwell cites the screenplay manual as evidence for his argument that: 'In formal design, today's Hollywood is largely contiguous with yesterday's.' So I haven't somehow reinvented dramatic structure from the ground

up; nor have I been miraculously inspired on some writerly road to
Damascus to overthrow thousands of years of storytelling in favor of the
'one true beat sheet.'
I do have a model, or to be precise a set of three models, to offer you,
of course. It doesn't have a cool name but, if you want to call it something
for politeness sake, call it **The VW Wardrobe Method**. Yeah, I know,
that sounds really lame, but it covers most of what you need to know
starting out, and it works for most stories. The three parts, 'V', 'W' and
'Wardrobe' all talk to one another. More than simple templates, they are
designed to help you connect different kinds of creative thinking and to
focus and prioritize your efforts in story creation.

The 'V' is a very simple, introductory model of story structure that
is designed to help us think our way from building story worlds to
making them work in storytelling. We will introduce it in Chapter 3.
The 'Wardrobe' is a way of conceptualizing the relationship between
theme, character, story and plot. We will get to it in Chapter 4. The 'W'
takes the simple 'V' model and makes it do its homework, to produce a
more complex and responsive way of thinking about structure. That's in
Chapter 5. There is also a long case study of the 'W' in Chapter 6.

My 'W' model of screenplay structure falls into the helpful piñata
category. It isn't intended to apply perfectly to every story, but it works
for many and teaches important lessons for most. It also develops
logically from the first principles of premise, character, story world and
theme we will be laying out beforehand.

In my experience, all that many aspiring writers want is a helping
hand and a friendly guide along the jungle path, rather than the company
of a master explorer who has not only cleared all the underbrush before
they get there but proceeds to tell them, at length and repeatedly, how
smart he is for having cleared that brush with his patented Universal
Imaginary Jungle Underbrush Clearer™ which is available for a small fee
from his website and by the way people paid him loads of green for the
privilege and now he has supermodels on his d.

You are reading this book because you are preparing for your own
adventure—let's keep this goofy jungle explorer premise going as long
as possible. All I am going to do is walk with you as you go, keeping up
a cheerful banter and checking your map and compass to make sure you
are still headed in the right direction. I'll be pointing out the odd pesky
snake on the trail ahead, but encouraging you to have fun and do your
own exploring.

And so we learn our first lesson about both character and story creation:
I, the writer, *need* you, dear implied reader, dear imaginary character that
you are to me, to have certain specific goals and needs. If you do, then

everything I write serves your purposes directly. If you don't, then I'm writing in a vacuum and have no real purchase on what I'm doing.

There is a whole section up ahead called: 'Why "my protagonist is kind of an everyman" often translates as: "I'm a lazy-ass writer".' Annoyingly I think I may have just stepped all over its point.

*[1. Writer's Chat] [Julian] Pfft, writing is hard/nerf imo.*

I have written a version of you into my book, following my assumptions. I have *characterized* you, made you into a character, knowing that I can in no way encompass all aspects of your personality in doing so. I'm working with the characteristics that will be useful for me to keep in mind as I write for you, and I'm ignoring those which are less germane to your engagement with this book.

I am sure that there are many other fascinating and quirky, endearing and lovable and even annoying and creepy aspects of your personality— just as there are of mine. Our friends and families care about them, or don't, but the work of this book can be undertaken without my knowing all of them. That means I get to not expend any more effort upon them.

As with this book, so with your screenplays, because this very job of prioritizing, discarding and foregrounding information that we have just been doing together goes to *narrative economy*, one of the most important principles of screenwriting.


## How movies work, only without the complicated bits

The principle of narrative economy influences many of the decisions you will have to make while writing your screenplays. It also helps to explain the basic operating model of mainstream cinema. Indeed, narrative economy is so important that I'm going to discuss it right up front as part of a little introduction to how movies work. This is going to be a very partial and personal view, and your film studies professor will most certainly tut and sigh, but it helps me work and it will get us on the same page fast. I want you to keep it in mind throughout all the other sections of the book.

Now, of course, films are really very complicated things. That is precisely why I'm going to spend the next few pages telling you how they are really very simple things. This is for our collective sanity and to help us have the guts to actually attempt to write one. That this simplicity is an illusion need not bother us for now—after all we are, each of us, already experienced professionals when it comes to accepting illusion for reality in so many aspects of our lives.

## The trinity

All I'm going to do to start with is to offer you up three principles of cinematic storytelling. Just as bell peppers, onions and celery are the 'trinity' of Cajun cooking, these three principles are my personal but, in detail, hardly original trinity of screenwriting: **narrative economy, narrative excess** and **show, don't tell.** They are the aromatic base that simmers underneath everything I write for the screen. Enough with the cooking metaphor? I think so.

What they are intended to do is help us to understand the rigor and discipline that is at the heart of screenwriting. This rigor and discipline should be there even when we are indulging our wildest fantasies and showing our readers the most incredible sights through our writing. This is really important and is a major pitfall for those who don't take the *craft* aspect of screenwriting seriously.

### A boring pair of everyday shoes: narrative economy

Narrative economy is one of the principles that underlie what film studies academics call Classical Hollywood Cinema. This refers to a system of filmmaking, associated historically with the output of the American studio system, which is designed specifically to hide the traces of its own construction so that the viewer is better able to avoid noticing and having to think about the film's inherent status *as a film.*

What narrative economy has come to mean in practice for screen-writers is that, in films like these, stories seem to unfold 'naturally' because every piece of information you give the audience has some direct relationship to the plot or the story. (We will discuss the relationship between plot and story in more detail later.) We may not know why we are being told something by the script at the exact moment that we are told it but, if we have been told it at all, we can be certain that it will be important later on.

Hence the 'economy' part of narrative economy: if some piece of information isn't vital to our understanding and enjoyment of your story, it isn't *valuable* enough to be in your script.

Techniques of cinematography, editing and sound design (for example) are used to complete this seamless illusion by establishing and maintaining visual continuity in the world of the film. The whole package is organized with the intention of keeping us happily in our seats and engaged with the drama, not with the filmmaking process itself. It has become what we might call the default technique of mainstream filmmaking internationally.

Here is an easy example to get us moving: The opening scene of *Die Hard* (scr. Jeb Stuart & Steven E. de Souza; 1988) takes place as Bruce Willis's plane lands at LAX. His neighbor, a frequent business traveler, notices that Bruce is a nervous flyer and offers him some friendly advice about relaxing.

```
SALESMAN
You wanna know the secret of
successful air travel? After you get
where you're going, you take off your
shoes and socks. Then you walk around
on the rug barefoot making fists with
your toes.
```

So the film opens with a conversation about jetlag? *Die Hard* is one of the great entertainment machines of the late twentieth century. We know it is going to be a great big beast of an action movie because we have seen the trailers, read the reviews and looked at stills of the lad Willis running around in a grubby old 'wife beater' vest. We know it will be all gunfights and explosions and possibly even yippe-ki-yeas. Let's face it, that's why we are in the cinema in the first place. Not to listen to Bruce talk about jetlag and the comfort of his little tootsies.

But we, the audience, have grown up seduced by the blandishments of Classical Hollywood Cinema. We are well trained in narrative economy, whether we realize it or not. We know that this is not just a scene about post-flight podiatry. We trust that not only will there be all gunfights and running about and explosions in the not-too-distant future (I'm looking at you, *Jurassic Park*, don't even think I have forgotten) but that this conversation about toes and rugs is leading to an event which will make Bruce's participation in those gunfight and running about and explosion related sequences ever so much more impressive. We don't know what it will be yet and we may not even be thinking about it actively, but somewhere deep down we know it is coming.

And of course it does. Eventually, a stressed out Bruce does take off his shoes, makes fists with his toes and finds, to his surprise and momentary pleasure, that the salesman was right. Only just then Alan Rickman and his eurotrash mates with criminal haircuts enter the scene and force him to fight with guns, run about and avoid being exploded by and with things … in a modern high-rise building … where everything is made of glass … in his bare feet.

Genius.

Anyway, the point is that, even when it is having fun with Bruce Willis's bare feet and huge broken panes of glass, the cinema we have grown up with is, somewhere in its heart of hearts, a utilitarian kind of fellow.

As with *Die Hard*, so with an Oscar-winning European art movie.

Ulla Isaksson's screenplay for *Jungfrukällen / The Virgin Spring* (1960) is based upon a medieval ballad ('Töres Dotter I Vänga' / 'The Daughter of Töre of Vänga' and other variants). It tells a deceptively simple tale of jealousy and murder which explores the futility and bankruptcy of revenge and tests the possibility of a rational belief in an omnipotent God. In the first ten minutes, every major theme in the film is established or foreshadowed. We see tension between Pagan and Christian beliefs in fourteenth-century Sweden. We are also given an introduction to character flaws in all of the key members of Max von Sydow's family which the story will go on to expose and punish. Specifically we learn about the tensions that surround the legitimate daughter of the house, played by Birgitta Pettersson.

So, in the first scenes of the film we are shown how old Max, who is a bit of an enabler, overindulges pretty blonde Birgitta. She is deeply resented by her dark foster sister (played by Gunnel Lindblom), who clearly wishes she could be a Scene Kid, only she's a few hundred years ahead of the trend. Besides, she just can't get her hair to fall that way. Frustrated, Gunnel resorts to general sullenness, Odin worship and calling down pagan curses on her sister, and we know that never ends well. Inevitably, Birgitta's naïveté and vanity will be catalysts for a tragic series of events that follow her chance meeting with three goatherds as she travels through the forest to deliver the virgin candles to a nearby church.

This is narrative economy at work again. The film helps us to catch up fast with all the issues we are going to need to be up to speed with and doesn't weigh us down or confuse us with random and thus useless information. We are introduced to the small, enclosed world of Max's farm and his extended family community, and learn nothing of the world around it other than the nearby forest where the fatal encounter between Birgitta and the goatherds takes place. Also we learn nothing of the communities and culture of medieval Sweden other than we can infer from what we are shown and told.

This is standard expository work, no matter that it occurs to help the audience understand and engage with the film's religious and moral symbolism rather than the need for its lead character to remove his shoes at an inopportune moment.

Here's another quick example, this time played for real poignancy. Near the beginning of *The Brothers Bloom* (scr. Rian Johnson; 2008), master con-man Stephen explains how to tell the difference between real and fake blood. Apparently real blood turns brown after half an hour. At the end of the film Stephen is shot and, in his final con, fakes out Bloom that it was all a setup and he is fine. Bloom believes him and escapes with his love interest, Penelope. We cut to them later in the car. Bloom glances at the bloodstain on his cuff. It is brown. He realizes Stephen fooled him and that he is almost certainly dead.

Johnson hasn't mentioned red and brown blood since that one moment near the start of the movie, and has just let it sit in the back of our minds, waiting for us to share a horrid revelation at the end. It works perfectly and is an example of really good writing.

In terms of narrative economy at least, the writer's job in *Die Hard*, *Jungfrukällen* and *The Brothers Bloom* is basically the same here.

> IMPLIED YOU
> Oh come on, screenwriting is a lot
> more complicated than this though,
> right?

> FRIENDLY ME
> Yes, of course—hence this book and
> many others like it.

> IMPLIED YOU
> I mean, not all films even attempt
> to follow the Classical Hollywood
> continuity model.

> FRIENDLY ME
> Yes that's right. Conveniently I'm
> just about to mention that in the
> next paragraph.

> IMPLIED YOU
> Wow, it's as if you'd planned it!

> FRIENDLY ME
> All right. Easy. Just keep
> reading.

Some films tell their stories through complex, non-chronological flashback structures (*Rashomon* 1950); others have multiple narrators (*Election* 1999); are non-linear (*Stardust Memories* 1980); or have elliptical narratives (*Lost Highway* 1997); but they all make use of narrative economy in their own ways. This says nothing of the particular traditions of certain genres, of 'national cinemas' around the world and the work of the surrealists, expressionists and other modernist and avant-garde filmmakers.

Focusing our minds on narrative economy is a solid starting point, however. Think of it like the relative who gives you a good pair of boring everyday shoes for your birthday. They are not very exciting and they are not the pony you asked for and you can't download MP3s or play video games on them, but sometimes everyone needs a good pair of boring everyday shoes. Once you have worn them in you can walk anywhere. This is a good thing. Just ask Bruce Willis.

Narrative economy is also about the concision and precision you bring to writing your scene descriptions or 'action.' Remember, typically you have a *maximum* allowance of only 120 or so pages—more realistically you should aim for 100 pages—with which to tell your feature film's story. For those outside the USA that is 100 8.5″ x 11″ pages. In filmmaking, we estimate that one page of script equates to approximately one minute of screen time. A two-hour movie would, thus, equate to 120 screenplay pages. Sitting in front of your blank computer screen, 120 pages may feel like an awful lot.

Trust me, it's not.

Remember the scene with Cobb and Ariadne in the café in *Inception* (scr. Christopher Nolan; 2010)? You know the one, the great set piece (see **narrative excess** below) with the dream world curling around and sandwiching back above us that ends with the café exploding? Here's the action description from Nolan's screenplay:

The restaurant VIOLENTLY FRAGMENTS, EXPLODING AND IMPLODING PARTICLES OF FURNITURE, WALLS, PEOPLE FLYING AROUND—Ariadne WONDERS at the MAYHEM WHIRLING around them—Cobb SHIELDS his head against the debris.

One sentence of description which gives us a context and—important this—plays the event straight back to character reaction. *Action is of no interest unless it affects our characters, so write it to character.* Nolan doesn't focus on the minute details, he gives us the information we need to get the plot function of the event and movies on. The micro management and visual development of a sequence like this in a big budget movie is for discussions with the visual effects team. The script version just gets us all up and running with the intent of the spectacle: concision and clarity are the keys.

A good test here is to start by thinking how long the sequence will take in real time. Assuming one page to a minute, work your description based on that equation. Actually I think Nolan could have afforded himself a few more words in terms of onscreen time in this case, but don't ever be redundant. Your choices should always be about keeping the read going smoothly. It's better to be a little out of sync than lose us in the minutiae of what this or that random explosion looks like. We've seen explosions before, so unless yours are somehow very different—in which case by all means knock us for six—assume we want to understand the story function of the action and move on. For complex and innovative action sequences, the trick is to encapsulate that innovation in short statements so we go 'wow!' Leave us amazed and impressed, not bored or confused.

Narrative economy is the principle that guides you to prioritize, focus and discipline everything you write. Just as with the assumptions I made about you at the start of this book, you need to decide which aspects of a character or situation are essential for the successful telling of your story. These need development; the rest are just wasting page space. All creative writing benefits from clarity of purpose, but in screenwriting there is a major economic imperative as well.

Here's an everyday example: I need to get home in a hurry in the rain so I try to hail a cab. I am on a street corner in New York alongside many other people with the same intention. Twenty minutes later, there I am, wet, unhappy, still waiting for a taxi.

Here's the screenplay version: I stick out my hand. A taxi stops. Cut to next location.

Unless, of course, some plot or story *beat* (another word to which we shall return anon) is being served by seeing me getting ever wetter and more unhappy on the street corner, we don't want to waste a single unnecessary second—to say nothing of twenty minutes—of our movie watching me try to catch a cab.

> IMPLIED YOU
> Really? The hail a cab example?
> That's a hoary old chestnut.

> FRIENDLY ME
> It's as current as you like. I just
> saw Tony Gilroy have Julia Roberts
> do it in *Duplicity* and that's one
> of the slickest, most knowing
> pieces of throwaway spyjinx you
> could ask for.

> IMPLIED YOU
> Right. Listen, are you going to be
> this annoying all the way through
> the book?

> FRIENDLY ME
> Yup. Pretty much. That was a beat
> just then, by the way. You shifted
> the subject from my example to your
> feelings about my 'I've got an
> answer for everything' attitude.

```
Of course that's actually what you
were talking about in the first
place, but you hadn't come round to
admitting it yet. I just thought
I'd mention it.

        IMPLIED YOU
Oh. Yeah, ok, I see what I did.

        FRIENDLY ME
Good dialogue often does that. It
moves from the surface to the
emotion. That's one of the ways we
reveal character.

        IMPLIED YOU
I'm watching you. That's all I'm
saying.

        FRIENDLY ME
Fair enough.
```

The principle of narrative economy reminds you that you need to *budget* your story and, like any personal or household budget, this means getting the most you can from a finite resource. It does not mean that you have to tell trite tales or oversimplify your ideas. Taken too far it can be an excuse for excessive self-censorship, but you need to keep it in mind.

In screenwriting, then, the lesson of narrative economy is that the following usually applies:

Clarity > opacity
Concision > verbosity

In my experience, the further from the mainstream—let's just say it, the further from Hollywood—aspiring writers aim their stories, the more likely it is that they begin to re-imagine > as <. This is almost always a bad idea. Clarity and concision do not automatically equate to mediocrity and blandness. Neither do opacity nor verbosity automatically equate to authenticity or artistry. *Remember that there is a big difference between being clear on the page and being blandly transparent on the screen.*

For now, bear in mind the obvious: unlike in a novel, your writing is where your movie starts, not ends, and making that movie will cost you, or hopefully somebody else, a great deal of money per page. What would you prefer to spend it on?

Basically, narrative economy is your friend and we will return to it often.

If you are feeling a little depressed at the mechanical, reductive implications of all of this talk of narrative economy, I sympathize, but remind you in turn that in some ways screenwriting is the most restrictive, rulebound kind of writing you can do. There are many reasons for that and many joys that compensate for it, and we will discuss them in a section called '*What is a screenplay and how do I get there?*'

Fortunately, there is another side to cinema which is always lurking somewhere in the wings, waiting for any chance to take its place in the spotlight. If narrative economy is the square sister who followed the family tradition and became an accountant, there is another sibling in the movie family tree who drank a very different flavor of Kool Aid.

## Staring open-mouthed at cool stuff: narrative excess

So much for utility, because films can also be joyously gaudy, freewheeling, surprising, hilarious, violent, perverse and, yes, fundamentally excessive works of art. They can break or ignore rules and sometimes don't care a damn for narrative economy, replacing its organizing principle with that of visual and emotional delirium.

At its most simple, excess is about you deciding to write moments, sequences or even whole screenplays in which your film will spend more time, effort, budget and style to say what you want it to say than can be justified purely in terms of narrative economy.

It means that you understand that cinema can be about much more than simple storytelling. It means that you understand that audiences have always gone to the movies with a complex set of motivations and expectations, not all of which are about sitting primly in their seats letting a nice, simple, unthreatening little tale wash over them.

It means that you have probably seen *El Topo* (1970).

Some genres, such as horror, science fiction, melodrama, the musical and, outside the scope of this book, certainly pornography, are almost by definition more 'excessive' than others, and some filmmakers—Alejandro Jodorowsky, Dario Argento, Douglas Sirk, Vincente Minnelli, David Lynch, Sam Raimi, Werner Herzog, Takashi Miike and … Michael Bay amongst many others—made their reputations from variations on the theme.

Most often, however, the opportunity for excess is what your parsimonious narrative economy buys you in regular doses eked out over the course of your script depending upon your budget.

What this also implies is that, as a screenwriter, you can address your audience in different ways, depending on what you are trying to say.

Sometimes a screenplay even signals to the audience when it plans to shift from one form to the other. You remember the scene in *Jurassic Park* (scr. Michael Crichton and David Koepp; 1993) which comes at that precise moment when you realize that you are five seconds away from getting up out of your seat and leaving the cinema because they *still* haven't shown you any dinosaurs? You know the one. The gang has finally arrived on the island and they are being driven to the main compound in tasteless Jeeps when suddenly Laura Dern becomes fascinated with a leaf.

She starts to coo over it and to gush about its properties in a paleobotanicalkillmenow sort of way, until Sam Neill sees something off-screen and registers awe. He stands up, mouth open, and stares off at whatever it is that we cannot see. Laura is still giving it full leaf until Sam reaches down and physically turns her head to look out of the jeep. Laura's jaw drops and she stares in stunned silence at something we STILL can't see. By this time, and by design, every member of the audience is inventing new rude words with which to curse Steven Spielberg through sheer force of will. And then, finally, we cut to the reverse and we see ... a deeply sucky CGI dinosaur in what must be one of the greatest visual anticlimaxes in movie history.

Yes, there will go on to be a Tyrannosaurus Rex who eats a lawyer, and a bunch of Velociraptors who eat Bob Peck, and they are, in fairness, pretty cool—even if they repeatedly fail to eat the annoying American children who are served up to them on a plate and thus deny the film's international audience one of its greatest pleasures. The point is that with this scene the screenwriters show that they understand two key things about their movie:

1 The audience came here to see dinosaurs. We really don't care about much else. We haven't seen any yet and we are becoming restive, thus the scene plays a little teasing game with both our patience and our excitement.
2 Films position their audiences in a number of different ways, and sometimes we screenwriters need to be helping our audience to forget about the story and just do a version of what Sam and Laura are doing in their Jeep: staring open-mouthed at cool stuff.

Why we need to pay attention to this scene is because it sets out to control a change in the way the audience watches the film. One minute we are following the story, the next we have forgotten all about that and are simply looking at CGI dinosaurs and trying not to drool. The story just stopped. The writers got their characters to put the movie on pause for a moment and, through them, said to us: 'Hold on a second everyone—look at this.' They waited politely for us to take it all in and go: 'Wow, cool,' or in my curmudgeonly case: 'Pfft, meh, pfft,' and then pressed play and got on with the story from where it left off.

It is an important lesson for screenwriters, as it reminds us that people go to the movies not just to be told stories but also to be shown *wonders*. Indeed in terms of film history the wonders pre-date the stories, and to a certain extent movies have always been about the content as a kind of technology demonstrator: film *as* wonder.

I remember that Professor Vivian Sobchack summed it up perfectly in a seminar on science fiction cinema back in my grad student days by saying: 'Films about the future are usually about the future of films.' *2001: A Space Odyssey* (scr. Stanley Kubrick & Arthur C. Clarke; 1968) is a perfect example. It is both an exercise in film-as-wonder—the story is basically one long 'Wow, cool' moment, even without the aid of drugs— and simultaneously a demonstration of what the combined technologies of filmmaking can accomplish. At least it is a demonstration of what could be accomplished in 1968.

Incidentally, that leafgasm scene in *Jurassic Park* isn't even in Michael Crichton's first draft of the screenplay, which really does leave it a very long time before we see all the dinosaurs. In one of the later drafts I have read, it is present, but orchestrated around a visual gag in which Sam Neill mistakes one of the Brachiosaur's legs for a tree trunk. Fortunately for our bursting sides they didn't shoot that version. In the end they simply directed their characters to prepare the audience for the shift as the film's story went on pause and it shifted from a *representational* (telling-led) mode to a (showing-led) *presentational* mode: look, dinosaurs!

The finale of *Close Encounters of the Third Kind* (scr. Steven Spielberg and others uncredited; 1977) is also one long, long neck-crane at space-ships. Hey, if François Truffaut is going to spend the last act of the movie watching the skies, that's good enough for me. Of course, the whole process takes far longer than is strictly necessary in 'hailing a taxi' terms: we play five notes of music; spaceships land; we meet the aliens; roll credits.

In this case, however, what the audience is asking of the climax is the emotional and spectacular answer to the mystery of alien contact that the film has been offering up throughout its considerable length. We have followed our heroes as they give up their families and their ordinary lives to travel, drawn to this spot for an answer, and we need that joint commitment to be *paid off* in full. It is a lesson Carl Sagan and company really should have learned before they wrote *Contact* (1997).

Movies do this all the time, even if they don't usually flag the shift to their audiences in quite so literal a way. Certain genres also allow, even expect, their writers to work in sequences of unabashed excess. Of course this has always been a key feature of horror films in different guises and styles throughout the genre's history. Just think of the operatically staged murders in Italian gialli and horror movies such as *Suspiria* (1977) and the slapstick gore of *Evil Dead II* (1987), *Sien Nui Yao Wan A Chinese Ghost Story* (1987), or *Braindead* (1992). Recently it has come back with a vengeance (ho ho) in the prolonged and bloody Grand Guignol of so-called 'torture porn' horror movies such as *Hostel* (2005). Not my taste, I have to say, but excessive they certainly are.

Excess—segue alert—is also really just the logical hyperextension of the oldest of old screenwriting mantras: 'show, don't tell.'

## Remember who you are writing for: show, don't tell

Screenplays are not novels. This doesn't mean they aren't literary works in their own right, but it does mean that they have different and in some ways more exacting sets of rules and functions than a novel does. One fast route into understanding this difference is through 'show, don't tell.'

I'm sure most of you have already come across this very important direction but, like narrative economy, it underpins your writing at every stage. It is another fundamental component of the rigor and discipline of screenwriting that I have begun to push on you, so we should include it in our up-front introduction.

Go down to your local tattoo parlor and get the nice inked-up bloke down there to tattoo the words: SHOW, DON'T TELL on the backs of both your hands in big bold letters. That way you can read them as you type.

Alternatively, and assuming you aren't a complete idiot, stick a note on your monitor or something.

This one is really simple:

1 Film is a visual medium.
2 The job of a screenplay (unlike a novel) is *only* to tell the reader what s/he will see on screen.
3 We can't see things like internal dialogue and motivation.
4 Don't write them as such.

What this means is that when you are writing your screenplay your job is to translate everything that is going on *inside* your characters' minds into its *external* manifestation. In movies we learn about characters' internal lives and motivations only through their actions, responses and interactions.

Here is an obvious 'real life situation' to make the screenwriting point: it's the big date when for the first time you—let's make you male and call you Bob for the purposes of this example—are going to tell your girlfriend—let's make her female and call her Jenny—that you love her. You really mean it, by the way. This isn't some cheap dick move to get some action; you can see yourself spending the rest of your life with this person. She is the Juliet to your Romeo; the Ramona Flowers to your Scott Pilgrim; the Kim Kardashian to your Justin B… hmm, well maybe not the last one. You think she loves you back, but her response is, of course, going to be a really big deal.

Jenny turns up. She looks beautiful, even after a full shift at the poultry farm, sexing chicks. Things are going well. Wine is drunk. Appetizers are eaten. You are pretty sure food isn't sticking to your teeth. Jenny just laughed very sweetly at your feeble joke. There is a natural pause in the conversation, filled only with some goofy smiling and general staring into each other's eyes. You suck it up. 'Jenny,' you stammer (see how pathetic I made you just to make this little point? Being a writer is great!) … 'I love you!'

Now see where we are? Jenny is going to react and respond. There are so many nuances, so many levels and so many ways your/Bob's suddenly deeply neurotic and paranoid mind will read every tiny aspect of her expression, intonation, words and actions when she does. Why? Because you desperately need to know what she is really feeling, *but you can't know that, other than from her words and actions and your interpretation of those words and actions.*

That's what it is like being a screenwriter. You have to write every scene with half your brain as Bob. *Don't tell us what your characters feel. Tell us what their feelings make them do or say.*

Look, here's an example of what not to do. Sadly things aren't going well for Bob and Jenny:

```
EXT. JENNY'S HOUSE — NIGHT
Bob collapses onto the front porch in tears, thinking of
all the lost opportunities and the time he saw her
kissing Chad at the ballpark.
```

*[1. Writer's Chat] Writers' Failbot: 'Bob fails at show, don't tell.'*

How do we know what Bob is thinking about? We don't, because all we *see* is Bob falling down and starting to cry. If we have already seen the moment when Bob saw Jenny and Chad canoodling we might make a logical assumption that this is what is on his mind. Even so, we can't definitively know his thoughts, but we can read his actions. Allow us to do this. Have confidence that your reader isn't a complete moron. Here's another example:

```
INT. JENNY'S BEDROOM — NIGHT
Jenny sits at her dressing table, brushing her hair.
Tears fall, but not for Bob. She is still upset over the
news of the terrible multiple streetcar pileup in Riga
yesterday. And just all the random cruelty in the world.
And how it's so unfair that Jennifer Aniston can't find
her perfect man. And all the abandoned kitties.
```

*[1. Writer's Chat] Writers' Failbot: 'Jenny fails at show, don't tell.'*

OK, an even sillier example; but hopefully the silliness drives the point home. Of course there are always exceptions to any rule. This is from *Away We Go*, which is full of descriptions of interior motivation [my bold]:

```
EXT. GREYHOUND TRACK BLEACHERS — AFTERNOON
In the center of the track, there's a brief ceremony
saluting U.S. soldiers wounded and killed in Iraq. A
local middle-schooler sings 'The Star Spangled Banner.'

Taylor is sitting in the front row of the bleachers,
holding a Crayola marker and a racing form, circling the
dogs he thinks will win. Ashley is sitting apart from
him, watching the action on the track, wishing she were
living a different life.
```

*[1. Writer's Chat] Writers' Failbot: 'Ashley fails at show, don't tell.'*

And again:

```
                   BURT
       He's gotta be sharp. Gotta be wily.

Verona winces and looks at him: Where does he get these
adjectives?
```

*[1. Writer's Chat] Writers' Failbot: 'Verona fails at show, don't tell.'*

If you are Dave Eggers and have already written *A Heartbreaking Work of Staggering Genius* you get to write quirky. Besides, quirky movies are kind of expected to 'read quirky,' *up to a point*. Mainstream genres tend to get read by mainstream readers in mainstream studios and companies, however. So if you are a quirky writer it helps if you can arrange it so that you spend as much as possible of your development life in the relatively nurturing world of independent film production. Good luck with that! For the rest of us, remember the difference between being an unknown writer with a spec script and a famous writer writing for a known or more accepting reader.

These may seem like tiny points, but to a producer, or more likely to the assistant who is reading scripts for them, it is like a great big siren going off in their head that shrieks: 'Pfft, noob!' Most importantly it is the kind of thing that makes all the difference between your script getting a read past page one or being trashed. Look, every writer makes that kind of mistake occasionally, despite their best efforts. That's why you mechanically trawl through your drafts to catch them.

Similarly, don't describe something in dialogue, voice over or with any other technique if we can actually see it happening onscreen:

```
EXT. HOTEL VERANDA — DAY
SNIDEMAN and REDUNDANT BOY join the CROWD gazing out at
the huge ERUPTING VOLCANO across the bay.

                    REDUNDANT BOY
          Whoa, check out the huge erupting
          volcano across the bay!

                    SNIDEMAN
          You mean the huge erupting volcano
          we are all already staring at?

                    REDUNDANT BOY
          Yeah, totally. Look at all those
          giant burning rocks it is throwing
          out.

Snideman and the rest of the crowd are already running
from the path of the GIANT BURNING ROCKS.

                    SNIDEMAN
          We see them.

                    REDUNDANT BOY
          That one looks like it's coming
          right for me. Do you see it? That's
          awesome!

With a resounding CRUMP a giant burning rock squashes
Redundant Boy flat.
```

*[1. Writer's Chat] Writers' Failbot: 'Redundant Boy fails at show, don't tell.'*

Typically, writers fail at show, don't tell when they are being lazy, not paying attention to detail, and especially at the start of scripts when everything and everybody is being introduced and the whole exposi- tional info dump has to happen somehow.

Exposition, basically the introduction of characters and situation that begins at the start of the story, is one of the hardest things to write elegantly, and we will come back to it in Chapter 5 in a section called (wait for it): *'Exposition.'*

## When format nerds attack!

Remember what I told you about screenwriting being one of the most restrictive and rule-bound kinds of writing you can do? Well we are about to dip our toes into the area where that can become the most annoying. We will deal with format issues on and off throughout the book, but in order to understand why this matters—and why I have included it in my introduction to how movies work—we need to take a moment to introduce you to the wonderful and supportive world that awaits the fruits of all of your creativity and sweat as a writer. There are flowers and rainbows and pastel colored ponies with long cotton candy manes that never get tangled there. Honest.

Let's keep it short and not very sweet:

1 Everybody has a spec script. This means there are many, many screenplays in the world and, even with rigorous gatekeeping, there are always too many scripts to read in Hollywood.
2 Almost all of these spec scripts either really suck (I have been a script reader and sadly I can confirm that this is really true—and when I say suck, I mean suck so much worse than your list of the worst movies ever made) or are just not what your reader is looking for.
3 All too often the mindset of your roll the dice and get a random reader is: anything that gives me the excuse not to read your screenplay is a bonus.
4 Being a format nerd is the fastest and easiest way to get to '3'.
5 Ergo assume everybody in Hollywood is a format nerd.

```
           IMPLIED YOU
What do you mean by a 'spec' script?


           FRIENDLY ME
That means a script that you wrote
'on spec.' Nobody asked you to
write it, you just had a story to
tell and now you hope somebody will
buy it. This means that you are
writing to be read by a 'generic
movie industry reader,' not
somebody who knows and loves you and
```

```
your wonderful, yet idiosyncratic,
style.

            IMPLIED YOU
But what if I have a wonderful, yet
idiosyncratic, style? In fact, it
just so happens that I do.

            FRIENDLY ME
Well the danger is that if your
style means that your screenplay
doesn't look and read how they
expect a screenplay to look and
read, readers may well latch onto
that as a compelling reason not to
read far enough to fall in love with
it.

            IMPLIED YOU
That doesn't seem very fair.

            FRIENDLY ME
Well it is and it isn't. Remember,
using proper format is also an
important way of showing
professionalism and respect
for your readers. Anyway, fair
warning.
```

**OK, let's recap.** I hope that this little discussion of my trinity has established some important ground rules about movies and screenwriting for you. We are going to backtrack in a moment and start at the very beginning of the writing process, but at least now we can move forward armed with a certain amount of knowledge:

1 Nothing is ever wasted in a screenplay. If your story needs it, it stays in. If not, kick it.

2 Audiences will expect you to 'pay off' scenes and ideas that do not have a transparent story function when you introduce them (Bruce's jetlag scene). They will feel somehow cheated or confused if you fail to do this.

3 Movies are not only about telling a story efficiently, sometimes they are about overegging that story or even putting it on hold and showing your audience wonders.

4 I cannot see your thoughts and feelings. I can, however, see what they make you do. It's the same with the audience for your movie.

5 If I can see something onscreen, don't waste my time telling me about what I already know.

6 If I can't see something onscreen and you feel you need to tell me about it, ask yourself: 'Why am I not just showing this?'

7 Write with half your brain as Bob.

Clear? Good. Now let's go back to the beginning.

## 'Write what you know': why this idea sucks and what to do about it

The worst thing you can do right now is sit in front of a computer screen, or a blank sheet of paper, with no idea for a story and just wait to be creative.

Go on. Try it. It's Sunday afternoon and I have been meaning to watch the pilot of *Studio 60 on the Sunset Strip* on Hulu. I hear it's really good. People tell me it's a crime that show got cancelled and I missed it thanks to my move from England to San Francisco, so I have time. I can wait.

I'm back. Are you back yet? Well I enjoyed the pilot and want to see more. Time well spent.

How did the automatic creativity experiment go?

OK, congratulations to the seven of you who got a great movie idea just then and proved me wrong. Yes, I counted—and, by the way, cool! I sold seven books! Go write it down now before you forget it. For the rest of you, those who proved the rule, we need to think this through a little.

```
            IMPLIED YOU
    That's ok; I get ideas all the time.
    I had one this morning about selling
    pre- fried eggs. It was great, I
    could make a fortune.

            FRIENDLY ME
    No. I mean you are going to need a
    movie idea. That's a whole
    different thing. Wait, pre-fried
    eggs?

            IMPLIED YOU
    I know. Why did you make me say
    that?

            FRIENDLY ME
    I don't know. I'm sorry. I'm just
    writing my way into your character
    at the moment. You're coming over way
```

```
      too random and first drafty on this
      page.

             IMPLIED YOU
      All right, I'll bite. Tell me what
      the difference is between a regular
      idea and a movie idea?

             FRIENDLY ME
      Mid six figures against high six if
      it actually goes into production.
      Sorry, I couldn't resist. That's a
      good question and we'll talk about
      it shortly, but first we need to
      think back a step or two. Writing
      is a creative endeavor so we should
      spend a little time prepping our
      creativity.
```

## Creativity today, or: 'Don't try this at home!'

Those who dream by day are cognizant of many things which escape those who dream only at night.

Edgar Allen Poe

We are caught between two lies in our culture. The first is the vapid self-help book assertion that inside everybody is a perfectible little nugget of genius just waiting to be smelted out of all our impurities. We can all make it to the stars as long as we have the guts to reach for them (and the money to buy the food or the book or the course that will open the magical doorway to get us there).

The second and more dangerous lie is that talent and creativity are what the other, strange people have and we should be content to sit back on the couch in our farting pants, with our pork rinds and beer cans readily to hand and just watch our stories and be thankful the strange people were there to tell them to us.

In fact the reality is that we are all at least minimally creative most of the time, and yet surprisingly people tend to discount, suppress and ignore their own creativity. Some of us are too far gone to care, but for many of us, even if we are too smart completely to buy into the fantasy of perfectibility, there is the will to try to learn and improve.

Unusually for me, I agree with the psychologist Abraham Maslow on this: 'The key question isn't "What fosters creativity?" But it is why in God's name isn't everyone creative? Where was the human potential lost? How was it crippled? I think therefore a good question might be not why do people create? But why do people not create or innovate? We have got to abandon that sense of amazement in the face of creativity, as if it were a miracle if anybody created anything.'

If you will forgive a brief medieval analogy (and with deep apologies to the eminent historian Caroline Walker Bynum), too often we have a tendency to take a lesson as if from the writers of hagiographies who encouraged their readers and audiences to wonder at, not imitate the miraculous deeds of the saints. In a more modern idiom: you can't be as good as [insert name of your favorite creative genius here], so don't bother trying:

*Professional writer. Closed train of thought. Do not attempt.*

Personally I put a lot of the blame onto the culture of reticent mediocrity our various structures of formal education and informal socialization tend to foster in too many young people, but that's a story for another time.

Much of what we do on a day-to-day level we don't think of in terms of creativity. In fact we spend a great deal of time automatically suppressing our creative impulses through established routines of thought and behavior. It is easier to do and to think what we always do or think in a given situation than it is to open ourselves up to allowing the possibility that other choices are available and that they might lead to … who knows where?

If that simple observation is more exciting than scary to you, then there's hope for you as a creative individual!

Many illustrious careers have been made studying creativity and I am certainly not going to leap blindly into the deep end of that pool. In the abstract, however, creativity is basically about making connections in ways and between things you wouldn't normally make and do. I suppose it's a kind of metathinking (thinking about thinking), but in a directed and at least partially disciplined way.

In screenwriting, for example, one manifestation of this metathinking frequently involves mentally putting yourself in someone else's skin, a character's in this case, and looking at the world you have created through their eyes.

Fortunately we come to the process of being 'intentionally creative' with a wide range of skills and experience that will all prove useful. There are only two problems.

1  We are not always aware of all of these skills and areas of experience as skills and areas of experience.

2  People who don't understand writing tell us that's where the sum of
our creativity is to be found.

*This brings us to that great crime against creativity which this book is
written in part to address: the advice to 'write what you know'.*

'Write what you know' is what bored teachers used to tell us when we
had to write a story in school. 'Write what you know' is what parents tell
kids when they are stuck for ideas—the parents, not the kids. It is what
students often tell me they have learned in (bad) writing classes. I bet
somewhere, sometime in your past, somebody has given you this little
mind-killer of an advice nugget at least once. Google it as a phrase and
you will see how often somebody blogs it as a homily.

The assumption here is that, if you stick to your areas of specialist
knowledge and direct experience, then you will find the task of coming
up with good ideas easier; the process of writing smoother; and the
stories you write will be more likely to come across as somehow
'authentic' … whatever that means.

Of course, like most clichés, it has a grain of truth.

Of course, like most clichés, it is also utter rubbish.


## Write what you know?

This is such a commonplace, reductive statement that it tells you
nothing.

How could you *not* do this as a writer? We each bring such a diverse
and personal range of general and specific knowledge, to say nothing
of our memories, hopes and dreams, passions and prejudices (big and
small; conscious and unconscious), to each and every creative undertaking that we might as easily—and just as reductively—say: 'write who
you are.'

You will. Up to a point you can't avoid it.

Indeed one of the tasks of a good writer is to bring a self-critical
perspective to exactly that inevitability. Good writing is as much about
carefully and selectively purging certain manifestations of your own
unique voice from your work as it is about celebrating and glorying in it.
For those of you who have already tried writing screenplays, ask yourself
this revealing question (as I have myself on occasion): 'Why do all my
characters sometimes sound alike?' The answer is probably because they
all sound like you.

## Write what you never realized that you knew?

Well now we are starting to get somewhere. Writing should be about pushing your own personal and creative boundaries, and the first step is to test out where those boundaries actually are.

This does *not* equate to writing = therapy.

That way, self-regarding, jejune, unfinished or unwatchable dross lies. Do writers work through issues with which they are struggling in their own lives in their writing? Of course, all the time, whether they know it or not. We'll even give some examples of this in later chapters. But for good writers, this is what underpins first-rate storytelling and innovative character development; *it is not an end in itself.*

Having said that, one of the true joys of writing lies in finding your untapped resources, making new connections, unearthing the long-forgotten and reinvigorating the once-vital.

There's one more step you need to take, however.

## Write what you *don't* know

You want to be a writer and, despite what everyone—including me—is telling you about the mundanities of narrative economy and show, don't tell, and the tyranny of the format nerds, your duty to yourself is first and foremost to be the best writer you can be.

The way to do that is to start by relaxing and not worrying about all that other stuff. There will be time enough for building it all back in later, if you need to and before anyone else actually sees your screenplay.

For now, writing should be an adventure, and your first tasks are to:

- Take creative risks.
- Experiment.
- Research.
- Learn something new.
- **Write what you *don't* know.**

That's what the next chapter is all about.

# 2

## Screenwriting: The Hardest Easy Thing You Will Ever Do

Actually, screenwriting is a really hard thing to do well. That's why so few writers break through out of all those who aspire. Like most professions, doing it well takes time and practice and dedication. That scares off most of the lazy writers after a while, because there are no real shortcuts for time and practice and dedication. Remember how we already talked about the importance of perseverance? Well, if you want to be a screenwriter you will surely be tested.

Having said that, screenwriters have something of a head start in learning their craft compared to their fellows writing for other media. For a start there are industrial rules and practices to follow. These are a mixed blessing, to be sure, but they do offer us checks and reminders when we need them. Also, writing a screenplay means producing far fewer pages than your average novel. Again that's a mixed blessing, but I suppose it can be an advantage. Besides, it must be easy, after all, nobody is releasing industry-standard formatting software for novels, right?

There's a comedy sketch in there somewhere, a Saturday Night Live style fake commercial perhaps. Go write and shoot one for the 26 people who will find it funny. Now where was that hotkey to [Insert Narrative Voice]?

Easy or not, we have to start somewhere, and the first step in overcoming the tyranny of the blank page is to get in the right mindset to be creative. To this end, this chapter is all about motivation, creativity and encouragement, with more than a dash of Public Service Announcement thrown in. If you are dead keen to start down the screenplay path immediately, you can skip ahead to the next chapter. You'll be missing some fun stuff—I make cheap jokes about *Twilight* for a start—but maybe you'll come back and check it out later on.

We have already introduced a few simple screenwriting concepts to help keep us honest. This chapter backs us up past them. It won't be the only place in the book where this happens. There will be a little pattern of retracing our steps so as to understand important stages in our journey towards a screenplay.

One of the hardest challenges you will face as a budding screenwriter is simply conceiving a script project in such a way that it will have a chance of working as a story. There are so many ways in which writers—even experienced ones—can make poor choices at the beginning, effectively shooting themselves in the foot and killing off any prospect of their script working down the track, that I am going to spend some time warning you about many of the common (and a few not so common) mistakes I tend to come across in my teaching work.

At times it may feel like a whole lot of negative criticism, but remember that we learn from history so as not to repeat it. Also there will be the usual dodgy jokes and the sad tale of a guy who, against my advice, wanted to travel back in time to kill Hitler. There will also be plenty of encouragement for all the good reasons you might want to write. I haven't forgotten my promise to point out the snakes on your trail, but most of these can be avoided with a little forethought.

This chapter is also about the challenge of **writing what you don't know**. For me, this is the very heart and definition of creativity. It is about turning old ideas around and making them anew. It is about thinking laterally and using that new perspective to see the world and your story afresh.

The novelist Donald Windham (*The Dog Star*) once wrote: 'I disagree with the advice "Write about what you know." Write about what you need to know in an effort to understand.' So **writing what you don't know** is also about engaging with subjects that will inform, enlighten and deepen your own understanding of the human condition. We write because we want to know more, even if that means increasing our understanding of a familiar subject. Of course we also write because we want to entertain, even if our definitions of what constitutes entertainment may be varied and personal.

**Writing what you don't know** is about being open to unsought connections and finding unique ways to use the ideas you already have. We will discuss what makes a good movie idea in much more detail later on; this chapter is more about ideas in general and where they come from. Before we start to write stories for a formula-driven movie world, we need to take a few moments to prepare our best formula-busting weapons. Even if we love the formulas imposed on us by genres, we need to find ways of making them feel fresh and alive; that's where **writing what you don't know** comes in.

**Writing what you don't know** is not about celebrating ignorance. Only a fool or a crazy person launches themself into completely uncharted territory without some kind of a map. For me, one of the great pleasures of **writing what you don't know** is learning enough about that uncharted territory to risk an adventure. Then again, our definitions of foolishness and lunacy are often pretty close to our definitions of creativity and genius.

I called my book **Write What You Don't Know** as an encouragement for you to push out beyond your comfort zone and to embrace new ideas and creative possibilities. Much of what is to come in this book deals with *accepted ways of doing things*. That has a lot to do with helping you speak a language your peers and colleagues in movie land will understand. There are usually good reasons why you should at least pay attention to those rules and strictures. They have accumulated over time as reflections by professionals on the experienced history and development of your chosen medium. They also make sense from the perspective of those to whom you will be submitting your scripts.

The danger in learning about screenwriting is that a young writer becomes overwhelmed or cowed by the sense they are somehow merely working to formulas, and kind of shuts down creatively once they have found false security in 'the answer' to 'how it is done.' My title is there to remind us that, in this rule-bound craft, there is always room for innovation, imagination and creative exploration. I won't always be pointing at it in the writing every few sentences from now on, I'll just trust that it is still waving at you from the background whenever you feel like you are getting formulated to death.

On that note…

### Kind of a pep talk: you should write a movie

The world is full of people trying to give you advice on *how* to write a screenplay.

                    FRIENDLY ME
          Hi there.

Yeah, him as well, if you let him. They all mean well, but most people just assume you want to write because … well, *why?* There are lots of reasons to write a screenplay, some good, some bad, some personal and some pretty universal. It is surprising that more isn't written about the why, because the answer may have a great deal to do with whether or not you actually manage to finish a draft and, if you do, whether what you end up with will be worth reading, let alone making into a movie.

Before we launch ourselves into the world of ideas, creativity, structure, format and all that good stuff then, let's take a moment to address the why of it.

In time-honored tradition, we'll have the bad news first. If you really want to be a screenwriter, you need to go into things with your eyes open. I want to be honest with you and, in the abstract, the prospects of success can sometimes look bleak.

Remember we talked about how there are too many spec screenplays in the world?

Most of them are terrible. I have read a great many and written or worked on a few dodgy ones myself, so this is not just me being arrogant; it is the basic and depressing truth.

Most of the decent ones will never get read by anyone who has the power to get a movie made from them, because their writers don't have access to the right people.

Most of those that do will never get reads from people who truly appreciate, desire, are courageous enough to risk developing or can afford their qualities and, thus, they will not get made.

A very few will go into development, and many of those will never actually get made (writers usually get paid something at this point, however, so yay writers). I've been there as well—we call it 'development hell'—and it is always painful.

Of the ones that do get into development, some are ruined by stupid development executives or simply by the often contradictory and perverse exigencies of the business that is show.

Some of that tiny proportion of screenplays that still remain are taken out of the control of their original writers and handed over for rewrites to other writers who are believed to possess whatever version of the 'Barton Fink feeling' the development execs think is missing from the original. Sometimes the new writer works with the old one and sometimes they work independently. By the way, I have also been that re-write guy, so I know how it works. This re-writing process often happens in parallel to the original writer's redrafting process—and usually without telling him or her, by the way. Studios will simply bring another writer or another team in to give new options and insights on the story without—or at least before—removing the original writer/s from the project.

And don't get me started on the myriad problems that emerge to scupper many of the tiny minority that finally do make it into production ...

                    IMPLIED YOU
          No. I'm not going to do it.

> FRIENDLY ME
> You're not going to do what?

> IMPLIED YOU
> This is a total set-up and I am not
> playing along. I can read you like
> a book by now, you know? Dammit.
> You know what I mean.

> FRIENDLY ME
> I'm sure I don't know what you
> mean.

> IMPLIED YOU
> Right. This is a 'pep talk,' but
> you start by whining about how
> writing screenplays is a hopeless
> thing to do.

> FRIENDLY ME
> Oh, I never said that.

> IMPLIED YOU
> Aha, exactly, aha! So now I say
> something dumb and predictable
> like: 'Oh, you're not being very
> encouraging' and you're all: 'Aha,
> my subtle and fiendish rhetorical
> trap is sprung,' and then you twirl
> your moustache and explain how
> actually this is all beside the
> point because here are all the
> great reasons why you should write
> a screenplay anyway.

> FRIENDLY ME
> Um.

> IMPLIED YOU
> Busted.

Implied You dances a little dance of joy and victory.

> IMPLIED YOU (CONT'D)
> We're doing scene description now?

> FRIENDLY ME
> Apparently.

> IMPLIED YOU
> Come on then. Dig yourself out of
> that.

> FRIENDLY ME
> Aha. Wait. Wait. Aha. No.

IMPLIED YOU
If happiness was a snake, I'd so be
an anaconda right now. Hmm. You
still haven't quite got me yet,
have you?

FRIENDLY ME
Working on it. Aha. Yes, aha. I
have a teaching moment and it comes
right from me working on your
character. OK, yes, I am going to
go on to talk about why you should
be writing. You were always going
to be my segue here, but I thought
I would take charge and have the
first lines and you would plug in
with questions like before.

IMPLIED YOU
But I surprised you.

FRIENDLY ME
Yes, you did, and that's a good
thing, for two reasons. Firstly it
means that I have internalized your
character enough by now that you
spoke up in my mind. I made you
kind of prickly and smart and a bit
bolshie and that meant you wouldn't
take being my patsy lying down.
When a character is starting to
work, writers often find that
character takes over their thoughts
as they write.

IMPLIED YOU
I like that—and the second reason?

FRIENDLY ME
Ah, the second reason is that your
mini revolution let me launch our
dialogue with a little conflict, and
an intriguing little hook that let
us bypass all the introductory
stuff and just get to the point.
This is a good lesson for writing
tight scenes. Of course we waffled
on afterwards, but we still learned
some stuff about dialogue.

IMPLIED YOU
Go on then, tell me why I should
write a screenplay. I'm so going to
anyway though.

```
                    FRIENDLY ME
          First I want to check you aren't
          doing it for all the wrong reasons.
```

## Bad reasons to write a screenplay

I want to spend a little time on this, because there are identifiable patterns of cause and effect with many bad scripts, and because exploring some of them will make all the hours one spends reading them a little more worthwhile. Stay with me, because there are useful warnings here.

OK here are some classics:

## When 'Write What You Know' attacks!

This is one of the major pitfalls of being too close to your subject. There is nothing wrong with using your life experience to inform your writing—we already established that you will do this anyway whether you are trying to or not. Where writers often get into real trouble is when they can't get enough emotional and critical distance from the personal experience that is driving their story. The biggest clichés in this broad category include the following:

1 The attempted romantic comedy which gradually turns into a bitter and twisted relationship confessional because the writer is still dealing with leftover crap from their last failed romance. Top tip: When you set out to write *Fluffy Wovey Bunny-Wunnies II: The Refluffening*, but end up with *All Men Are Bastards* or *All Women Are Witches*, you are in no shape to write a romcom. Give it up or turn it into the horror movie it clearly wants to become.
2 *Teen Suicide Is Awesome*. No it isn't.
3 And neither is its close relative, *Endless Spiral Of Depressing Crap My Protagonist Can't Escape From Because That's What Life Is Really Like Man And I Know Because I'm On Pills For My Nerves*. Unless you are Ken Loach or Mike Leigh. And then only maybe.
4 'Sid ... where's the drugs?' Movies about drug culture and people overdosing, made under the assumption that simply showing people smoking dope or shooting up is somehow radical or transgressive. It's not big and it's not clever and you are not being Alex Cox or Dennis Hopper or Darren Aronofsky, and you have no imagination. Write a proper story and don't make me slap you.

## When 'Write What You Don't Know' attacks!

Yes, I'm afraid this can go horribly wrong as well. It's all very well to want to challenge yourself to move out of your writerly foxhole, but going over the top without the body armor of at least some detailed knowledge of your subject is often kind of silly.

1 Oh dear, oh dear, it's a gangster movie. American version: *Say Hello to My Little ... Clue*. Not for nothing, with all due respect, but you haven't been to a sit-down outside Satriale's and you don't know your badda from your bing. English version: *I'm A Cockney Geezer, You Muppet*. No, you are an upper middle class, public school educated wanker (it takes one to know one) and I feel I must apologize to everyone on behalf of the land of my birth for the many crimes to cinema committed in the wake of *Lock, Stock and Two Smoking Barrels* (1998). At least that one was fun.

2 The same kind of problem happens with most genres, but I just want to offer one specific cautionary tale here: never write a script about some random guy who goes back through time to kill Hitler before he comes to power. This is a dodgy idea at the best of times, but even more so when you know nothing of time travel, Hitler, history and politics in general or even basic European geography. I had this one in front of me from a student once and, no matter how much I warned the writer, he just wouldn't be told. In fact he ended up shooting a battle of the Somme 'trench warfare' sequence in the beautiful, sunny New Forest with a stoner-looking bloke playing Hitler wandering around in Vietnam-era green fatigues amidst the pathetic wisps coughed out by a small, asthmatic disco smoke machine. Hey, I tried. [Note to the non-British amongst you: The New Forest is an ancient National Park involving significant numbers of trees, ponies and pubs in the south of England. The Somme was a hellhole of mud, blood and fire, slightly worse even than the scene after closing time outside British pubs.]

We'll spend some more time thinking about the importance of research in a section called '*Learning something new: the joys of research. Yes, really.*'

## 'I want to make lots of green'

This can happen of course with your first spec script but, in the scheme of things, it is very unlikely. This is especially true if your contacts in movie land can be summed up by the amazing coincidence that your second cousin's girlfriend's labradoodle's vet's receptionist kind of knows this flaky production assistant she met this one time in a bar and his name was Chad or Sven or Sanjay or something and maybe he gave her his number but she'd have to empty out her purse to check.

Usually it takes a long time, a number of 'training scripts' and a lot of hard work to improve your writing to the point at which you should be shopping it around. Screenwriting is not a reliable get-rich-quick scheme. As a motivation for creativity, money alone—hey, we'd all like some cash—is really shallow and won't sustain your effort very long unless you have some other source of commitment to back it up.

### 'I want supermodels on my d'

Clearly you have never heard the oldest filmmakers' joke:

> Did you hear about the ambitious actor who had no clue?
> He slept with the screenwriter.

Stranger things have happened, but unless you already possess the skills and talent to entice the aforementioned supermodels onto your afore-mentioned d, this is a doubly stupid reason to start writing.

### 'Pfft, I could do that, it's just some car chases and 'splosions, how hard can it be?'

I know I say screenwriting is the hardest *easy* thing you can do, but there is a reason for the *hard* part of that sentence. Car chases and 'splosions are not the only things you will have to write. Pesky subtle and compli-cated things like story and characters always get in their way—or at least they should.

By the way, writing a *unique and compelling* action movie is one of the hardest things for a screenwriter to do. That's why anyone who can do it well *is* paid lots and lots of green and may just possibly have actual supermodels on their actual ... well, you get the idea.

While we are on the subject, there has been a trend towards the replacement of action with ACTION in movies in recent years. The former is all about advancing the story in a dynamic, exciting and spectacular way while the latter is about ladling more and more kinetic gravy onto your serving of roast plot until empty kinesis drowns the meat of the movie ... (Tonight on Fox: 'When Mixed Metaphors Attack!') This is how the two 'T2' movies of the last 20 years might put it, if asked:

*Terminator 2: Judgment Day* (scr. James Cameron & William Wisher Jr.; 1991): 'Story, meet action. Get to know one another because you're going to be working as a team.'

*Transformers: Revenge of the Fallen* (scr. Ehren Kruger & Roberto Orci & Alex Kurtzman; 2009): 'Dude, we're totally gonna blow shit up!'

By the way, you might be wondering about the difference between 'and' and '&' in the screenwriting citations I use in this book. The distinction comes from the way in which the Writers Guild of America distinguishes credits for screenwriters. Basically '&' refers to members of a writing team (x *&* y wrote together), whereas 'and' refers to writers who worked on separate drafts (x *and* y both worked on the script but y came in to rewrite after x was fired, or similar). There is a complicated procedure used to decide who gets credit for what. Some movies will have had many more writers working on them than get an actual credit. A famous example of this was *The Flintstones* (1994). The writing credits went to Tom S. Parker & Jim Jennewein and Steven E. de Souza, but it is rumored that up to 60 writers were involved at one time or another. I'll leave you to judge the fruit of their labor.

## Copying the 'hot' concept, or: 'Amagawd, I totally got off on *Transformers 2*!!11one'

Talk of the devil. Now this is an appalling admission for anyone other than a hyperactive, sugar rushing, intellectually challenged ten-year-old (of any age). I feel I should somehow be made to sit sheepishly on the White House lawn, putting up with Joe Biden's hail-fellow-well-met jokes and pretending I drink Pabst Blue Ribbon just for saying it. It hints at another *really* bad reason to write a screenplay, however: copying the 'hot' concept instead of finding one of your own. It's all too common and, along with its friends above, sums up much that is wrong with the average screenplay written by an untrained or unimaginative writer.

Let me tell you about the way these guys will usually write. I have read enough screenplays of this sort to know they could not possibly have been written any other way.

They will typically follow whatever genre or format is currently hot, not realizing that it was actually hot a couple of years ago when there were competing projects in development at the studios or on TV. That genre or format is almost certainly no longer hot now. The movies have come out, most have flopped, the executives who green lit them have been fired or promoted and those now on the inside are already onto the next big thing or the one after that, because their professional survival depends on it.

As I write these words, the 'hot' format our wannabe writers will be picking up on might well be ghastly, anodyne, sexless, tween vampire romances (not to be confused with Buffy and Angel who are, of course, still awesome). There are other options but, whatever they pick up on, by the time you read these words it will certainly be something else.

The problem is that the 'supermodels on my d' kind of writer typically believes that slavish adherence to the hot format is their key rather than the uniqueness of their concept—or at least the uniqueness of their take on an established concept—and the quality of their character creation and storytelling. They are not out to write a work of real imagination that takes their chosen genre forward like *Låt Den Rätte Komma In/Let The Right One In* (2008), or even *Bakjwi/Thirst* (2009) have recently done for vampire movies. Rather, they are just out to write a stale second-order sucky Sookie or smelly Bella clone, even if they don't realize it at the time.

They will note key scenes and situations and write their screenplay by focusing on cramming as many of those scenes and situations into it as possible. If you cup your hand to your ear and turn it in the direction of Los Angeles on a quiet night (try it now) you might be able to hear the refrain from thousands of these hopeful writers telling their friends: 'I'm writing a movie, bro. It's going to have all this cool stuff in it.' This is what we might refer to, in technical terms, as an 'ass backwards' approach to screenwriting.

Their screenplays will have all the key moments you would expect from this kind of movie. Now, although I'm a huge vampire movie fan, I stopped watching *True Blood* pretty fast (the vampires were lame) and I refused to go see *Twilight* (2008) (the vampires were lame) despite comedy prodding from various friends and students. This means the following list is the product of guesswork and decoding random hormonal explosions in class (translation: occasional unwarranted gushing about Robert Pattinson—yes, that means you, Morgan) because there are some things I just won't research. My admitted slackness notwithstanding, I'm willing to lay Really Small Amounts of Money that this invented *Twilight* plot outline will be close enough for government work. Ah, low hanging fruit, my favorite kind of fruit:

*Contains Mild Pining:* mawkish whining; mawkish diary writing; being randomly pale and possessing floppy hair; complaining about how hard it is to be emo—sorry a vampire—sorry a tediously self-absorbed teenage girl; random standing on a treetop in the moonlight; la la la you like truly understand me and see into my soul / lack of soul and shit and like complete me and stuff so I'll let you open-mouth kiss me because that means we are like in love and stuff la la la; awkward snogging; bigger vampires came; you shan't have her, you just shan't; I won't fall for your clever kidnappy schemes—curses, you tricked me; oh noes, I appear to be in Mild Peril; don't worry, I'm coming to save you using my emo vampire super speed and shit; woe is me, evul vampires bit me; emo vampire v. evul vampire douche-off; suck out that contagion—giggle, I said suck; make me a vampire because I'll love you like forever and ever and not just until the next boy band arrives; more awkward snogging; roll credits to Death Cab For Cutie or similar. Per se.

Now, the original was very successful and clearly hit every hormone it aimed at in its intended audience. Good for the writers and the cast and the crew. The point is, the clone movie written by the 'supermodels on my d' guys will have all those moments—all that 'cool stuff'—only it will read like the prose equivalent of a Xeroxed photograph (in other words, see my fake outline above, only minus the attempts at humor). It kind of looks the same, only all the life and energy and joy has been flattened out of it and nobody, I mean *nobody* who writes like that, is ever going to get a script sale.

Apart from That One Guy.

I don't exactly know who 'that one guy' is, but there is always some exception to the rule whose unlikely success after doing things exactly the wrong way serves as sufficient justification for every other hopeless hoper to try the same thing. Of course, the reason it happens is usually linked to a unique multi-car pileup between luck, pluck, timing and raw talent and is, thus, functionally unrepeatable.

Don't you just hate That One Guy?

Fortunately you are not merely a hopeless hoper, dear implied reader. How do I know? Well for a start you are reading books about how to actually *do* that whole screenwriting thing. That puts you one big step ahead in your thinking already. See—there is actual pep in this talk after all.

## Good reasons to write a screenplay

So why should you add your clutter to the already cluttered film world with yet another spec script? Well, first and foremost it's not my place to tell you what you should or shouldn't do. My job is merely to inject a little realism into the discussion, help you with some common challenges and warn you about where people have gone wrong in the past. Let's start with how some of you are probably feeling right about now:

### 'I don't know exactly but I love movies and it's my dream and I don't know—wait, I already said that ...'/blush /facepalm /hide

Good. Don't be embarrassed. Keep reading. Everyone starts from somewhere and you love movies and you dream of writing one. That's a brilliant start because it gives you all the best reasons to write: subject knowledge and personal investment. Hopefully this book will help get you going, but you already have the most important tools to help you persevere.

### 'I have something really important I need to say'

Ah now, that's a good reason in the making. I don't care whether the subject of your story is personal or political; moral, emotional, intellectual; or all of these in a crazy mixture and more. What's important right now is your need to tell it. What you have to find is the personal discipline to be able to step a pace backward so as to view your subjectivity with some objectivity. Without it you are in danger of shouting random heartfelt stuff into the void.

This is really important because, if you are writing about a political, philosophical or historical issue, or a person about whom you feel passionately, the way to kill your story for a general audience is to be over-reverential. That can turn it all too quickly into another instance of *When 'Write What You Know' Attacks.*

I mentioned the term 'hagiography' in the first chapter. This refers to a genre of medieval narratives recounting the life and miraculous works of saints. Hagiographies were really catalogues of good deeds, not juicy tell-all tabloid biographies, and were typically uncritical of their subjects. If you are writing a biopic, for example, you would do well to keep it as far away from being like a hagiography as you can while still being fair to your subject. If you don't, all the lovely conflict and tension that comes from having real, flawed and often contradictory human characters and gives your story impetus, emotional truth and depth will be hard to find. It is very hard to like General Patton as he is presented in the 1970 biopic that bears his name. He really was an appalling nutter. One of his biographers even writes: 'We admire Patton the captain, we relish Patton the legend, but we are, at the very least, uneasy with Patton the man.' Nevertheless, the combination of a strong, unflinching script from Francis Ford Coppola and Edmund H. North, and an Oscar-winning performance from George C. Scott, mean that it is equally hard to come away from the movie without some kind of grudging respect for the man and his accomplishments.

*I take a deep breath and prepare to duck and cover ...*

I really don't want to get into a whole religious thing here, but a challenge that comes up fairly regularly in class in the US is helping and advising students who identify as Christians and who want to write stories which deal directly with their faith and its doctrine. I mention they are Christians only because, to date, I have encountered no instances of people of other faiths wanting to do the same kind of writing. Make of that what you will.

Now of course people are perfectly entitled to write about whatever catches their imagination. In this particular circumstance, however, the writers usually find it very difficult and in some cases impossible to get much of a perspective on their ideas beyond a conviction that they are right. Look at it like this: whatever your beliefs, you have to decide who your story is aimed at—who your primary audience is. If you want to help other people come to understand, respect and find value in what you believe, you need to find a means and a language to communicate at a level beyond preaching to the converted. What this means is that you need to understand and be able to reflect upon your political philosophy or your religion at a level of subtlety, fluency and complexity far beyond the ability to simply spout its doctrine in the language and with the vocabulary of that doctrine.

That brings us back, once again, to the issue of **writing what you don't know. Writing what you don't know** does not mean changing your philosophy of life—although, who knows, sometimes it just might. Rather, in this case it means being open enough in your own mind to see outside of yourself and understand that, because not everyone thinks like you, you have to try extra hard to find an approach to storytelling that will open them up to your way of thinking, not close them off from it.

The more you speak your political or religious story *as doctrine*, the faster you shrink your audience. The more you speak *the same story* in human terms, the more people are likely to be engaged with it and with the issues of faith or politics which inform it. C. S. Lewis understood that when he wrote the *Chronicles of Narnia*, and so did George Orwell when he wrote *Animal Farm*. Even though ostensibly they were both writing about talking animals, 'human terms' still very much applies.

Incidentally, if any of you are now curious about hagiography after that little aside, you could do much worse than take a look at Abbot Ælfric's *Lives of Saints*. For those few of you who join me in not being fluent in Middle English, modern translations are available. Enjoy.

Indeed, the lives of saints and mystics have frequently given good value as the inspiration for a wide range of films from *Simón del Desierto/Simon of the Desert* (1965) to *A Man for all Seasons* (1966). In fact I happen to have a talented grad student working on a very promising screenplay which deals with the stories of three of the more unusual 'saints' of the US / Mexican border region right now. To tell you that one is Jesus Malverde, the patron saint of Mexican drug smugglers, might give you a sense of it.

Remember, **writing what you don't know** is also about learning new things. I'm not suggesting you all go off and write a biopic of Christina the Astonishing but, then again, the very wonderful Nick Cave wrote a song about her, so it's not as far out as you might imagine. After all, if you had asked me a page ago if I was going to mention Abbot Ælfric in this book, I would have laughed at you.

### 'My story is so visual it just needs to be filmed'

This is a great reason to write a screenplay. In fact it is one of the best reasons, and yet so many aspiring writers still write radio plays with FADE IN at the front. Yes, you can offer *My Dinner with Andre* (1981) and so forth as counter-argument, but the general point still holds. Film is, first and foremost, a visual medium, so one of the defining reasons to write for that medium is to communicate in visual terms.

Who cares about the difficulty of getting it made? If your idea screams for a cinematic treatment, it would be foolish to work in another idiom. Indeed a wonderfully visual story is more likely to get positive attention.

By the way, when talking about visually rich scripts I don't mean just costume dramas and effects-laden, blockbustery epics. Take, for example, a smart and thoroughly charming little film like *(500) Days of Summer* (scr. Scott Neustadter & Michael H. Weber; 2009) which I happened to see this week. Not only does it play entertaining games with chronology, taking us back and forth within the titular (500) days of the Quirky Relationship™ between characters played by Joseph Gordon-Levitt and Zooey Deschanel (the eponymous Summer), but it uses a range of cinematic devices to keep us buckled into the emotional roller-coaster that is Joseph's side of the relationship. These range from simple graphic intertitles, through a split-screen sequence at a party with the screen halves labeled 'EXPECTATIONS' and 'REALITY', to a joyfully knowing public dance sequence (à la *Enchanted* 2007) the morning after the relationship is consummated.

In an interview with Katey Rich, Neustadter explains the writers' choices like this: 'I think we're really inside his head. From the minute we start the movie, there's a narrator, and there's flashbacks to him as a kid. There's discussions [sic] of movies and music and all those things. We're saying, this character is going to be telling you this story, but he's not the most reliable guy, because he is so warped by pop culture. I think that because we decided that very early on, we sort of have to stick to that logic and those rules; we are able to do some of that fun stuff. Otherwise it would make no sense.'

The relationship portrayed in the film is based on a real romantic disaster in Neustadter's life. Impressively he had the strength and perspective—or the friend and writing partner to help him find the strength and perspective—not to turn his story into *All Women Are Witches*.

## 'I have an idea that I love for a story, but I don't know whether it should be a novel or a screenplay'

This is a common question, especially if this is your first attempt at writing a long form narrative. If it could work as a screenplay we get to the core of the 'hardest easy thing' issue.

Here is a fast test to see if your idea would work better as a novel or a movie. Ask yourself these three questions:

1  *How do you imagine your story's voice?* Is it essential that the narration (the mechanism for the telling of your story) works through internal dialog? If so, a novel might be the best format to support that. There are always exceptions, one of which has been the hardboiled detective who always seems to be talking through voice over. Characters that are overtly disturbed, solipsistic or narcissistic also frequently get a

free pass—think of *Dexter* or *Gossip Girl* on TV. Typically, despite those examples, many genre stories have external catalysts rather than internal: *Halloween* (1978) lands on the young community of Haddonfield because of Michael Myers. They don't go searching for him. Likewise, Luke Skywalker would still be kicking his heels at Uncle Owen's moisture farm on Tatooine if a certain two droids hadn't come across his path. Yes, yes, destiny blah, blah. Mention midichlorians—or attempt to correct my spelling to midi-chlorians—and I won't be responsible for my actions.

2 *What is the visual scale of your story?* In a novel you can write: 'All the legions of Rome appear over the hill,' and all it costs you is a little ink. In a movie you suddenly need to pay, feed, costume, transport and house those legions or, more likely, pay some animators a lot of money to CG them in. Either way, that little line just unleashed hell on your budget. It goes the same way for locations. Each one costs money in a movie and nothing on the page. Add them all up and they can really add up. These aren't exactly 'right or wrong' issues for either a novel or a movie (after all, sword and sandal flicks have been around almost since the start of cinema, although I meant the example more generally), but you do need to give them some thought, especially in a first spec script.

3 *How badly do you want to be able to control every aspect of your story?* If your answer is 'very badly' and your clout in movie world is less than zero, maybe go write a novel. If you value the collaborative nature of a movie project and can get your head around the possibility that collaboration might come to mean that it gets taken entirely out of your hands and given to someone else, then keep reading!

## 'I want to be a director'

So does everybody else and their labradoodle's vet's receptionist. But, unlike many directing wannabes, you realize that directors need something to actually … direct. Well done. The best directors, even if they are not themselves writers, have a vision of the world or an agenda that they want to explore and communicate. Otherwise what do they think being a director is all about?

```
                    IMPLIED YOU
        Having supermodels on your d?

                    FRIENDLY ME
        Indeed, but I think it's time to
        free those poor supermodels. They
```

```
      have played their part in exposing
      the mindset of the movie doofus,
      and we are grateful. Now they
      can venture out, blinking in
      the sunlight of a new dawn and
      enjoy all of the non-d related
      activities this wonderful world
      has to offer.

                   IMPLIED YOU
           Bye, supermodels, have fun.
```

The best way to realize your dream of directing is to write your own scripts and make your first films. Unless you have a parent who is running a major studio or is successfully blackmailing somebody who is, nobody is going to give you a shot at directing professionally without some kind of track record. A track record could start with the shorts you made at film school, the webisodic comedy you post on your blog, or even the low-tech but brilliantly imaginative rock videos you made independently. Whatever you make, somebody had to write the scripts.

Maybe you have a friend or partner who is a great writer. Even so, you still need to collaborate with them and understand what they do. At the very least, directors need to know how to talk to writers and communicate their ideas and problems in terms writers will understand. What better way to learn this than to have written yourself?

Of course, you will still need a great idea.

## Ideas and where the pesky things hide

Creativity is a huge topic and much of it lies well outside the scope of this book. I do want to address it, however, because students often admit to being stuck for ideas right at the beginning. Often their solution is to ask me impossible-to-answer-in-a-way-that-applies-to-anybody-other-than-myself-type questions like: 'How do I get my ideas?'

This is officially the naffest question you can ever ask a writer because it really translates as 'how can I be you?' Obviously you can't be me—sighs of relief all round; you can only be you. For that very reason, of all the subjects I am going to cover in this book, this is the most contingent, partial and probably doomed to failure before I even begin. I'm still going to give it a go, however.

The secret to creativity is being creative. Helpful, eh? While I can't hope to tell you anything about how to do the *you* parts of your own creativity, I can talk a little in the abstract about how people have tried to address or illustrate the subject. We're going to go on to talk about movie concepts properly in Chapter 4. This section is just a kind of introduction to creative thinking in general, with some movie examples to give us a little focus. Along the way we are going to try and simplify and encapsulate it as the intersection between the **write what you know** and the **write what you don't know** impulses you will be bringing to your writing.

Let's start by offering ourselves a basic model. How basic, you ask? Well, it's going to be pretty much scraping-the-bottom-of-the- barrel-because-I'm-not-a-psychologist basic. Basic enough, indeed, that we get sold it all the time in the movies!

### Creativity in the movies

Ilan Mitchell-Smith and Anthony Michael Hall are nerds.

What's worse for them is that they are nerds in *Weird Science* (scr. John Hughes), a movie made in 1985, before the advent of geek chic or whatever the young people are calling it these days. This means they get picked on by everyone including Robert Downey Jnr.; can't get a date to save their lives; have Bill Paxton for a nemesis; and, to top it all off, they are forced to dress in mid-1980s suburban mallrat teen drone 'fashions.' I haven't seen the movie for many years but I have the horrid, partially repressed memory of jackets with rolled up sleeves being involved at some point.

At least, as nerds, they have the hots for science and huge amounts of excess adolescent hormones on their side, and these twin impera-tives push them to use a computer to create a digital composite of their ultimate woman as some presciently pre-internet virtual porn. Not enough processing power? No problem, hack the government's computers. And then the lightning storm happens. And then they can't turn off the machines. And then—boom bang pfft (but mostly pfft)—they have created something unexpected because a real-life Kelly LeBrock appears in blue pants and still won't have sex with them (swizz). She has special powers instead (swindle) and various and sundry pranks ensue until eventually, thankfully, the movie ends and, if you are anything like me, you are left with Johnny Rotten's famous aside ringing in your head: 'Do you ever feel like you've been cheated?'

This, then, is one standard movie model for creativity. Let's call it the **Mad Scientist Model**:

Obsessive intention + unique knowledge and experience + (optional)
serendipity = creativity

There may be more blue pants involved, but *Weird Science* is just
teening up the creative process of *Frankenstein* (1931), along with its
life-giving lightning and overreaching scientists. Here, instead of being
soundly spanked by the plot for their impertinence as they would
have been in a horror movie, our heroes get to go through the whole,
biting-off-more-than-you-can-chew-until-you-grow-a-pair-and-learn-
to-chew-better, teen movie redemptive ending.

We get a comedy pet-related version in *Frankenweenie* (1984), a
teen-gothic version in *Edward Scissorhands* (1990) and even a feminist
science fiction version in *Making Mr. Right* (1987), in which the android
creation becomes more emotionally responsive than its cold-hearted
scientist creator and switches roles with him, having found true love
with Ann Magnuson. As you do.

Another well-trodden movie path links creativity, usually expressed
as 'genius,' even more directly with mental instability or at least
insecurity in one form or another. We are presented with masochistic,
driven obsession in *Lawrence of Arabia* (1962); a lust for glory in *Patton*
(1970); random eccentricity and bad hair in *Back to the Future* (1985),
wherein Christopher Lloyd is the shorthand of the shorthand of the mad
genius; schizophrenia in *A Beautiful Mind* (2001); surpassing loneliness
in *Tideland* (2005); and generally being a mopey, tortured, epileptic,
post-punk popster in *Control* (2007).

The second, but adjacent movie shorthand for creativity, which we
can call the **Mad Genius Model**, would go something like this:

Obsessive intention + unique knowledge and experience + catalyst of
serious mental instability + (optional) serendipity = creativity

Of course there are other models, but clearly a lot of movies are
telling us creative people that we are deeply tweaked. I wouldn't go quite
that far, but I do think creative people are 'different' in as much as they
are more likely openly to celebrate their own obsessions and less likely
to deny or repress their ideas and instincts. Certainly this can make a
creative person seem unusual or eccentric in a world that tends to reify
conformity.

And then some of us are just deeply, joyfully tweaked and there's no
point denying it.

Back to the movie model. If we dig down through the surface excess
of Gothicism and general emotional hyperbole, we can find a reasonably

realistic vision of the creative process lurking within. I am assuming, just for the sake of argument, that you are only a mad creator in the way of most writers and not actually capable of making the alchemical leap from simple galvanism to horrific demiurgy. Nonetheless, don't be afraid of a little obsession. Don't be bashful about of a lot of subject knowledge, although try to wear it lightly in your writing. And certainly do not ignore serendipity when it comes a calling.

Indeed I believe that you should actively open yourself up to the unforeseeables, the uncertainties, the chance encounters and collisions of circumstance and thought. Revel in them because they can lead you in directions you would never have traveled otherwise. Sometimes lightning will strike and you will get a new story idea, born almost fully formed from a moment of inspiration, but more often you will find a connection that lets you give your old idea a novel twist, some added depth or a new direction. This is all part of what I call **writing what you don't know**, and I believe that it is fundamental to your development as a creative person.

Creating imaginative new worlds and managing them in story terms is a major undertaking to say the least (see Chapter 3). One thinks of this as being the task of the fantasy or science fiction writer, but in fact *every story involves world creation and all characters are built for their story worlds* (or vice versa). We will discuss this in a section called '*Story worlds: their creation and destruction.*'

The history of literature is well stocked with examples of writers who have explored the nature of creative thinking. The great fictional detectives like Dupin and Holmes are masters of finding meaning in that which others ignore or are not even aware of. Their genius lies in *not* seeing the world as others do. As one of my favorite authors, the great Edgar Allan Poe, writes in *The Mystery of Marie Roget*: 'Experience has shown, and a true philosophy will always show, that a vast, perhaps the larger portion of the truth arises from the seemingly irrelevant.'

Opening yourself up to finding relevance in the seemingly irrelevant, and making creative connections to chance and uncertainty, can be powerful stuff. It is similar to the creative state the Romantic poet John Keats wrote about in 1817 in a letter to his brothers when he coined the term 'Negative Capability': '... that is when man is capable of being in uncertainties, mysteries, doubts, without any irritable reaching after fact and reason.'

Someone else who revels in the world of uncertainties is our old friend Alejandro Jodorowsky, splashing around in the deep end of **writing what you don't know**: 'I am extremely attracted to what I don't understand. My intuition tells me that there is something important to study. In cinema I cannot create an idea; it has to come to me. I plant seeds in my unconscious, go to sleep and then images emerge. I don't have ideas. I wait for them to appear. It's a different approach. It's like the thirsty explorer in the desert, imploring the heavens for a little rain. At night, I plead for my unconscious to work so I can have the idea that I need the next day. And they come.'

The famous French bande desinée artist Jean Giraud (aka Moebius) describes Jodorowsky's brain working 'like 3,000 crazy computers.' That might be just a few too many for easy management for the rest of us. I think his basic model of psychological openness and freedom of thought, of reveling in the unknown as much or even more than the familiar, is nevertheless a seductive one.

Fortunately we have another model for creative thinking all around us. It is simple and very powerful and most of us use it, or at least appreciate it, in one form or another in our everyday lives.

## Some kind of comedian

The eminent neurologist Vilayanur Ramachandran explains: 'Jokes involve juxtaposing seemingly unrelated ideas, seeing something from a novel vantage point, and that's the basis of all creativity.'

The other day, quite by accident, I came across a website offering advice on how to spice up a business presentation with humor. The author was 'David Granirer MA, North America's "Psycho" Therapist / Stand-up Comic,' and it occurred to me that anyone who reinforces his claim to wackiness with both quotation marks and italics must be onto something. Sure enough, he comes up with a decent structural definition of a basic joke: 'A joke must have at least one of two elements—exaggeration or surprise. So a good way to tell if a joke will work is to ask yourself if it contains some sort of exaggeration of reality, some sort of unexpected twist, or both.'

So a joke works as a model for creativity and is also just another example of **writing what you don't know**. To write a good joke you need to be able to see beyond the obvious and the literal and take the world and twist it somehow, giving your audience a new slant, a new perspective on your subject.

Look, here is one of my favorite schoolboy jokes:

An elephant walks up to a naked guy and asks: 'How do you breathe out of that thing?'

*'I thank you, ladies and gentlemen; I'll be here all week. Don't forget to tip your waitress.'*

Now I'm going to explain it—because that's always the way to squeeze every last drop of funny from something … To get the joke you have to understand that the elephant has mistaken the guy's penis for a trunk—in other words, his nose. With me so far? Following the complex thinking? I thought so. How does it work? It makes us see elephants as ourselves and ourselves as strange. It transforms our world, or shows us how we might look from an 'alien' perspective. It's an example of **writing what you don't know**. In fairness, it's also a dick joke and they never get old. Here's another:

Why did the pigeon fall out of the tree?
Because it was dead.
Why did the squirrel fall out of the tree?
Because it was nailed to the pigeon.

Let's not get carried away, but for a brief second that little joke turned your world from sweet to sour and then repeated the turn for full effect: world of life, meet world of death. It opened a veil and offered you a glimpse of the larger truth of mortality in our strange and cruel little world. And yet we also made funny because we made unexpected. Add some Three Stooges gags, Bruce Campbell's chin and a camera nailed to a 2 by 4, and you've got *Evil Dead II* (1987).

Culturally we grossly undervalue comedy, even though—perhaps because—it is one of our greatest sources of cultural pleasure. And yet we keep shying away from taking fun seriously. Of course humor can be powerful, subversive and even palliative. It is also the best training for any kind of creative thinking. Sadly, the lessons of comedy are all too often lost on our schools. As the educational pioneer A. S. Neill, founder of Summerhill School, once remarked: 'We do not know how much creativity is killed in the classroom.' Too often children are educated, both formally and informally, by creatively neutered people. Typically they mistake maturity for the ability to wear a tie and, thus, they train us into viewing seriousness as serious and frivolity as frivolous, whereas it is frequently the other way around.

What this leads to is limited, authoritarian thinking. And Republicans.

On the other hand, think of Tex Avery, breaking the mold of animation storytelling with his wonderful modernist cartoons populated with brilliantly realized characters like Bugs Bunny and Daffy Duck. Here was a funny man who truly understood **writing what you don't know**. In his cartoons, anything could happen and usually did. In my opinion, Avery (whether he is viewed as an individual or as the personification of a creative team) stands as one of the true creative geniuses of the 20th century. As a creative writer you want to work with half of your mind as Bugs: when you put your hand behind your back you can pull out anything that you can imagine. All you have to do is realize that you can and then open yourself up to the possibilities of doing it. In the next chapters, we will think about this kind of transformation in terms of movie genres. For now, let's think about how we might help you train your brain.

## 'Le cadavre exquis boira le vin nouveau'

The Surrealists loved playing games and undertook a wide variety of experiments in writing and art designed to help liberate the creative mind from the shackles of the everyday. They used automatic writing and collage and découpage (cut-up, similar to that later found in the work of William Burroughs) as exercises, and all of these are available to you if you want to use them to jog your synapses a little.

The most famous of their techniques is probably the 'exquisite corpse', named after one result from the first time the game was played: 'The exquisite corpse will drink the new wine.' In this game each player in turn writes part of a sentence, folds the paper and hands it to the next. The text that results marks the strange melding of several minds and, besides being fun and often ridiculous, can expose interesting and often perverse connections. Oh how André Breton and those naughty boys must have smirked and giggled.

Incidentally, the idea of the exquisite corpse turns up in one form or another in movies every now and then. For example, Hedwig sings a moving song entitled 'Exquisite Corpse' about feeling all cut up by life and relationships in *Hedwig and the Angry Inch* (2001).

Games like the exquisite corpse and the others played by the Surrealists offer a very good model for creative brainstorming. You don't need to play parlor games with poseurs in Paris to think creatively, however. Here are a few simple everyday things you can do and mini creative adventures you can have to open yourself up to new ideas and ways of thinking. These are just to get you started. I'm sure you can come up with much better ones yourselves:

1 *Change your routines.* From the time you wake up in the morning, think actively about the way you prepare for the day and all the other little ruts you don't normally think about. Decide to make small

changes just for the sake of making them, and pay attention to all the curious little newnesses that come into your life. Even something as simple as driving a different route into work can open you up to new sights and break familiar patterns of thinking. The key here—and with all the suggestions which follow—is to be aware and actively engaged with your choices and decisions.

2  *Take public transport.* If you don't usually take the bus or the subway, get out of your car and do so. Look and listen and people-watch.

3  *Have a day of opposites.* Decide that at every moment of decision today you will at least consider what it would mean to do the exact opposite.

4  *Have a pretend parallel universe 'evil you' day.* This is like the day of opposites, but this time you get to think about the evil alternatives to all of your normal actions. (I suppose if you are already evil you would need to be good for the day!) Note: please don't actually do anything evil. That would be horrid.

5  *What would ... do?* Pick somebody you know very well—a friend, relative or partner—and consider all your choices today as if from their perspective.

6  *See the world as a child.* Spend a day doing things you haven't done since you were a little kid. Don't over-think it, just try to have fun. Review at the end of the day. If you have eaten a single vegetable (except chips in the English definition, not the American) = epic fail.

7  *Eat a new dish every day for a week.* They don't have to be complicated or expensive, just something you have never eaten before. New sensations are very evocative and can lead to new areas of knowledge if you research them and their ingredients a little. A friend of mine told me the history of Worcestershire Sauce the other day. Fascinating and potentially story-worthy.

8  *Learn something new.* This could be something you have always wanted to know or it could be a complete turn-to-a-random-page-in-the-encyclopedia chance. Keep it manageable; the point isn't to start a PhD, just to give your brain new food.

9  *Make up ten stories in a day.* Divide your day into ten segments and find a twist and a story hook for each one. Use some of the ideas above to get you going if you want. How could your ride into work, your job, your friends, the cute boy/girl who works in the coffee shop you go to for lunch be involved in an adventure, a fascinating relationship, a nefarious plot? Take the basic character of people or situations you know intimately and give them some new spin. What if your best friend was actually a bank robber? A werewolf? A terrorist? Your brother/sister? Suffering in an abusive relationship?

In love with you (careful here)? Now you have a character you know well and a situation you would never have ascribed to that character. Have fun and **write what you don't know.**

10 *Play the location game.* This is similar to the ten stories except you have to pick ten locations you encounter in a day and make up stories to fit around them. The trick is that all of the stories must use their locations in a way other than for their primary function. The bowling alley story is not about bowling. The hospital drama has nothing to do with sick people (or doctor–nurse soap opera romance). Flip the obvious meaning of some of your places. The pawn shop is actually the moral center of the neighborhood. The funeral home is a place of joy and relief. Why? Because the people who work there make them so. Now you have characters also. Go off and **write what you don't know.**

In an interview with Patrick McGilligan, Larry Cohen talks about playing the location game with the Chrysler Building in New York, which led to his screenplay for the wacky and wonderful *Q* (1982):

I kept staring at the Chrysler Building and saying to myself 'Well, the Chrysler Building should have a movie about it. Why should King Kong and the Empire State Building get all the attention, when the Chrysler Building is so much better looking?' The Chrysler Building definitely needed its own movie. I saw all those birdlike gargoyles on the sides of the towers at the Chrysler Building and I told myself, 'If a giant bird flew over New York City looking for a nest, it would certainly head directly for that feathered pinnacle that shines so brightly over the city in the reflection of the sun.'

Add the reincarnation of an Aztec winged serpent god and Michael Moriarty in a bad hairpiece, and joyous B movie history was made.

I played ice hockey for many years before middle age, general slackness and moving to America put a stop to it. As a goalie, most of the drills I used to do involved repetition after repetition of breakaways, reacting to variations of offensive plays and, of course, stopping shots. The idea was to train my body through this repetition to do much of the work involved in moving and reacting to shots automatically. When the shot came, my body would know what to do: block, catch, kick save, butterfly, poke check, stack pads or, all too often, fall over and randomly flail about in the hope that something connects with the puck … We call this training body memory.

The point of exercises like those above is to set up the mental equiv-alent of body memory so you fall more easily into creative patterns of thinking, listening, noticing and connecting. A few months ago I was chatting with Gary Whitta, writer of *The Book of Eli* (2010). He told me he got the original idea for the character of Eli, post-apocalyptic wanderer and preacher, while planning his costume for a Hollywood party. Ideas can come from anywhere, but you have to be ready to recognize and capitalize on them.

Good story ideas turn the world like good jokes, and it takes practice to find the personal fulcrum that will let you do the turning.

Here's a silly one I just sparked on while writing the previous section—in fact a fun bunch made up from a single premise. I offer them as a bit of fun, just to get your thinking going.

Start with this: a nice, but deeply repressed guy/girl (we can work out their backstory reason for sucking at life—hey, it probably involves parents or childhood trauma in some way) is fed up being the butt of all their friends' jokes: too boring; so predictable; all those ridiculous routines; no sense of adventure; can't hold a long-term relationship together because their partner always gets frustrated or loses interest.

Add this: In desperation, perhaps after their latest romantic calamity, they are advised by their therapist, or the random, eccentric mentory type person they meet at their moment of great despair, or by their inevitable creative friend (who doesn't *have* to be gay, it's not actually the law and anyway who says the lead character isn't gay and their friend straight?), to find ways of—wait for it—teaching themselves to become fun!

It is a counter-intuitive response for the audience because it argues against the spontaneity we tend to associate with having fun; but it plays to character because that's how our hero/ine thinks right now. Enter exercises and mini adventures similar to the ones above. They feel foolish. Zany fish-out-of-water-related pranks occur. Gradually they begin to have some fun and loosen up. We probably insert a romantic subplot right about now, as someone dreamy is attracted to the newly goofy side of our hero/ine.

Horror/comedy version: it's ten stories in a day time and they pick 'your best friend is actually a werewolf.' Well, wouldn't you just know it? Better start running.

Zany screwball comedy version: it's parallel universe 'evil you', or see the world as a child day, and a bump on the head or a paranormal occurrence occurs. We wake up with a headache and possibly also temporary amnesia and, you guessed it, evil or kid version strikes!

Romantic comedy version: so many possibilities here, but the gift is the day of opposites which slots right into the person we meet falling for our character's uninhibited, creative side ('I wish I could be like you') which they then have to sustain somehow 'because I really, really like them and they won't want the old boring me'—but who will we become in the process? These are hardly earth-shattering ideas, although they could be polished up somewhat I suppose. At least it illustrates why you need to have your 'idea hat' on all the time.

In my own writing, I have two familiar modes when I am approaching a new project: slow cooking and flash frying.

'Slow cooking,' only ever used for personal spec scripts with no deadlines apart from those casual ones I impose on the work for my own reasons, allows me to develop a concept slowly over time. I mull it over, happily leaving it 'on the shelf' for periods—years even—and neither hurrying it nor forcing connections and detail.

I might start with an image, a character or a situation, and build from there, or I might have a clear idea about the emotional core of the story but be searching for an appropriate context in which to tell it. Boy can meet, lose and possibly regain girl in song, a spaceship or South Dakota, after all. I've never tried song; I might have to do that one of these days. See how tiny baby ideas can come from anywhere?

Part of being a writer is being open to story ideas, whatever their source. When I was a kid my parents bought me a recorder and some lessons. Middle-class British children still tend to get at least a try-out on an instrument at some point in their youth. I am ashamed to say I made it halfway through 'Three Blind Mice' and that was it. End of parental scenarios leading to 'My son, the musician.' I really am pretty tone deaf and I know nothing about musicology, so I think it's very unlikely that I will ever write a musical romance, even though the idea sparked briefly as I wrote it just above. You never know where that spark might lead, however, how it might be transformed, flipped or re-imagined at some point far in the future.

In general, however, I have confidence that the details of a story will gradually filter in as the overall concept simmers away in my head or, if they don't, then it wasn't meant to be. I almost always carry a little notebook in my pocket and squirrel away interesting nuggets here and there. At any given time I have a number of these ideas gestating. Some will never get written; others may be the catalyst for quite different scripts or even stories in a different medium. Most of the writers I talk to have a similar story bank that they keep with them. Maybe it's genetic.

My friend Amanda Avanzino is, in this as in all things, much better organized than I am: 'One thing I do, to keep those old ideas circulating through my mind or even just to update them, I take them from my notebook once every few weeks and transfer them to my computer.

Sounds redundant but it's interesting how just by going over them after a little break, you can sort out those that have potential from those that are total crap. I even go as far as to organize the types of ideas in my computer. I have a page for titles that I am fond of (which often imply a story), characters that I've played around with, and stories themselves, which I organize as well.'

When I am working to a deadline, or when happy circumstances conspire to inspire, I go into 'flash frying' mode. You might imagine inspiration as being not unlike conception (apart from all the fun activities leading up to it). Potential story ideas are swimming around you all the time, but they need to find or force an opening into your creative mind …

> IMPLIED YOU
> OK. Enough with that analogy, please
> —and by the way: eew. I think I know
> where you are going with it anyway.
> You mean it takes receptivity and
> a link to something that inspires
> or interests you to make a creative
> connection happen, right?

> FRIENDLY ME
> I think so. At least that's what it
> feels like to me. Creativity is a
> very personal thing, so here I'm
> just trying to give an example from
> my own experience as an
> illustration, not a rule.

I find that a promising idea will typically emerge from a collision between something I am already interested in and something that I know nothing much about, but am intrigued by. Basic story ideas don't change—a boy still meets a girl, revenge is still best served cold and monsters still hide under your bed in all their colorful variety—but inspiration comes from the creative interaction between those genres, story types and areas of knowledge and experience. *It's all about seeing the familiar in unfamiliar ways.*

In an interview conducted by his brother Jonathan, Christopher Nolan talks about exactly this kind of fortuitous collision of genres in the writing of *Inception* (2010): 'I'd been dealing with the world of corporate espionage and so forth, but as soon as you want to present the subtle art of conning somebody, of fooling somebody, then you enter the world of the heist movie. And that is when I consider this script to have begun, when I figured out that I was going to use a heist movie structure to wrangle these ideas in …'

To reinforce the point, here's a slightly embarrassing story against myself. One of my own 'just for fun' screenplays is a horror comedy: *The Evil Shed*. From the title you might assume that it involves both evil and a shed in some combination and you would be right. Its genesis is typical of the interaction between **write what you know** and **write what you don't know**.

By the way, I relish my 'just for fun' screenplays. I bite on an idea (flash frying here) and write a fast draft, usually in a few weeks, and see where it takes me. They are a kind of short-term creative release for me and usually don't get shown in public—hence the slight embarrassment over this story. This is a very different process from the planning and preparation I undertake (and that I am encouraging you to undertake) for most of my writing projects. The spontaneity and excitement keep things rolling and I make a point of not allowing these projects to take too much of my time.

I encourage all of you to allow yourselves to write for the sheer fun of it sometimes, even if what results may be unlikely to get made. Writers should never be ashamed of writing what they want to, just for the love of doing it. Besides, it refreshes our motivation and commitment to the writing process. One day I may even go back to *The Evil Shed* and beat it into better shape.

The idea, which I fully admit is deeply silly but appeals to my slightly warped imagination, came one night when I was visiting with two close friends. Jo Bushnell is the talented director of a contemporary art gallery, and her partner, Roy Brown, is an up-and-coming British artist with whom I collaborate on documentaries and video installations. Let's break it down quickly:

*Stuff I brought with me to the evening (the* **write what you know** *bits):*

- A longstanding love of Hammer Horror films and the 'Poe Cycle' of Roger Corman.
- A worryingly detailed knowledge of the weird tales of H. P. Lovecraft.
- An interest in the world of contemporary art.
- A more than passing familiarity with the local contemporary art 'crowd,' some of whom I found, in my arrogance, to be pretentious and annoying and deserving of a kick in the ass.

*Stuff that lubricated the little grey cells:*

- Alcohol, in moderation. (Too much and you won't remember the great idea you had.)
- Good food. Roy is an excellent cook.

- Stimulating conversation. (Seek this out wherever and whenever synapses are required to spark.)

*Stuff that was going on in my friends' lives at that moment:*
- Roy was in the process of getting two great big sheds put up in their back garden for use as a studio.

*Stuff I knew nothing about but that went 'ding!' when I heard it (the* **write what you don't know** *part):*
- 'Shed Art.'

Now I don't remember all the details of 'Shed Art' anymore, but Jo and Roy were talking about a contemporary art show or a series of shows that were either held in garden sheds or used sheds as the base materials—or maybe both. We got to talking about the variety of works people had produced for the show, and the potential for others. This turned us to the idea of the ordinary garden shed as a space of suburban British gothic.

What a wonderful setting for a wryly comic version of an old-school British horror movie with a contemporary twist, we thought. (This is about how ideas come, so I am going to account for *The Evil Shed* in the terms in which we discussed it that night, not as a pitch-ready premise.) And so we tossed around a plot idea that opened with an 'historical' sequence full of nostalgic reveling in the style of 1960s and 1970s British horror movies, like the great *Witchfinder General* (scr. Tom Baker and Michael Reeves; 1968) and had fun with the notion of possessed building materials taken unknowingly from a place of evil and turned into an artist's studio. This gave us a literal take on the tortured artist and a chance to deliver a satirical poke or two at the British contemporary art scene.

Jo and Roy would be the inspiration for the artist and his wife whose relationship is tested to breaking point as his work in the eponymous evil shed turns him ever stranger, and 'Shed Art' would give us the impetus for the creation of a truly deadly art exhibit which destroys its public while the critics assume that the growing pile of corpses is all part of the transgressive show. The script was written back when Jake and Dinos Chapman were all the rage, so you get the idea.

There are other subplot elements, including an evil Familiar, borrowed in part from the terrifying Brown Jenkin of Lovecraft's *Dreams in the Witch House*, which allowed us to move the horror out of the shed and was just the right size to murder the neighbors and terrorize the couple's young child. Members of 'The Sealed Knot' play rude mechanicals throughout, and help to save the day at the end, so, yes, the whole enterprise is meant to be pretty camp.

[Random Fact about British Eccentrics alert: 'The Sealed Knot' is a curious British institution, being a group dedicated to re-enacting our Civil War (in other words the war of 'Roundheads' and 'Cavaliers', not that of 'Johnny Rebs' and 'Billy Yanks'). It involves a great deal of musket, pike and general historical accuracy related activities and an even greater deal of beer related activities, as far as I can tell. Three cheers for The Sealed Knot. I'm certain that the world would be a poorer place without it.] So the idea combines elements of the old and the new; the very familiar and the newly encountered. It blends different subgenres of the horror film and elements of satire and broader comedy. Of course you may hate the idea and we didn't take it very seriously ourselves, but it illustrates how creative ideas merge **write what you know** and **write what you don't know** in new and interesting fashions.

*The Evil Shed* did not require much in the way of research before I got into the writing. I think I looked up one Sealed Knot website and briefly considered joining 'Lord Saye and Sele's Regiment of Foote' (Parliamentarian, of course), impressed by their claim to have a '... determined and experienced pike division.' Then I didn't.

Research can be one of the great pleasures of screenwriting, however, and is very much a part of **writing what you don't know**.

### Learning something new: the joys of research. Yes, really

Years ago I wrote another 'just for fun' screenplay, a lighthearted caper movie of sorts. Titled *Methuselah's Last Ride*, it was based on the premise that *it's never too late to get a life*. The story follows an old and rather rubbish outlaw who ends up in the world of B-movie westerns in 1920s Hollywood, becomes a minor star, and gets his revenge on some old enemies he finds there. (Oh, and before you ask, no, it's not much like *The Grey Fox* (1982).)

The idea for this script came out of a chance conversation with my old friend and former colleague the excellent Mr. Tony Moon, while waiting for a group of slacking students to appear for a script meeting. Initially I had no interest in writing any kind of a western, being measurably less American than your basic Budd Boetticher. I mean surely there must be a statute in Texas banning anyone named Julian from even thinking of writing a cowboy flick. Of course, by the time I got home from work that day not only had I convinced myself that I was going to write the story but that it would be a very good exercise for me to attempt something so far out of my usual comfort zone.

**Write what you don't know** had come a-knocking and I was all for answering its call. All it needed was the usual developmental work on character and structure (of which more later) and some research into the world of B-movie westerns in the 1920s. 'Hoorah!' I thought, in a worryingly *Five Go Mad in Dorset* (1982) and distinctly not very *Seven Men From Now* (1956) sort of way, and began to attack the books.

Again, *Methuselah's Last Ride* is one of those **write what you know/ write what you don't know** collisions. I knew something of silent cinema and the history of the American movie industry, having studied it as a grad student. I knew a good deal about westerns as both a fan and a student of cinema. I knew something of riding and the world of horses, having grown up around them in—here it is again—The New Forest. Yes, the road from Beaulieu to Brockenhurst is hardly the Chisum Trail, but a horse is still a horse, a fetlock is still a fetlock and a stirrup is still a stirrup.

What I knew nothing of, however, was the discrete world of the 1920s movie cowboy. How he lived, how he spoke and how he understood his world. Even though my screenplay was going to be a lighthearted, adventurous romp rather than a realistic historical drama, I knew it still needed to pass my *three key tests of movie research*:

1 *The 'be accurate enough' test*: Don't put anything in your screenplay which is so wrong or out of place that it will bring the audience out of the movie. You don't want them to be noticing the throw of dancing light on the pattern of heads in the rows of seats in front of them. That is never your friend. Some of the most frequent and most egregious failures of this test are nothing to do with the writer—yes, I'm looking at you American tanks with German markings in almost every war film before CGI (kudos to *A Bridge Too Far* (1977) here)—but writers still need to be on their toes. Let's not replay the whole *U571* (2000) fiasco here, but we Brits cared even if Americans didn't.

  This may be slightly unfair, but whenever I watch *Gettysburg* (1993) I can't help noticing the ranks of chubby Confederate extras, who must be re-enactors for reasons of budget if nothing else. They go through their oh-so-accurate and, thus, somehow conspicuously unlikely drill moves and right shoulder shifts and whatnot in their perfectly researched uniforms. These men and their gear have not been on campaign with the Army of Northern Virginia and are clearly no more than a 30-minute drive from the nearest Dennys (I clearly have no life, so I did some research and yes, there is one in Chambersburg PA which is about 20 miles away from the battlefield, so that's doable with decent traffic—and yes, the film was shot at least partly in the historical locations). Let's have some more bare feet and butternut, people. Again, not the writer's fault, but I wanted a chance to rant about it because it pissed me off—and don't get me started on the cannons firing blank charges with no recoil ...

2 The *'story beats history' test*: On the other hand, you are telling a story. Don't overload it with historical or institutional detail to the point that the story gets lost in discussions of the manufacture and proper application of saddle soap in 1863. This is the test that pats the 'me' of the previous paragraph gently on the head and sits him down on the couch with a long cool drink and this month's issue of *Military Minutiae*. Apparently it has part one of a two-part special focusing on the increasing likelihood that he will never have sex again.

3 The *'history is cool' test*: This should be the upside of research, both for yourself and for your audience. Has your research led to the seeding of your screenplay with the kind of really interesting little nuggets of information and 'color' which help your audience feel they are in safe hands but also give them the joy of learning new things? Accuracy is not the only reason to research a script; the pleasure of discovering the new in the world of the old is just as—if not more—important, both for you and for your audience. Did you know, for example, that cowboy stuntmen in the 1920s called the bags they kept their equipment in 'idiot bags'? Did you know that a 'Running W' was a horribly dangerous stunt in which the rider tied wires around his horse's front legs and pulled them up at full gallop, crashing the horse in a spectacular but often fatal fashion? Did you know that a lazy cowboy who talked a good game was called a 'scissorbill'? Well neither did I before I did my research for *Methuselah's Last Ride*, and I learned a lot more besides. It is all in the script and it just goes to prove that history is cool. I defy you to disagree.

What this test reminds us is that there are two main categories of empirical research. We can refer to them very loosely as *academic* and *experiential*.

Academic research is the kind of book research I did for *Methuselah's Last Ride*. It is the kind you would do if you needed to know about police procedures, the history of the Triangle Shirtwaist Factory fire of 1911 or the rules of cricket for your screenplay. It may involve online, library or archive research of texts, images and sound or moving image materials.

There are shorthands to help us with some of this, especially with institutional and procedural research, as publishers have brought out a number of useful books and guides either directly for writers or as introductions for the general novice. I use Lee Lofland's *Police Procedure & Investigation: a Guide for Writers*, for example, when I want to check some basic issue, and there are many more like it.

Interviews with participants and people connected to events can also be important research activities. Paul Greengrass prepared for writing his screenplay for *United 93* (2006) by reading the 9/11 Commission Report, but also by interviewing military and civilian participants in the events and by working with many of the relatives of those lost on the plane. In this way not only did he gain impressions of them as people from those who loved and knew them best, but he learned more of the phone calls and final communications made from the plane during the events leading up to its crash. *United 93* is a remarkable film and a brave one from a writer's point of view, in that its success hangs on a knife-edge combination of the accuracy of empirical research and the plausibility of imaginative extrapolation about a raw and controversial and all-too-recent event.

Sometimes you even get funded to do this kind of research. When Stephen Gaghan was developing the screenplay of *Traffic* (2000) for Edward Zwick, he tells Stephen Soderbergh, 'they authorized a research trip, a really expensive one. I went to Washington and New York. I spent a long time in D.C., using any contacts that Ed or I had. I ended up at the Pentagon, at the Office of National Drug Control Policy, the Council of Police Chiefs, the head of the Council of Mayors, people at think tanks, people advising policy makers about the War on Drugs. And at the same time I was reading a lot of different books, anything I could find that seemed relevant.'

Experiential research basically involves doing something or seeing it happen to learn about it. I could write convincingly about the experience of being an ice hockey goalie preparing for a penalty shot because I have done it repeatedly. This is using **write what you know** in the service of a higher calling. How do I really know what it feels like to be in a rowdy crowd at an English football match unless I have been there?

As a fan of Norwich City Football Club I used to go to Carrow Road and stand (back when one still could) at The River End chanting rude things about Ipswich Town fans ('… here's your father's gun; go shoot some Ipswich scum; it's City for me, my son; que sera sera …'); singing 'On The Ball, City'; feeling the sway and the press of the people around me; having snatched conversations about the prospects of the team, or the quality of the opposition, or the best place in town for a kebab, or the techniques and aesthetics of slip glazing in contemporary Latvian pottery— broken off as a new attack flowed forward; joining in the surge against the metal bars to see a goal and the despairing collapse of thousands of shoulders all at one moment when the visiting side scored, heads thrown back, eyes imploring the cold uncaring heavens.

By the way, is it just me, or do Americans really need to come up with some funnier and ruder sports chants? I mean 'D—Fence,' 'Go Area Team' and 'Out-Of-Area-Team Sucks' are just … not really trying. You don't have to go down the whole hooliganism route—indeed, please don't—but let's try and liven things up a bit, shall we?

Anyway, research is also one of the most important things you can do to provide a secure foundation for the exercise in creative world building involved in any kind of screenwriting. That is the subject of the next chapter.

# 3

## Screenwriting is *For The Birds*: A Simple Model for Cinematic Storytelling

This chapter is about making the first big move from your idea towards your story. We will think about the way many new writers approach the challenge and offer our first structural model to support us as we go. Logically, we should probably be discussing big important terms, like: *premise, logline, treatment, beat sheet* and *script breakdown* here. Those are all useful stages of story development and draw out and focus what movie land thinks is important in a story idea. Indeed, if you have read or been taught anything about screenwriting before, I'm sure you have some if not all of those words circling in your brain already. However, I don't think we are ready to make full use of them yet, so I'm saving them for the next chapter.

In my experience there is still a lot of work to do before we get there. In order to go to work with the language of story development, we need to understand the assumptions about story that lie behind it. You have to be trained in a certain kind of thinking about the relationship between stories and characters to be ready to use them. This chapter will help us prepare, because many of us start our creative thinking from a very different place.

### Story worlds: their creation and destruction

#### Working in film student order

Even the most talented students are not always completely logical and organized. They often find it hard to arrive in class with a coherent idea of what their story is really about. Quite understandably, they tend to start by pitching at the level of the flash of inspiration, not the well worked premise. That means their concept will usually be expressed as the externalization of an internal problem or challenge *that they have yet to identify as such.*

What I mean by this is that a student will give a pitch that is full of ideas for events in a *story world*. It will likely flag some major plot points, but will not yet be understood through character. We can tick off some likely suspects easily. Kill the dragon. Get the boy or girl. Win the big race. Rob the bank and get away with it. Survive the zombie plague. Save the Galactic Federation from invasion by the Evil Cyborg Empire of Spang.

In some ways these are promising; after all, at the simplest level you can design your screenplay as a test for your hero/ine. Unfortunately they only address the surface of movies, not their depth. Even good genre movies need a little depth, otherwise you end up with *Skyline* (2010). The ideas don't yet speak clearly enough to the biggest challenge of storytelling, and that is writing about real human feelings and motivations. What do we search for to make sense of ourselves and our world? Why do we do the crazy things we do? How do we overcome our own limitations? Characters in these pitches will be the people 'doing things.' They will not, as yet, be the *reason* for all the 'doing.'

```
        IMPLIED YOU
This is why we haven't talked about
what makes a good movie idea yet,
isn't it?

        FRIENDLY ME
Exactly. Film student order. Don't
worry, we'll come back to pitching
in the next chapter and develop it
further.
```

Students who pitch like this are not working in the order in which most other screenwriting manuals expect them to work. Students start from whatever story world their imagination has transported them to. Manuals, on the other hand tend to be written by professionals for budding professionals, and assume their readers need to start by attending to important and sensible things like logic and professional working practices. The problem is, logic isn't always immediately visible from the surface of Planet Spang. Let's compare:

*'Professional' Manual Order:*
Premise → character → story → plot → acts, beats and all their mates
(With minor variations.)

*Film Student Order:*
Cool stuff → generalized idea → vague world → plot(esque) → 'sorry dude, I had to move house because my girlfriend's parrot died, I'll get

it to you next week' → character(ish) → story → acts, beats and all
their mates
(With more or less parrots.)

Of course, dear reader, you would never approach a story this way
because I imagine you to be all kinds of cool and smart and sexy and not
wearing any Ed Hardy. But just in case ...

My challenge as a teacher is to bring my students from where *they*
typically start their creative thinking to where their story is hiding.
I always try and accomplish this without imposing too much of my
own interpretative story making onto their understandably wooly 'just
starting out' thinking. Sadly, in a classroom situation it can be hard to
say what needs to be said without offering a strong intervention. That's
because one has a limited time to work with each idea as it emerges.
Happily, in book form we have more time and space, so let's try to make
that journey together. We will start by walking backwards ...

What we will need to do is reverse our conceptual thinking from
story world towards character, because stories hide in the human. In
class, I often begin by asking students to focus their attention more
critically on the story worlds they have already begun to create. By inter-
rogating the hidden dramatic potential of these constructions they come
to understand better what they are trying to say.

## Understanding story worlds

Let's start by thinking about what story worlds are and how we should
use them. You can approach this process from opposite ends, depending
on whether your story idea started with a character or a theme. Either
way you will end up in the same place.

**Either:** build your story world around a theme you want to test out,
and train up your character to be the best person who could possibly be
tested by your theme in that world.

**Or:** build a character who needs something only a very particular
kind of story world can provide, and design that world specifically to
make him or her earn it the hard way.

```
              IMPLIED YOU
    What do you mean by 'story world'?
    A fantasy world like Middle Earth?


              FRIENDLY ME
    Possibly, that's one model we can
    look at. But it can be a world that
```

```
is like ours in every respect only
all of the parts of it we show are
those parts specifically designed to
test out our character and help or
hinder their progress.

         IMPLIED YOU
That's narrative economy again
isn't it?

         FRIENDLY ME
Yup in a different context. Every
story has its own story world, but
not every story reminds you of it
with scary aliens and talking
animals.
```

We all know that fantasy, horror and science fiction movies often involve the creation of wild, weird and wondrously alien worlds so as to show us impossible sights we can only dream of in our everyday earthbound lives (here we are back to **excess** from Chapter 1, of course).

Not all films in these genres use worlds which are visually different from our own, indeed many horror films are all about scaring us by showing an invasion, corruption or perversion of a particular manifestation of our normative reality, but all of them require some work on the part of their audience to compare and contrast their understanding of that reality with the world of the story. If they didn't, they wouldn't be horror, fantasy or science fiction films, after all.

Those are the obvious story worlds, because they tap the audience on the shoulder politely (*Alien* 1979) or just yell in their ear (*X2* 2003— *Bamf!*) and introduce themselves as different and thus important to understand. When done right, they kind of come with their own instruction manuals in cinematographic bold print at the start of the film and usually leave us in little doubt how we need to work with them.

*The Lord of the Rings: The Fellowship of the Ring* (scr. Fran Walsh, Philippa Boyens & Peter Jackson; 2001) starts with an extended history lesson: 'The world is changed. I feel it in the water. I feel it in the earth. I smell it in the air. Much that once was is lost and none now live who remember it.' We learn of Middle Earth and, more importantly, the narrative of the magic rings of power that will be at the center of the trilogy. 'It began with the forging of the great rings ...' By the time we come to the opening of the present-day plot in The Shire and meet all the little Hobbits with hairy toes, we already know this story world is all about magic and magical races *as well as* the perils of the temptation of power and the importance of strength of will. In other words we understand both the basic operating rules of the story world and have been introduced to an internal theme. In other-other words, we have passed Tolkien 101.

The sneaky story worlds are the ones that pretend to be just like our own, but really aren't because they have signed the same contracts with us as their gaudier fantasy cousins and are only pretending to be normal. Take this opening description:

```
EXT. CENTENNIAL LANE — DUSK
JUNO MacGUFF stands on a placid street in a nondescript
subdivision, facing the curb. It's FALL. Juno is sixteen
years old, an artfully bedraggled burnout kid. She winces
and shields her eyes from the glare of the sun. The
object of her rapt attention is a battered living room
set, abandoned curbside by its former owners. There is a
fetid-looking leather recliner, a chrome-edged coffee
table, and a tasteless latchhooked rug featuring a
roaring tiger.
```

Juno's world is our world, only not. There are no orcs and dragons, no starships and spacemen, but Diablo Cody has written Juno a world that is in some ways just as artfully artificial, just as rule-bound and partial as Middle Earth or Hogwarts. We will see only what she wants us to see and only what we need to see. Cody even sets the film in a 'nondescript subdivision,' its bland generality playing off Juno's uniqueness, just to show us that in movies normality is really only 'normality.'

*Juno's story world is designed only to tell Juno's story.* It does so by presenting us with information—showing us things—that will help us catch up with her and understand the challenges she will face. So why does the film open with an image of Juno staring at abandoned furniture?

```
            IMPLIED YOU
    Ah, I've seen this one. She just
    found out that she's pregnant and
    she's thinking about when she had
    all the sex in the chair in Michael
    Cera's basement.

            FRIENDLY ME
    Exactly. Chair A reminds her of
    Chair B. Now, for extra credit,
    work that through narrative
    economy.

            IMPLIED YOU
    OK, the story is all about how Juno
    deals with her pregnancy and so the
    first thing we see links us to that
    theme.
```

```
              FRIENDLY ME
Pretty much. And what does she do
next?

              IMPLIED YOU
She takes a pregnancy test?

              FRIENDLY ME
I mean before that. Even the props
are working the story — you remember
the orange juice?

              IMPLIED YOU
Oh, right. She's drinking juice
from this huge carton and we don't
know why.

              FRIENDLY ME
Everything in the story world
speaks to Juno's problem, so …

              IMPLIED YOU
Yeah, it seems kind of random until
she goes to the store and buys
another test. So then we understand
that she's drinking all the juice
so she will be able to pee on the
new pregnancy test. It's like you
were saying about Bruce Willis's
bare feet. It's a set-up that pays
off later.

              FRIENDLY ME
Juno's world again, everything we
see is motivated by her situation
and her emotional needs.
```

'My world is changed. I feel it in my water. Much that once was is lost and one now lives inside me who won't remember it. It began with some … forging in Bleeker's basement.' Think of it like this: *stories are all about change.* They are the enemies of stasis and that's why most basic stories start with a problem or challenge and end with a solution. Of course there are other ways of conceptualizing stories, but as a first working model this will serve.

In *Juno* the furniture symbolizes this structuring logic in that it reminds her of how she got into the mess in the first place and also points her towards her big choice—what to do? The furniture on the lawn is a symbol both of home and responsibility and also of dispos-ability—it is now unwanted. In the same way, Juno's baby, conceived in a chair, is also unwanted. Thus it also sums up Juno's initial choice for what to do about her baby.

In movie terms, therefore, we think (and pitch) change through character: some*one* has a problem or challenge ... but we haven't got that far yet in following the film student trail.

## The 'V': build a world, break it and then fix it again

This book is about giving you starting points. The models we use are not designed to answer every structural question for any possible story. They are intended to help you get a clue quick, understand priorities and start to write. This section, for example, is about how we can build character and theme into a really basic model of storytelling when we apply it to our story world. We are going to start by introducing our first structural model. This one is very simple; we'll develop it into a much more complex version in Chapter 5.

To start with, imagine your story as a great big letter 'V'. This is the first part of my little 'V W Wardrobe Method'—I'm excited, are you excited?

Pfft, suit yourself.

Anyway, when read from left to right the 'V' has a down slope followed by an up slope. These two slopes or *angles* will correspond to the two principle *story events* we are going to use. In this first model, we start by showing our audience a world, usually in stasis, always with an overt or underlying problem or vulnerability. We then introduce an event which *disrupts*, threatens or destroys that stasis—changes that world—usually by exploiting the underlying problem we identified at the start. The story resolves when we *repair* or move past the problem and end with a *different* world. Good stories never simply restore things to how they were. If they did, that would mean nobody learned anything from experiencing the process of destruction and recreation and the audience would quite rightly be asking themselves: 'What was the point of that?'

So in this basic storytelling model the most important idea is that the world you end up with is not the world you started out with. Imagine our letter 'V' with the second, or 'up,' angle of the letter slightly longer or shorter than the 'down' angle, to represent relative success or failure. Things may have got better or worse for the characters—in movie terms we may have had an 'up' or a 'down' ending—or they may simply be different, but they can never be as they once were. This means *you* the writer need to manufacture that change. Welcome to the rest of the book.

The next step is to see characters as the agents of change and work

# THE 'V'

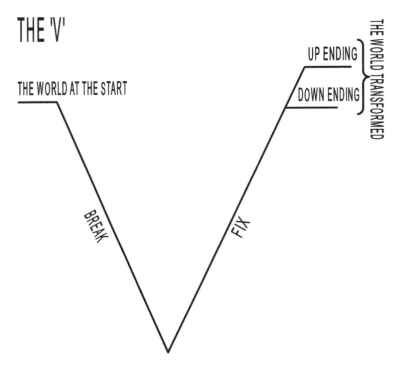

THE WORLD AT THE START

UP ENDING

DOWN ENDING

THE WORLD TRANSFORMED

BREAK

FIX

our story ideas through them. The story doesn't change, just the way we understand it, express it and are able to apply it. Juno's life in her bland suburban world is 'broken' by her unexpected pregnancy. She takes steps to 'fix it' by taking responsibility for what happens to the baby, and we follow her path in doing so. In the end she has learned a lot about responsibility, love and parenthood from her experience, and has worked out that she doesn't need to rush into adulthood and that what she really wants is to try out Paulie Bleeker as a real boyfriend. In fixing her story world she has changed *herself* and, thus, her world.

We can see how this relationship between character and story world works in more detail in a wonderful short cartoon from Pixar, *For the Birds* (scr. Ralph Eggleston; 2000).

The story world at the start of *For the Birds* is very simple: a line of telephone wires beside a country road. These wires are the habitual perch of a flock of little birds. We should note here that they line up at one side of a length of cable, near a telephone pole. This will be important later on.

Already we have a world that is defined both through *use* and through *character*:

> *Use*: the birds need somewhere safe to roost, away from the rabid weasels that, no doubt, live in the fields below. I mention rabid weasels because at one point the Pixar creative team played with the idea of rabid weasels eating all the little birds at the end. It would have been great fun for all the cynical adults, but perhaps not for some of the small children in the audience!
>
> *Character*: the little birds show a number of important impulses. When we meet the birds as they land on the wire one by one it is clear that they define their community through status—literally by pecking order—as they fuss and push and squabble for space along the wire. They muddle along as a flock, but some are also given basic individual personalities. 'Bully,' 'Chipper,' 'Snob' and 'Neurotic' are the first to land, and their interactions in establishing this pecking order serve as a model for the whole community.

The world is there to do a job for characters, not to work in the abstract. Who cares about phone lines in the middle of California or Kansas, or wherever, otherwise? We have been introduced to the cause of the flock's eventual downfall at the start of the movie by establishing the cliquey, status obsessed, inward looking—we could even say 'nativist'—behavior of its population of Mean Birds. *We* may not realize it yet (Juno's juice carton, Bruce's shoes), but the seeds have been sown.

All we need now to get the story moving is the catalyzing event that breaks the world. It comes in the form of a Big Goofy Bird who just

wants to be friends. Big Goofy Bird is … big and goofy and also guileless and well meaning. This means we like her immediately and the Mean Birds do not. She lands on the nearby telephone pole and tries to start a conversation, but the Mean Birds only tease her. Then they take the (literal) step that will doom their world as they know it. They snub Big Goofy Bird by shuffling along to the middle of the span. At this point the shot widens to show the whole span of wire as it wobbles a little with the flock's movement and gives the audience the first hint of what is to come.

*Remember, the Mean Birds' move is motivated by their character.* They have already shown they are intolerant, both individually and as a flock. Moving away from Big Goofy Bird just confirms it.

Big Goofy Bird doesn't take no for an answer and flies goofily after the flock, landing in the middle of them and putting far too much weight on the wire. It is pulled taught and dips almost to the ground. All the Mean Birds slide down the wire towards big goofy bird at the center.

Their world is broken, as is their pecking order, as the wire makes a great V shape, just like the shape of the model of storytelling we are working through.

Implied You acknowledges this stunningly brilliant synthesis of structural model and story with a slow golf clap.

Oh noes, what to do now? *There is only one choice consistent with their character.* Remember that we are trying to move from world to character in understanding how to express our story ideas. The Mean Birds haven't learned their lesson yet. They haven't changed, they have just been annoyed. So they start pecking at Big Goofy Bird's claws to make her let go. There is wonderful gag timing here from the Pixar team as we realize what is going to happen, followed by one of the birds who tries to warn the others. The rest of the flock then gets it just before the two pecking birds, but it is much too late. The last claw releases. Big Goofy Bird drops a couple of feet to the ground and the telephone cable fires like a great bow, shooting the whole flock of Mean Birds into the air in a cloud of feathers.

The point here is that the Mean Birds are the cause of their own downfall. Character traits and motivations (insularity, snobbishness, fear of the outsider) lead to character actions (they move away from the newcomer to the center of the span) that turn their world from a comfortable convenience to the engine of their own destruction. The 'V' of our story model has resolved itself and the Mean Birds, landing naked on the ground minus all of their feathers, suddenly find a use for Big Goofy Bird as a fig leaf for their modesty. They all hide behind her. Their world has certainly changed, at least until they grow their feathers back and can fly again. They might need a powerful ground running friend like Big Goofy Bird now, and they have certainly received a lesson.

Let's recap. Why *For the Birds* works as a story is because everything that happens is motivated by character. The little birds' society is fragile because they are not open to change. The story plays on that weakness

and their world is destroyed because of it. In the new world of the ground they will certainly have to adapt, to accept change and deal with it. It's either that or get rabidly weaseled.

Our little 'V' model of world creation and destruction is really a model that centers the storytelling process on character and motivation.

What you have to do is find a way to speak your story worlds through, and to, character. This will make them into proper movie ideas. Before we move on to deal with that in more detail, let's think a little bit more about how movie worlds work.

## Rules of story worlds

Story worlds need to operate *and be understood by the audience to operate*, by a set of rules and principles. These rules and principles define the world's purpose in story terms as well as giving us enough contextual information so that we don't keep asking ourselves awkward questions about why and how something happens and can just enjoy the story. What this means is that, as a writer, you need to know what makes your world tick and your audience needs to know enough and see enough of the mechanism to feel confident that *you* know the rest.

### We don't need to know everything

To use an example from a cinematic fantasy, you don't need to give us a lecture to explain the exact physiological process which allows Harry Potter to focus magical energies with his mind through his wand to make something Leviosa when he Windargiums it, or whatever. In fact, please don't. It is enough that we accept the general premise that, in the story world of the film, magic is real and can be focused and directed with training, and that we see Harry in class learning to do it. Do we know how it is that Hedwig and the other owls can carry heavy parcels to and from magical households and fly for hundreds or thousands of miles with them? No we don't, but we do understand that it is a system that helps the characters communicate at vital points in the story, as well as making delightful 'sense' of the day-to-day operation of a magical world, and thus we go along with it. Fans love Harry Potter not just for his battles against Lord Voldemort or for his friendships with Ron and Hermione and all the rest, but for the feeling of being immersed in a detailed, coherent world where, *in that world's terms*, the nonsense makes sense.

*The rules of your world do not have to be complex ...*

In fact some of the best fantasy story worlds operate by the simplest and most elegant of rules. Take one of the best British children's television programs from when I was a kid: *The Clangers* (scr. Oliver Postgate; (1969–72), a stop motion animated show which tells charming stories about a community of pink, knitted, whistling, mice-like aliens who inhabit a barren little planet far out in the universe.

The show's creators clearly decided that they had to answer one simple question to satisfy the everyday curiosity of their young audience: How could the Clangers survive on a barren planet with no food? Their answer is strangely logical in its absurdity. It is also funny and elegantly simple: the magma at the core of their little planet is replaced by hot soup. This single idea leads 'logically' to another: How do the Clangers get to the soup? Why, they get it from the being that lives in the soup: the Soup Dragon. Of course they do. I mean, who else would live in the pits of magma soup?

Various pranks ensue, some involving the wonderful Iron Chicken who lives in her metal nest in space and whose eggs give birth to notes of living music, but the soup-centered ecology of *The Clangers* has a second, metaphorical purpose because soup is comfort food. I remember the experience of watching *The Clangers* as being like sitting warm and snug in my favorite chair, wrapped in a blanket made from the prime wool of a thousand heavenly lambs with an intravenous Cadbury's Dairy Milk chocolate IV drip pumping sweet pleasure into my very soul. Ah, nostalgia. In other words, the show is the best kind of comfort food for kids and the soup is the expression of that purpose in the stories.

What a wonderful example of **writing what you don't know**: take a real world fact (planets have hot molten cores), twist it elegantly (magma becomes soup) and, in one stroke, you have invented the ecology of the world of *The Clangers*. Not only that, but in true Pavlovian fashion I had to have some soup for dinner after writing that. Kind of sweet, or kind of sad—you decide.

*... but they should be consistent*

In other words, once you establish a story world, you establish its rules and systems. If these seem to change without us knowing (through a plot incident, for example), we will be confused or uncertain. Fortunately help exists in deeply anal and generally trollish websites like: www. randommistakesInoticedinmoviesthatyouwouldhavenoticedaswellif

youactuallycaredandhadnolifelikemeandnowIfeelmarginallyvalidated
butamstillgoingtodiealone.com.

Think of it like the famous 180° rule you learned in Filmmaking 101. You know the one; it has to do with matching eye lines and making sure that there is visual continuity in a scene. Once you establish the 'line of action' in a space or between characters you need to keep it consistent, otherwise it will look like somebody just turned their head around through 180° when you cut to them. That's why you get taught at film schools *never to do it* on pain of patronizing and dismissive comments from your professor. Then you watch some movies and think a bit and realize you can do it in certain circumstances *if you know what you are doing*.

But, getting back to our little analogy, in non-Tony-Scott-related film language you can only change the line of action in a scene by having—*and showing*—characters move in relation to one another or by moving the camera in relation to those characters. If we see either or both of those things happening, we will not be confused by the way you are organizing your space.

It's the same principle with your story world. In *For The Birds*, we see the telephone wires being pulled down by Big Goofy Bird and so we understand why the Mean Birds' world has changed. In *The Clangers*, we establish that there is gravity on their little planet and would be confused if they suddenly started to float off the surface, unless your story is about the Perfidious Gravity Cancelling Device that Major Clanger has invented. Similarly, every Brit of my generation would be scandalized if the Soup Dragon started serving lemonade from the soup pits without us knowing the reason. Actually for any reason; it's just wrong.

### 'I just do eyes, just eyes': outside-in story world creation

*The Clangers* presents itself as an example of what we might call 'top-down' or 'outside-in' or 'macro-to-micro' world creation. In this way we create the general overview of how our world works and then start to focus on details important for particular elements of the story.

*Outside:* How does the world work? The Clangers live off the soup at the centre of their planet.

*In:* In the fourth episode of the series, the Iron Chicken's egg hatches into notes of living music. The hungry Soup Dragon eats all but two of the notes, so one of the Clangers plants the remaining notes. With a little help from the Little Cloud, who rains when asked politely, they grow into music trees. The episode ends with a concert as the happy Clanger conducts the music trees in performance.

We don't need to have invented the Little Cloud, or worked out how to persuade it to rain or that notes can be planted to grow into music trees, in order to understand how the Clangers live in their world. These micro rules come later and as needed for a particular story. The soup pits are constants of the entire show and are established in the very first episode. They are shown repeatedly to help reinforce the audience's appreciation of the daily life of the Clangers. Tasty, warming soup is always near to hand.

Let's take as a more complex example *Blade Runner* (scr. Hampton Fancher and David Peoples et al.; 1982), the movie adaptation of the novel *Do Androids Dream of Electric Sheep* by Philip K. Dick (1968). One good reason for picking it is that the film is, amongst other things, another reworking of the Frankenstein story we have already discussed when we worked on models for creativity.

This time the 'mad scientist' story is refracted through a near future world in which cybernetics has advanced to the point at which the boundaries between the human and the artificial are being blurred. The film asks the question: 'What does it mean to be a sentient being?' This is the 'outside' of Blade Runner's world that will apply to everything else as we work our way further 'in,' because, as we should already understand, the story world should be designed to help us explore and answer that question at every level.

So *Blade Runner* goes about this by setting up its story world of Los Angeles in 2019 as a kind of narrative *alembic*, which is the kind of chemical or alchemical refining apparatus you might find in the lab of a good mad scientist. What I mean is that that the film's story world is designed specifically to articulate, illustrate, refine and distill the problem of identity—of what it means to be human.

It takes that central idea and crumbles it into bird feed for the rest of the story and the world, scattering it into a whole range of story contexts. These are uncovered by the detective plot as Harrison Ford's Rick Deckard pursues cyborgs through this future city.

It does this in visual terms by continually reinforcing the idea of hybridity—cultural, architectural and physical—as an image essay, arguing against easy meanings and definitions. Everything in *Blade Runner*'s Los Angeles was, is or will also be something else. Language was once culturally specific and is now the mishmash of 'Cityspeak.' Umbrellas are also fluorescent lights. Buildings are also advertisements.

Cars are also aircraft. People are also machines. Machines are also people. Sean Young is also 'maintain eye contact; back away slowly.' Allegedly.

In story terms, the world/alembic of *Blade Runner* contains a controlled reaction between its hybrid genre (science fiction and film noir) and its hybrid population. This cast of characters is designed to embody individual aspects of, consequences of or approaches to the problem of what 'life' means.

Sean Young is Harrison's mirror image—the unknowing cyborg ('replicant' in the film's language) whose situation educates the audience in preparation for the questioning of Harrison's own identity. William Sanderson gives the metaphor of untimely decay a human twist—how would we feel? Daryl Hannah allows the audience to indulge in the cheap fantasy of having our own 'basic pleasure model' cyborg, only to slap us down into guilty reflection by proving the possibility of real love or at least affection (and thus 'humanity') between replicants—and thus for Sean and Harrison in the future.

And so on.


### 'Now that's our ball now, right? And we're playing here': inside-out story world creation

The same applies in all stories, not just fantasy. The only difference is that the worlds do not always draw attention to themselves in the same way. Take a film located entirely in the 'real world', *This is England* (scr. Shane Meadows; 2006) is set in and around a depressed council estate (public housing) in Yorkshire in the early 1980s. The film follows a young lad called Shaun (Thomas Turgoose) who is adopted into a friendly skinhead gang. Later on, he is exposed to extreme racist politics when their former leader, Stephen Graham's 'Combo', is released from prison. Violence follows and Shaun ends up rejecting the world of British working class white supremacist politics, throwing his Cross of St. George flag into the sea at the end.

The story world of *This is England* presents itself as an example of 'bottom-up' or 'inside-out' or 'micro-to-macro' world creation. This is to say that we don't need special knowledge to understand what is going on here, and the script shows us only the details of environment needed to help tell specific story elements. We extrapolate from these to create an overall picture of the story world. In this way we build up a picture of Shaun's broken world, his depressing home and especially his bare room and the pictures of his dead soldier father.

This theme of absent fathers will be important as the story develops. Shaun is welcomed into a new family—the gang—by their leader, Woody, who is a surrogate big brother. The emotional void at the center of Shaun's life needs a father to fill it, however. This explains why he is tempted by Combo's analysis of the 'meaning' of his father's death and begins to look to Combo as an alternative father figure until he is proved unworthy through his violence and intolerance.

From Shaun's house we move out conventionally to parts of the estate and his school, and then, when he encounters the gang, we start to see the expanding urban environment as something to be reinvented and made your own. For the gang it is a great playground, and they inhabit the spaces in between destinations and those forgotten to the ravages of time and nature.

This may sound obvious and literal: we see the places the characters go to, so what? Well, for one thing, the story world of *This is England* gets recycled halfway through the film. The run-down spaces that the multi-racial and welcoming gang members inhabited and made into their own funland take on a much more sinister meaning as they become colonized by the racist gang later in the story. There's a graffiti-covered brick wall with a set of painted goalposts where early on the group messes around and plays football. We return to the same space later, when Combo threatens three Pakistani kids with a knife when they play football there.

*So this method of world creation can be about taking the ordinary and transforming it through the interpretations placed upon it by different characters. The world doesn't change, only its meaning.*

*This is England* is in part a film about making the most of what little you have. It sets up a series of bleak houses, shops and cafés and exterior spaces transformed first into happy places by virtue of the people who inhabit them and then back into unwelcoming spaces of fear and threat. (Shane Meadows plays a similar game with location in *Dead Man's Shoes* 2004.) The town, for all its problems, offers at least community, whereas the countryside is the source of hatred in the form of National Front meetings in an isolated pub. The end of the movie takes place on a bleak beach with a disgusted Shaun casting his flag out to sea, thus 'kicking out' from England the hatred it represents, just as the National Front wants to kick out members of ethnic minorities. This is *not* England, Shaun is telling us.

## Playing story worlds to character and theme

**Narrative economy** teaches you that whatever you invent should have a story function. **Narrative excess** teaches you that whatever you invent may also be the spectacular payoff for a stage in the development of that story. **Show, don't tell** teaches you to put the story functions of your world on display for us all to see and absorb. As we now know, all of those lessons are missing their targets if you don't aim them at character.

A story world operates and should be thematically consistent at every level of magnification. World creation in *Avatar*, for example, has been planned to be consistent and holistic. We see this from the level of the entire planet Pandora, through its geography and topography, through its flora and fauna, through the level of its culture to individual creative choices about technology, tool use, habitat and social customs, and so on down the line. But the sense of natural interconnectedness that permeates the story world is also a key marker for character development.

Paraplegic depressive Jake Sully's future depends upon the interaction between the human technology that allows him to become an avatar and the alien culture and ecology that offers him a physical, spiritual and moral rebirth. The world on its own cannot do it, as Jake has no effective access to it without the avatar technology. It is not enough to design a planet. It is not enough to design the avatar device. Without a character with Jake's particular situation, skills and psychology, the story world is just so much window dressing.

*Avatar* is a science fiction movie and, as such, works with and develops a range of situations common to other science fiction movies. We are offered contact with aliens, the extrapolated potential of future technologies and the ambivalence of science, to name but three. What makes it unique is the interaction between those hackneyed tropes (**write what you know**) and the story world of Jake-avatar-Pandora (**write what you don't know**).

One of the old maxims of academic film studies is that genre stories are organized around patterns of repetition and difference. Every western is like every other ... apart from all the ways in which it is new and different. This is important because we paid for a ticket to see a western and will be annoyed if you start to show us a romantic comedy. Unless it is a western-themed romantic comedy, I suppose. *Along Came Calamity Polly* anyone? Maybe not. Also we will be expecting our western to excite and surprise us with its new and original take on standard genre formulas. It's the same with world creation.

Take an animated superhero story like *Megamind* (scr. Alan J. Schoolcraft & Brent Simons; 2010). It has to work both as an animation and as a generic superhero movie so as not to disappoint the basic expectations of its genre fans and core audience demographics (**write what you know**). On top of this, *Megamind* is telling the story of how a supervillain finds his inner hero, thus turning many genre clichés on their head (**write what you don't know**). To this end much of the world creation is reasonably 'generic'. What evil supervillain would dare to show his face without some form of death ray and a big evil lair built into an abandoned factory, for example? The film, which is self-aware throughout, often plays with the *expected* nature of its own generic tropes. Remember the scene when habitually kidnapped Sassy Reporter Roxanne Ritchi anticipates and is bored by all of Megamind's nefarious torture devices?

Go one level deeper, however, and the story world design begins to play more directly to Megamind's character. His dastardly supervillain technology is all about *doing cool stuff with brains*, which supports the primary concept of his super identity. Thus he has an army of 'brainbots' who fly around, doing his low-level minioning. His primary minion— helpfully called 'Minion'; I told you it was meta—is a talking fish in a tank on a robotic body. The fish, which really should have been a brain, breaks the theme for comic purposes. So here we have a generic level of character specificity in the world creation.

But then there is a final level of world design that plays to the heart of Megamind's theme, the technology of *disguise and pretence*. The movie's opening sequence shows us that he was a wannabe hero turned super- villain by circumstances during childhood. He is hiding his true nature from the start, even though as an adult he has committed to his new villainous persona. But how are we going to give our blue skinned super- villain a sporting chance of getting anyone to talk to him long enough to help him understand and nurture his heroic potential, let alone to fall in love with him? Aha, cue disguise changing wristwatch! So our villain's powers are expressed through technology in the story world while at the same time that technology—that story world—facilitates his inner story of transformation: heroes aren't born, they're made.

## Plots and stories: why everything comes from character

Everything in your world should be part of your overall mechanism of storytelling. Every location, design choice, rule (magical or mundane) and principle of your story world needs to be serving some aspect of your story. Specifically they should manifest part of the central problem or challenge of your story and its hero/ine.

Here is Terry Gilliam discussing his creative process in writing *The Imaginarium of Dr. Parnassus* (2009): 'These kinds of worlds are me just allowing my imagination to run. I pretend I'm whoever the character is in there and I just go with it. Or I have an idea that already I'm trying to force onto the film and *I make sure the character becomes something that serves the ideas* that I've already wanted to get out of my system and get up on the screen' (my italics).

Take that wonderful adventure *The Princess Bride* (scr. William Goldman; 1987) with its Cliffs of Insanity, Rodents of Unusual Size and Fire Swamp, all of which signify their challenge in their names. Or *Labyrinth* (scr. Jim Henson, Terry Jones et al.; 1986) with its, well, labyrinth—oh, and who could forget the Bog of Eternal Stench and David Bowie In Tights, both offering a fate worse than death for its teenage heroine.

Remember, *Labyrinth* is about a girl who resents having to babysit her brother in the real world and has to get her priorities straight and learn responsibility when the King of Goblins steals him away. The labyrinth of the story presents her with a series of tests of character and judgment—a process of maturation if you will—that earns her the right and gives her the inner strength and the skills to save her brother in the end. It is the world that does the work here. It is the lesson plan for Jennifer Connelly's heroine, prepared most carefully and *to character*. In other words, the world is designed by the writers to test out and expose her personal flaws and weaknesses. It is not a random collection of 'cool stuff' crammed into a script. The former creates satisfying drama, the latter is just stuff that happens that we get to watch (see: *Resident Evil* 2002).

This is why we talk about *story* worlds rather than *plot* worlds.

### *Story* worlds, not *plot* worlds

One of the most difficult parts of the screenwriting process is to change your mindset from valorizing events (plot driven) to prioritizing motivations (story driven). This is the most important step on our film student road from generalized idea back to a workable movie concept.

By now it should be pretty clear what has to happen. Our discussion of story worlds has focused on how the world needs to work to and for character. Now we need to express that work in terms of a story concept rather than a plot concept.

Put another way, we need to stop thinking about *what* a character does, but *why* she does it.

Every movie has both a story and a plot. Stories are about the *internal challenges* our characters face, the changes they go through and the lessons they learn or fail to learn. Stories drive the events of the plot, and without a story a plot has no real meaning or emotional significance for the audience.

In filmmaking terms, therefore, plots are simply the *external mechanisms* we use to tell stories.

So how does this work in practice? Well, we just talked about *Labyrinth*, which is about a girl, Sarah, who needs to grow up, take responsibility and put the welfare of others first. The story of the film is about her learning to do that. It is an internal struggle for her as a person. We can't see internal struggles (remember **show, don't tell**?) so we need a plot to show us the process by which she gets from where she started, selfish and immature, to where she is at the end, a good sister and a more mature individual all round. We are given final evidence of this transformation when Sarah passes on her beloved teddy bear, Lancelot, to her newly rescued baby brother. In symbolic terms, of course, the teddy bear represents the parts of her childhood she is now ready to leave behind.

*In the plot* Sarah meets other characters and has all kinds of labyrinthy adventures which help her *get to* the final plot event when she faces the naughty Goblin King and his worrying haircut.

*In the story*, those characters and adventures form parts of Sarah's learning curve. They transform her from a spoilt brat to a clear-thinking young woman (she finally remembers her spell) who is capable of actually *defeating* the lad Bowie and his worrying package.

So plot and story in *Labyrinth* are two parallel journeys, one traveled by the feet and the other traveled in the mind and personality of the character.

*Plots get us into our seats; stories keep us watching.*

All of our examples in this chapter have stories as well as plots. Every film, even the most obviously plot driven films like *2012* (scr. Roland Emmerich & Harald Kloser; 2009), has a story. As a screenwriter, however important your plot and spectacle are to the final success of your concept, if you try and pitch without a story you will get nowhere. We will cover this in detail in the next chapter, but as a taster this is how Roland Emmerich describes his approach to *2012* in a video interview posted at Movieweb.com:

I realized that, you know, in disaster movie format you have two things. You have very big images and you have very small, intimate stories and that's a great combination. The heroes are normal people like you and me. They don't have to have special talents or anything. They only have to have the will to survive.

So in *2012* there are parallel, macro and micro plot tracks, the global Noah's Ark plan to save (the richest members of) the human race and the personal struggle of John Cusack's character, Jackson Curtis, and his family who understandably want to be among the saved rather than the drowned. Both of these tracks are *run by stories* that suggest you have to earn your own redemption. In the global plot, the story has Chiwetel Obamiofor—sorry Ejiofor—teaching Americans to basically suck less: 'The moment we stop fighting for each other, that's the moment we lose our humanity.' In the family plot, Jackson Curtis earns his redemption as a father and as a husband by proving he can be more than the obsessional flake who drove his wife and kids away before the start of the movie.

Both of these stories come from and play to character. Jackson Curtis is 'flawed' and needs 'correcting', just as the human race—or at least the American part of it, personified by Oliver Platt—needs a metaphorical smack on the nose with a rolled up newspaper: 'Bad America, no biscuit!'

How seriously are we expected to take these stories? The answer is: not very. My old friend, the brilliant film academic Martin Stollery, put it like this as we were leaving the cinema (I paraphrase slightly): 'Don't you feel that at the heart of all his films Roland Emmerich is just taking the piss?'

Nevertheless, the stories are there so that plot can be hung upon them in a functional sort of way.

Cue California sliding into the sea …

*… so that John Cusack can prove he's a good husband and father.*

# 4

## It's All About the Concept

I always wanted to write a 'Ping!' movie. That's a submarine movie to the uninitiated. Maybe I will someday, although knowing my sense of timing I will write one just as submarines are replaced by Virtual Teenage Nuclear Cyber Naval Attack Squid (Marxist Leninist). Now there's a movie concept in the making …

Of course, all it needs now is to actually *be* a movie concept, rather than random words slung together for the pleasure of the eight-year-olds amongst us. That's what this chapter is all about. Not the Virtual Teenage Nuclear Cyber Naval Attack Squid (Marxist Leninist) part; the turning *stuff* into a *movie concept* part.

I have to warn you that we are entering dangerous waters. It has all been relatively plain sailing up to this point. We have been cruising calm seas, inventing nice little story worlds and playing around with ideas in a general sort of way. What comes next is, without any question, the simplest and yet somehow also the hardest phase of the wandery film student odyssey that eventually leads to a screenplay. Clarity is hard. Simplicity is hard. Being clear and simple while expressing narrative complexity is incredibly hard. Nevertheless, this is what we have to learn to do next. We have to take what we have learned so far and work out how to express it clearly and simply as a script idea.

Be warned that this is also the most important part of the screenwriting process, because without a properly understood and expressed pitch statement (the concept and story of your movie encapsulated in a couple of sentences) you are bound to get in a mess with your structure and it's so much easier to unpick short statements than whole script drafts.

Oh, and also, if you can't pitch your idea effectively, there is very little point writing your screenplay, because then why would anybody want to read it?

## No ifs. No buts. It's the law. You just have to get this part right

I am trying to make this a friendly book. I hope you are already feeling the friendly and encouraging vibes as they struggle to escape through tiny chinks in the armor of my naturally cynical Britishness. The spell check just tried to change 'Britishness' to 'brutishness', which kind of makes my point for me and also explains the British Empire ... Anyway, the whole **write what you don't know** idea is about freeing you creatively and encouraging you to follow your muse. That means whenever we come crashing up against a wall of screenwriting 'law' I get frustrated. I don't like having to tell you there are some absolutes. Being friendly, however, can also be all about laying some home truths on the line, and here we reach a biggie.

If you don't think this is important, if you dismiss it as being 'mainstream' or 'formulaic', or if you don't apply yourself to the contents of this chapter above all others, you are just wasting your time. You might as well go take that Techniques and Aesthetics of Slip Glazing in Contemporary Latvian Pottery class you were thinking about back at the start.

I checked with that nice Ms. Eglītis and there are still places.

Go ahead and free your creativity, in other words. **Write what you don't know.** Indulge your imagination, but learn how to get the rest of us on board with it.

In this chapter we are going to talk about a whole knot of statements you have to prepare which are vitally important when it comes to talking to anyone else about your movie. Unhelpfully they are also kind of similar ... and yet importantly distinct. Confused? We'll try and unpick it all in the next few pages. What's more, these statements are there both for you to keep your head in the game and focused on your priorities as a writer, and also for the start of the selling process of your screenplay, which can begin before you have written word one of the script itself.

Even if you are just in a screenwriting class and are a world away from actually meeting and greeting potential producers, agents or investors, the first thing you have to get your head around is that you will need to be able to *pitch* your idea. Out loud. To real living human people. To be a screenwriter you need to be able to convince with your spoken as well as your written word. It doesn't matter how smart and creative you are, how well organized and prepared you are in your own mind. If you can't communicate your idea orally—even to your professor and fellow classmates—then you are not ready to write your screenplay.

A pitch is basically a short statement that outlines your story. It doesn't explain all the twists and turns but it lays the groundwork such that any significant detail that comes up in later discussion will fit snugly into place without further explanation. When you know how the story works, you also know how any individual part fits with the whole. Imagine a pitch like a magical, endlessly expandable version of one of those cool cases assassins in the movies have for their sniper rifles. You know the ones, they open up and all the pieces of the rifle and the telescopic sight are laid out in their own perfectly fitting holes in the foam insert of the case. Your pitch will be designed to hold any and all pieces of information that could possibly be attached to your movie idea in comfort and security and without having to cut new holes in the foam.

We will talk in more detail about what makes a good pitch a little later on, but we are going to work our way into what is the *pre-writing process* of screenwriting by looking at the way pesky film students tend to approach it. We will follow this pre-writing thread all the way to the finish in a section called: '*What is a screenplay and how do I get there?*'

Remember that the reason why we have chapters in books like this is for when you meet other professionals. They will quite reasonably expect that you are at least an aspiring fellow professional and will, thus, make an effort to speak their language. What we are all teaching is in part etiquette and professional courtesy. Don't waste people's time, be prepared, and give them what they need to work with you, clearly and up front. You're the one who wants to sell them your story, after all.

But wait, I hear the sound of little fluffy paws approaching. Let's go and see who is coming.

Ooh look, bunnies!

### First steps, or when bunnies attack!

We talked a little about pitching in the last chapter and I want to pick up on this now and go into more detail. Let's recap briefly. I'm sorry to say that all too many *first* pitches by a film student in an introductory class go something like this:

'*There's this world where "ooh look, bunnies" and then cool stuff happens. Oh and there's this dude.*'

In other words they have thought a little bit about the story world in which their story is set—it may or may not involve actual bunnies, they are just an example. They also have some ideas for (cool) stuff that might happen in that world, but characters and their little problems are still kind of an afterthought. This should all be familiar from the previous chapter. Anyway, after I have broken down and cried in the middle of the classroom and then begged the students to follow the principle of character leading story, their *second* re-pitches will go something like this:

*'There's this dude in a world where "ooh look, bunnies." Cool stuff happens.'*

They then smile in triumph, expecting awestruck praise from a proud and teary-eyed professor. Well at least they get the teary-eyed part. What follows is that they discover they are standing in my void zones and they wipe. Battle rez won't save them. Many deaths occur. Bloody, terrible deaths which send the poor students all the way back to the graveyard out in the hallway, before the start of the raid … um, the class. Remember kids, in screenwriting as in life, save early and often. They now promise they will rework their ideas with actual *story connections* between 'this dude' and 'ooh look, bunnies' which are played out through *story-appropriate* 'cool stuff' happening:

*'[Character] is [problem] in a world where "ooh look [problem embodied]."'*

In the same goofy language, here is the problem of *This is England* to show how it should work: 'Sean misses his dad in a world where "ooh look, false surrogates."' See his problem? And here it is in *For the Birds*: 'The Mean Birds are insular in a world where "ooh look, there's a causeway."' See their problem? If we are really lucky, the *third* re-pitches will start something like this:

*'There's this dude who is afraid of bunnies in a world where "ooh look, bunnies" …'*

So far so good, they are working hard at it and starting to get somewhere. There is a 'dude' and he has a potential problem that comes from somewhere inside him and not just from the outside world. This internal problem *gives him* an external problem because the 'ooh look, bunnies' story world is now designed to make him something of an outsider, with all the potential uncertainties and trauma that can lead to. We can actually make some kind of a story out of this. How 'we' then proceed to do so in the third re-pitches tends to split like this:

*Either:* '... and the dude learns that he has to find a way to get over his fear of bunnies so that he can live happily in the "ooh look, bunnies" world.'

*Or:* '... and the dude learns how to kill all the bunnies. With special bunny eating acid.'

```
                IMPLIED YOU
      Aw, don't hurt the bunnies. I like
      bunnies.

                FRIENDLY ME
      OK. Good to know. But these are only
      imaginary bunnies. They feel no
      pain.

                IMPLIED YOU
      How do you know? I don't trust you.

                FRIENDLY ME
      Ask the bunnies.

                IMPLIED YOU
      Don't be silly. Bunnies don't talk.

                FRIENDLY ME
      They are imaginary, so they can do
      whatever we want them to. 'Write
      what you don't know,' remember? Oi,
      imaginary bunnies, any of you feel
      pain?

                IMAGINARY BUNNY 1
      No guv'nor.

                IMAGINARY BUNNY 2
      Not me.

                IMPLIED YOU
      Oh. Fair enough. Bring on the acid
      then.

                FRIENDLY ME
      Whoa, not so fast there. You can't
      change that easily. What would we
      do for the rest of the movie?
```

So both options involve the 'dude' changing himself. In the first he has to find a way of coming to terms with the horror that is bunnies for the greater social good, to be able to make his way in the world and, no doubt, just for the sake of his own sanity. In the second he has to learn how to '... crush the bunnies, see them hopping before him and hear the lamentation of their does.' In so doing he is also a changed person because he has overcome his fear in becoming The Bunny Destroyer. In both these cases he will probably need help from friends or a love interest to talk through his problems and manage and support his change and, thus, we discover what **B Stories** are all about (of which more anon).

Alternatively, maybe your hero/ine is 'allergic to bunnies in a world where "ooh look, bunnies."' Now maybe we have a discovery plot—we need a cure or an antidote—oh and maybe a 'clock,' we need that antidote *right now*. Clocks are always your friends in screenwriting. Give your hero/ine a deadline to chase or a countdown to beat and suddenly your dramatic pace just picked up.

And so, through a process of sheer hard thinking, lots of examples, many wipes and epic fails, as well as a little common sense and creativity, our prospective screenwriters get to a simple statement about their story idea which has *someone with a problem doing something to change herself so she can overcome that problem and change her world*.

It's kind of that simple.

Here's an example of how that sort of discussion works in practice. Imagine the scene: it's a Sunday afternoon and I'm on Facebook catching up with a friend back in England. Suddenly a student starts a Facebook chat and wants my input on his new script idea. This is a true story, by the way. Now this is cheeky, I mean Sunday afternoons are my sacred slack times—it's the law—and not to be interrupted for any reason, especially work related. Nonetheless I'm in a good mood and I indulge him. Here's the actual transcript of our Facebook chat, with apologies for the 'online grammar' and with thanks to the student for agreeing to let me use our chat for the book. I joke because of the whole FB/Sunday afternoon thing, but his questions are perfectly sensible:

*Student*
Hello Professor Hoxter, how are you?

*Me*
Good thanks, you?
*[Top notch material this!]*

*Student*
I'm good. I have a logline for a script I'm trying to put together.
*[I have a bad feeling about this—by the way, we'll talk about loglines later in this chapter.]*

*Me*
OK...

*Student*
Could I run it by you?
*[I consider whether to kill him with my remote controlled student-killing
UAV (all professors have one, by the way, so be afraid). Decide I'll let him
live—for now.]*

*Me*
OK

*Student*
An ex cybernetics expert tries to find the terrorist responsible for
releasing a mind control virus he helped to create.
*[Translation: 'There's this dude in a world where "ooh look, mind control."
Cool stuff happens.' But at least he has a notion that his hero should be
implicated in the problem, which is a good start.]*

*Me*
OK, the basic idea is clear, now play it more to character. In other words
why do we care about your character?

*Student*
Why do we care about the effects of the virus or why do we care about
the guy stopping him?

*Me*
All stories are human stories, doesn't matter how plot driven they are at
the heart is a human struggle so play your pitch to the human struggle
that leads the plot.

*Student*
Should I include the fact that the guy is infected with his own virus?

*Me*
Possibly—but that is still plot. Why should I care? Who is he and why
is the story about him, not some other scientist? What motivated him
to create the problem and how will he have to change/develop to solve
it? Stories are about character development; otherwise they are just stuff
that happens that we get to watch.
*[Yes, it's a catch phrase of mine.]*

*Student*
OK, so I should think about the change of the main character?

*Me*
Does he learn from his mistake? What led him to create the problem—didn't think about the consequences? How does he learn to find new priorities etc. etc.? The pitch can be plot driven, but you must answer the human story also. Remember, if your hero has no personal challenges your film will be very boring—just dodging bullets or whatever. Think of it this way: Why can't he solve the problem at the start (if he can = no story)? Why can he solve it at the end? How does he become the guy who can (= story)?

*Student*
Oh! Okay that's helpful.

*Me*
Good—think it over and apply story to your plot and I'm sure it will improve ☺
*[He thought for a minute or two and then came back on. Pop quiz kids: what was my fatal error? Those of you who wrote 'you stayed on Facebook, you idiot' get extra credit. By which I mean: no extra credit.]*

*Student*
So I should think why we should care about the guy and his struggle.

*Me*
Yup, exactly. Your plot sounds like it can be fun but you need to link it to a human story to make it a real movie idea.

*Student*
Like learning from your mistakes—would that be a human story?

*Me*
Exactly—more than that though, think about how your hero is 'broken' as a person at the start (puts science before people/can't see beyond the end of his nose or whatever) and how he learns to fix his humanity—or whatever your story will be about. Link it to the plot: mind control—he's in control of his *own* mind, he thinks discipline and control is what people need to stop the chaos of the world (why is this important? Give him a motivation)—hence developing the virus—but learns he has to relax that control and be human and let his mind wander and be free in

order to learn how to escape the power of his creation. Something like that? See what I mean?

*[Yeah, it's really wooly but hey, Sunday afternoon!]*

**Student**
Yeah! I see. Or might it be the other way around?

**Me**
I'm just riffing—it's your story, go work it out ☺
*[Subtle eh?]*

**Student**
Hahaha, I know. Might it be that he tinkers too much with peoples' minds that he's lost the concept of limits?

**Me**
Yes, that makes him an archetypal overreacher—a common and powerful scientist character type, like Dr. Frankenstein or Dr. Faustus or Dr. Moreau.

**Student**
Is that bad or cliché?

**Me**
Only if you write it badly or clichéd …

*[Please note: just because this chat got into the book doesn't mean I want you all to FB me on a Sunday afternoon for critiques of your story ideas. I will be grouchy and 'release the bunnies!']*

By the way, ensemble stories fall into a slightly different context and we will give them some love in Chapter 7.

Now we just need some character development, and that's coming up in a moment. If you can express your idea through character and plot, you can pitch it. If you pitch it like this, your pitch will be taken seriously. This doesn't mean anyone will want to make it, but at least they will be thinking: 'OK, this is a screenwriter who understands their job.'

'So what,' you say, 'big whoop?'

So this: you are now part of the tiny 0.01% of *potential* screenwriters who do understand their job. Yes, I counted. That is job one. That is how you get on the nice list and stay off the naughty with the producer, the company, the agency or whoever you were pitching to. Even your screenwriting professor has a nice list. Who knows, she might hear of a job, an internship, a project that needs a *you* to fill it.

Being on the nice list means you get a chance of future jobs. It means word gets round in a good way that you are someone with potential, someone to take seriously. It means—drum roll please—people will want to read your *next* script. These are all very important things. They are toes in the door and those toes are connected to a foot. Your foot; their door.

If you read back and thought: 'Oh noes, I can't express my idea like this,' that means you are currently lurking in one or both of these two unfortunate positions:

1 Your idea still needs work.
2 You can't see the premise in your idea.

Of the two of them, the cure for the first case is relatively easier because it implies that at least you understand where you are trying to get to. The second is where most of the problems lie, and we will spend some pages working through it.

First of all, let's define some terms. We are talking about stage one of the pre-writing process. In this stage you will come across a number of similar steps that have a direct bearing on the screenplay development process. Of these, 'concept,' 'theme,' 'premise,' 'pitch statement' and 'log line' will probably be the most common.

## The theme

*The theme is the heart of the problem or challenge your lead character will face.*

It is also the handiest marker by which the audience will be able to follow her as she changes, through the action of the theme on the story. It is not yet a premise or a pitch statement, but it will be a major influence on both.

The easiest, but by no means the only themes to work with are one- or two-word encapsulations of a character's challenge. They are big ideas, like: love, courage, fatherhood, responsibility, loyalty, commitment and friendship. These are so big and broad that there is endless scope for all of the fascinating detail and character work you are going to invent to exist happily within them. Just as no two relationships you have had were exactly the same, no two movie love stories are the same, even if they share a number of *tropes* (common themes).

*Your theme will not change as you tell your story, but your hero/ine's attitude to the theme will develop and transform as the fundamental articulation of their story.*

To take the love example, let's go ahead and Aniston it up a little. Your heroine starts the movie jaded. She's fed up with all the game playing of the 'dating scene' and she tells her friends she has had it with love. Sure enough … well you can fill the rest in yourselves. Love is still the theme; just your character changed their mind about it all of a sudden.

Remember, there are many stories you can tell about this character—let's call her, oh, I don't know, how about Jennifer—who gave up on love and then found it when she least expected it. Jennifer could have any number of fascinating challenges in her life, both before and after the love story you just worked out. It doesn't matter how great they are, they are all *different* stories with different themes. That means they are different movies; don't mix them up by changing theme in the middle.

In other words, your theme keeps you on the straight and narrow. This is the funny story of how Jennifer changed her attitude to *love* when she found the right girl, not the really sad but ultimately uplifting one about what happened after her poor sister died and Jennifer got left with the twins and suddenly had to work out how to deal with *motherhood*. Go write that one next.

If you are not certain what your theme is, ask yourself this question first: *how does my story world spank my hero/ine?* The answer to that question should always imply your theme or at least offer a clear choice of themes, depending on how you want your hero/ine to face up to and overcome that problem.

This means that, until you have figured out the job your hero/ine has to do for your story, your theme will most likely be kind of fuzzy. This also means that answering that question is now your top priority, because every other structural and conceptual question relates back to the theme. When we know what it is we can hang everything else on it with security.

Yes, it's true, some heavily plot-driven action and adventure films don't really have big articulating character themes—but I bet many would be improved if they did. The fact that you *can* write a screenplay that points at explosions for two hours and says 'Look, explosions' and not much else (*Transformers: Revenge of the Fallen* 2009) is not an adequate excuse to do so. If that is what you want to do, put this book down, because it will be of very little use to you. Yes, I like a good explosion as much as the next geek, but I also like my action movies to have a heart and to be about something more than just giant space robots having an endless cat fight on a pyramid.

Take another kind of adventure movie, like *Conan the Barbarian* (scr. John Milius and Oliver Stone, adapted from the stories of Robert E. Howard; 1982) and you can see how the theme of a high genre movie can be integral to the drive of the narrative without getting in the way of all the sword fights, giant snakes and Hyborian hippies jumping off cliffs at the whim of James Earl Jones. Yes, it's a bunch of over-the-top sword and sorcery hijinks with the lad Arnold prancing about in leather, furs and a dodgy mullet, but you didn't think a filmmaker with the prodigious talent and eccentric obsessions of John Milius would deny you a theme, did you? It's simple and straightforward and narrowly Nietzschean, as befits the thought processes of its hero and the politics of its main writer. Anyway, here is Milius in an interview with Nat Segaloff:

> I took the things out of R. E. Howard that I wanted to use and chose a primal story of *revenge*. I had the idea of doing a trilogy. The first one would be about strength—'that which does not kill you makes you stronger.' In the end, Thulsa Doom [James Earl Jones] tells Conan [Arnold Schwarzenegger], 'I'm the reason you're here. I'm the reason you're Conan. What will your world be without me?' [my italics]

And here we get our first glimpse of the importance of the relationship between your hero/ine and their opponent, antagonist, villain/ess, rival, dark power or whatever you are going to call the force in opposition to their overcoming the problem of your movie's story: Thulsa Doom kills Conan's family and condemns him to a life of slavery. This hardship turns the boy Conan into the bulging Arnold we knew and loved. So the villain, Thulsa Doom, directly provides Conan with his theme (revenge) and indirectly with the weapons (his comedy muscles) to carry it out.

We will deal with this hero–villain relationship in more detail in the next chapters, but villains are your dear friends as a screenwriter and you should cultivate them early in your story thinking.

OK, so if your world is 'ooh look, bunnies,' your theme will be the reason that poses a problem for your hero/ine. If they are scared of bunnies (for which we read 'the world': this character is timid and can't get anywhere because they can't face up to the pressures of adult life— they need to grow up), finding *courage* (or embracing *adulthood* because maybe bunnies actually = grown ups) might be your theme. Then you play out the theme through your character and—ta da! Welcome to the beginning of structure.

We'll work this out in much more detail in the next chapter, but for now a cheesy example may be enough to keep you on track. Yes, ladies and gentlemen, we are going back into Nakatomi Plaza to hook up with the boy Bruce Willis, who is still running around in his grubby wife beater. Don't say I never give you anything.

In thematic terms, *Die Hard* is really little more than a basic manual for species evolution. Let's call it *Sentience for Dummies*. This is because the theme of *Die Hard* can be reduced to simple *adaptation* (*learning to adapt to change*).

It plays out throughout Bruce's story as he is forced to second guess himself, think laterally and anticipate in terms of mastering the *action plot* while he learns to recognize and value his wife for who she is and what she has achieved in the *relationship story*. Bruce is pretty good at thinking on his bare, bloody feet when the bullets are flying, but he really sucks at it when it comes to his view of the world and his relationships:

*'Bruce is a dinosaur in a world where "ooh look, your wife's a mammal."'*
*See his problem?*

At the start of the movie, Bruce plays a knuckle dragging, antediluvian, smirkingly superior, ignorantly conservative cliché of an almost man. In other words he is broken but he barely even notices. He can't deal with the success and independence and general not being barefoot and pregnantness of his wife. He can't deal with air travel, let alone Christmas in California. He even finds it hard to come to terms with the basic existence of Los Angeles. (OK, maybe we're with him on that last one.) Pretty much every problem he has is externalized: it's *your* fault; not mine.

*Your theme articulates what are often referred to as your character's core beats of change in the story.*

Typically, movie heroes find it hard to accept change—hey, if they didn't there wouldn't be much of a story. Indeed they tend to **reject** it outright to begin with (first beat). John McClane, for example, starts *Die Hard* in full-on superior East Coaster in La La Land mode: California bad. California lead wife astray. Me fix wife.

He then alienates his wife by demonstrating his emotional stasis: 'Didn't we have this same conversation in July?' she asks him. He knows he is blowing it ('Schmuck!') and **accepts** that he has to make a meaningful effort or he will lose her (second beat): hmm, wife better than Hart Bochner. Him Californian douchebag. She just work there. Me no want lose wife. Me fix self. Ooh, toes feel comfy on carpet—wait, what that bang bang noise?

Finally, after entertaining struggles to accommodate and finally to embrace the required change, a movie story sometimes asks its hero/ine to **sacrifice** the benefits of that change for a higher moral purpose:

now you want it, give it up (third beat). In *Die Hard*, McClane realizes that, even though he now understands how to save his marriage, he has to risk himself utterly to save the lives of his wife and the other hostages: Me learn lesson. Me be good husband now if can only survive Eurotrash haircut holocaust. Hmm, me think saving others more important. Me go get fire hose. Break more glass. See, me evolved.

Of course, in potentially sacrificing himself to save the others he also gets back as a reward what he finally offered up to providence for a higher purpose: his chance to save his marriage. In other words, it's an 'up' ending.

I didn't make this change beat system up, by the way. It's a pretty standard model for character development and you can find it in different language in many screenwriting books. For example, Vogler writes in terms of the 'Refusal of the Call,' 'Crossing the Threshold' and 'The Ordeal' as beats on the Hero's Journey. Anderson uses a three part 'Reject,' 'Embrace' and 'Sacrifice' model for her articulation of the 'character arc.' Snyder talks of the 'Debate' over whether or not to deal with the story problem and the 'whiff of death' that attends the character's greatest crisis.

While we are talking about Snyder, he has a nice little catch phrase that reminds his readers of the importance of change in storytelling. Good movie ideas begin with their characters facing the problem: 'Stasis = Death.' The best movie stories are attempts by their protagonists to avoid that fate, literally or metaphorically. Think of young Luke Skywalker itching to get away from his uncle's moisture farm on the dead-end world of Tatooine near the start of *Star Wars* (1977). Clearly here are only so many Womp Rats you can bullseye in your T-16 before, you know, meh.

Give your hero/ine that little stasis problem and you can bet they'll want to be somewhere different.

Here's a first rate example: in *Brick* (scr. Rian Johnson; 2005), Brendan starts the movie locked into a cynical, destructive loop. He is in self-imposed exile from every aspect of his high school community. His girlfriend left him because he wanted to take her away from that world and lock her away in the box of his love. Now she is dead and he has to re-engage with the world to solve her murder. True to the best Hardboiled Detective tradition: 'Brendan needs to uncover the truth in a world where "ooh look, everybody's corrupt" ...'

John McClane certainly faces that primal choice at the start of *Die Hard* in terms of his marriage and then in real life-or-death terms as the plot develops, in the shape of Alan Rickman and his bunch of butch Brunos. It proceeds to give Bruce/McClane an ultimatum: adapt or die.

Through the course of the movie, he gains the mental equivalent of opposable thumbs. Lives are saved and the McClane marriage stumbles on until he forgets all of his lessons just in time for the sequel. Nobody said he was a bear with lots of brain.

So as not to scare the more knuckle dragging members of its core audience, the need for adaptation is expressed through the hyperbolic action as a problem of masculine determination, something like: 'How far would you go for love?' What the film actually means—what it actually requires of Bruce's John McClane—is: 'How much would you *change yourself* for love?' See why the trailers focus on bare feet and bullets, not the results of the sensitivity training he is actually undergoing?

> IMPLIED YOU
> That's kind of reductive though,
> isn't it, adaptation I mean? After
> all you are always saying that any
> good movie story is about character
> change?

> FRIENDLY ME
> Good, you've been paying attention.
> In fact that's exactly why I picked
> Die Hard again for this little
> example. Don't get me wrong, it's
> a great action script, but it's so
> basic in thematic terms that it
> plays like some kind of ur-story.

Now we can apply what we learned about theme to your premise.

> IMPLIED YOU
> Wait. I'm getting lost in all these
> terms. Can we recap a little?

> FRIENDLY ME
> OK, think of a movie like the
> contents of a wardrobe.

> IMPLIED YOU
> Ooh, is this the famous 'Wardrobe' of
> your 'VW Wardrobe Method'?

> FRIENDLY ME
> Yes, but don't be snide. The idea is
> so simple it's easy to visualize.

With both eyes shut, Implied You takes a deep breath and concentrates.

> IMPLIED YOU
> Bring on the easy visuals.

## The wardrobe

> FRIENDLY ME
> OK, imagine the theme of your story
> as a big solid wooden wardrobe.
> Everything else will fit comfortably
> inside it if you do your job right.
> Also your theme will not change
> throughout the story so the image
> of a strong, heavy piece of
> furniture is kind of appropriate.
> Are you with me so far?

> IMPLIED YOU
> Yup. Wardrobe. Theme. Consistent.
> Go for it.

> FRIENDLY ME
> Good. Now inside your wardrobe is
> a rail that goes all the way
> across from one side to the other.
> This rail represents your main
> character's journey during the
> film. Notice that both ends of the
> rail are anchored firmly to the
> wardrobe. In story terms, your
> character is locked to the theme.

> IMPLIED YOU
> Without the theme there would be
> nothing to hold the rail in place.

> FRIENDLY ME
> You got it. Now imagine a bunch of
> clothes hangers on the rail.

> IMPLIED YOU
> How many hangers?

> FRIENDLY ME
> Like we were discussing before, it
> depends rather on how small you want
> your story elements to be for easy
> use.

> IMPLIED YOU
> OK. And the story is basically my
> heroine working through her changes
> as she struggles with the theme?

FRIENDLY ME
Yes, it deals with her internal
world. It's Bruce learning that he
has to adapt his old view of gender
roles to the new reality if he
wants to have a real marriage and
family.

IMPLIED YOU
And it's the decisions he takes
before and after he has done that
learning?

FRIENDLY ME
It's how a character experiences
the effects of their decisions in
an ongoing process of personal
change and development. The point
is that your story is nothing
without your main character and
it all falls down without a
consistent theme. Now let's imagine
all your best clothes hanging from
those hangers. Also, most of your
hangers can hang multiple garments—
like the ones you can buy for ties
or trousers or shoes.

IMPLIED YOU
In my mind I have such cool clothes.
They are my plot, right?

FRIENDLY ME
Yup, and they are making
everything look good.

IMPLIED YOU
Because they are all the cool
events and encounters that come out
of and are driven by the story—
the stuff that we actually see on
screen?

FRIENDLY ME
Good job. But remember, they would
just be a crumpled pile of cool
stuff on the floor without a story
to attach them to your heroine and
a theme to keep her moving in the
right direction.

IMPLIED YOU
Worryingly, that actually made
sense.

```
                    FRIENDLY ME
     Good. Now let's introduce some more
     terms to confuse you again.
```

## The premise

*A premise is a short, one sentence statement encapsulating the plot or story or at least the central story problem of your movie. It's the minimum information you need to know to 'get it':*

- 'Human-sized cockroaches terrorize the New York Subway.' (*Mimic* 1997)
- 'A terrible massacre underlines the tragedy of a young democracy caught between dictatorships.' (*Katyn* 2007)
- 'A divorced workaholic learns that fatherhood can be his finest accomplishment.' (*Kramer vs. Kramer* 1979)
- 'A supervillain transforms himself into a superhero, learning that heroes aren't born ... they're made.' (*Megamind* 2010)
- 'A maverick detective finds his moral limits when vigilante cops take the law into their own hands.' (*Magnum Force* 1973)
- 'A party animal has to grow up when a one-night-stand leads to a pregnancy.' (*Knocked Up* 2007)
- 'A bourgeois man transforms himself into an agent of genocide.' (*Spalovac Mrtvol/The Cremator* 1969)
- 'Cartoon monsters discover that laughter is more powerful than fear.' (*Monsters Inc.* 2001)
- 'Emo vampires and evul vampires have a douche-off.' (*Twilight* 2008)

Once again, if you can't do this for your idea then it still needs work.

Note that with heavily plot driven movies, as in *Mimic* above, a premise statement that sets up the problem can be enough to start with. It goes without saying that there will be a bunch of killings and then the forces of law or good or science or whatever will get down to some variation of monster spanking. So for *Jaws* (1975) the statement: 'A small town is terrorized by a giant shark ...' tells you enough to 'get it.' It's not like the film is going to play out as '... and everyone stayed out of the sea and hung out at swimming pools until it swam away.'

Well maybe they do in *Jaws in Revolt*, the quirky indie remake starring Michael Cera as Quint's bookish, thalassophobic nephew, Paulie Quint, who has to create his own cool, shark-like alter ego to help him get over his irrational fear of the sea (for which read: girls) the idea for which just forced its way into my screaming brain for some unknown reason.

*'Curse you, Michael Cera!'*

Anyhoo … this comes back to the other purpose of a premise, and that is *selling your idea*. Much as we like Mira Sorvino and Jeremy Northam, their characters' stories are not the selling point of *Mimic*; the giant cockroach guys in the subway are. Of course, when we dig deeper, we find that it was Mira's actions in developing an über-roach spray that led to the current crisis. This is important, but not as much as '… in a world where "ooh look, six-foot-long cockroaches"'. Where you need it is in the follow-up to your premise, your pitch statement.

## The pitch statement

*A pitch statement is the premise worked up into a slightly longer but still very short encapsulation of your story.*

By the way, some of these terms are kind of floating. For example, what I am calling a pitch statement many people call a **logline**. I'm calling it a pitch statement for the purposes of this book because it reminds us of its function in its title, unlike the rather abstract logline. No matter which term you use, it is the statement that sells your idea to other people and, as long as you are familiar with both terms, it doesn't really matter that much. The premise is shorter, pithier and more sales-pitchy. The pitch statement/logline is somewhat longer and speaks a little more to structure over concept.

Easy peasy and/or lemon squeasy.

Your pitch statement often, but not always, adds important story information that helps us to understand how your plot-driven concept is motivated and carried along at a human level. 'Ooh look, six-foot-long cockroaches.' *Because* Mira's bug spray had six-foot side effects. *And now* she has to redeem herself by putting things right. Cue giant roach stomping … You need to work it out fully in order to write your story coherently.

Some people will tell you a pitch statement can be a short paragraph of two or three sentences. Others will say it must only be a single sentence. I come down firmly on the side of the latter. Work your concept and your sales pitch into one sentence, but have well organized and prioritized supplementary information waiting for an opening. In other words, your pitch is your first statement, but you have prepared a second and a third to fill in details directly alluded to in your opening pitch.

We have seen that working out your premise is a process of paring down and focusing in on the key theme your screenplay is going to tackle. When you have found that key idea, your first job will be to express it clearly and in terms people can quickly and easily relate to. More importantly you need to keep in mind that, in spec world, the person to whom you are pitching or (especially) sending an enquiry letter has a very low level of investment in what you are about to tell them. You have to grab their attention and make them want to know more.

Your second job will be to apply your theme to your hero/ine in such a way that it defines their function in the story. This function is what some people call a *character arc* because the character will be transformed by the theme; bent to its will.

Your third job will be to nail your story fast to the trajectory of your character's arc and your fourth will be to express that story through plot.

## The top ten ground rules for a good movie pitch

1 *Your movie idea is now your pitch statement.*
   What, you thought your idea was a precious little jewel and the pitch was the horrible mucky commercial thing you had to cheapen it into to get it made? But why would your idea be different from your pitch? Remember, your pitch statement is also a check for yourself that your idea actually works and that you know how to develop it into a screenplay.

2 *Your movie's story is about somebody with a clear and consistent problem or challenge.*
   We have covered this previously. Remember, your wardrobe is designed to hold your clothes rail, not to accommodate multiple branches. If your theme changes—if your hero/ine's problem changes—your story just changed and this tends to make what came before narratively redundant and thus, in movie terms, a colossal waste of time and money.

3 *Your pitch will show or at least imply that this challenge manifests both internally and externally.*
   This is because the story world you create will be designed to force the internal challenge into the open so the audience can understand it and follow as your hero/ine deals with it (scared of bunnies/world in which 'oh look bunnies'—remember?).

4 *You will pitch through the story—through the trials of your hero/ine—not through all the cool stuff you have planned for the design of the spaceships' laser turrets.*

I'm looking at you: Half The Class ...

Yes, if you are writing a science fiction epic we will want to know at some point what sells your particular vision of the future. This will be important for some aspects of your storytelling and certainly for production design, marketing and publicity. But remember our example from *Mimic*, the premise is the six-foot-long roaches, but the story involves Mira facing up to the consequences of her actions ... which led to the six-foot-long roaches. In your pitch you need to play this out, even though your premise was doing just fine pointing at six-foot-long roaches and saying 'Cool, huh?'

Joss Whedon could have pitched the wonderful and much lamented series *Firefly* (2002) to Fox executives with a firm nod towards the words 'cowboys in space' (although all evidence suggests they weren't listening properly), but try summing up the science fiction concept of a new adaptation of Frank Herbert's *Dune* as efficiently in three words: 'Giant wormy jihad.' Meh. 'Feudal space bondage.' Hmm. 'Guild spice ... pranks.' Grr. Aha—here's the easiest gag: 'No Sting. Result!'

Now I feel cheap.

5 *Tell us who your hero is in a well-chosen phrase and link that description into the meat of the story or plot.*

Here's a rough attempt at a story-heavy example: 'After he is dumped by his girlfriend, Summer, Tom Hansen, an aspiring architect paying the rent as a greeting card writer, has to examine the five hundred days of their relationship to figure out where he went wrong.'

By the way, we know this is a story-heavy pitch because it focuses on introspection forcing action rather than action forcing introspection. This speaks directly to story rather than plot.

Now this one is a tough pitch. There are still a bunch of unanswered questions begging, but at least we have a hero with a double problem implied here: he needs to understand why he couldn't make his relationship work (internal) and he needs to find a way of getting on with his career (external). In solving the former, he will also see his way clear to solving the latter. If he doesn't, he's stuck as Mopey Loser Stasis Boy so let's hope his emotional exploration of those *(500) Days of Summer* works it all out for him.

This might be the subject of your follow-up pitch statement.

The pitch also implies the non-linear structure of this film. Of course, our hero needs to think his way backwards and forwards through the (500) days. How else is he going to make sense of it all?

This might be the subject of your third pitch statement.

Here's a plot heavy example: 'In the 1930s, Indiana Jones, a globetrotting archeologist, has to outwit the Nazis in order to prevent an all-powerful mystical artifact from being used for evil.' Yup, you guessed it, that one was for *Annie Hall* (1977).

As you can see from the examples above—ok, I lied, the second one was *Raiders of the Lost Ark* (1981) just in case, for some unfathomable reason, anyone is reading this in the year 2467 and no copies of the film still exist—you can pitch to plot. Ideally you still need to do it as much as possible through your characters and their human problems. What does my hero have to do to be able to survive and thrive?

What this particular pitch doesn't do is discuss Indy's little personal problems up front because there's a great big whopper of a problem that is already apparent. Be ready to talk about his internal problems, fear of snakes and being kind of unprepared for the reality of the supernatural, in a subsequent statement. For this pitch, pesky Nazis tells us all we need to be told.

You see how the worlds work variously to story, plot and character in these very different examples? To use the language of our previous discussion, *Raiders* is set in a world where 'ooh look, Nazis' and *(500) days* is set in a world where 'ooh look, other people don't always feel the same way you do.' That's Tom's problem, he is crazy in love with Summer but she is never really in love with him. What's more, she is honest about it from the start but he doesn't want to hear it. That's why their relationship is doomed and that's what he has to come to terms with in his critical self-examination. That's the problem in the world; the trap written into the fabric of the story.

6  *Give the name of your hero/ine in your pitch.*
You should name them because then everybody has a shorthand for discussion and we aren't working our dry, nervous lips around terms like 'protagonist' and 'main character' in a pitch meeting or class. Also names have power and can boost the punch of your idea. He's an archeologist—hmm, could be really dull—but fortunately he isn't doddery old Professor McSchwardflovskinheimowitzberg, he's Indiana Jones. Yup, he's a cool professor and we are going to have fun following his cool exploits. Did I mention the whip?

Also in the other pitch it is very important that we know right up front that Tom's ex-girlfriend's name is Summer, otherwise nobody will understand the double meaning in the title.

7  *It is a very good idea to specify the general location and period in which your story is set, if it is not obviously 'Somewhere Cheap' and 'In the Present.'*

In other words, your pitch should give some indication of your film's projected budget, especially if the budget will be high. A setting in the past, even the fairly recent past, will ramp up the budget, and exotic locations will also cost a lot of money, to say nothing of complex action and special effects. *Raiders of the Lost Ark* is a period piece, with countless locations and loads of good old Nazi spanking action—expensive stuff. *(500) Days of Summer* is set in the present and needs some offices, a karaoke bar, assorted contemporary houses and apartments, a bench in a park, a train and an IKEA if I remember correctly—pretty modest.

Don't hide this stuff from your audience. They are certainly not expecting you to quote a dollar amount, but they will expect you to be an honest broker. Let them know the kind of project they are potentially signing on for. If you sell a quaint little character piece featuring a touching romance between a retired landscape gardener and the owner of a cake shop, and only when you submit the first draft does it become clear that you have written an epic three-hour Victorian steam punk romance with half the film taking place in the great sunken seaweed gardens of Atlantis and the other half on the Bakery Planet of Brioche 9, you will not be a popular person to say the least.

8 *Don't pitch the* **B Story** *up front.*

But make sure you know what it is and how it works for the inevitable follow-up. We'll talk more about *B Stories* later, but it probably involves your hero/ine in a significant amount of snogging and being told to get a life.

9 *Leave them wanting more.*

Don't try to anticipate or answer every question about your story in your pitch. Entice them, don't overwhelm them with detail. Indy needs to stop the Nazis from using the artifact—cool, how does he do that? Tom needs to find out what went wrong with Summer—cool, what did go wrong? Now they have questions to ask you. Now all your additional planning pays off because you can go 'Aha!' and launch into the second and third levels of plot and story detail you had prepared but not blown in one enormous info dump straight off. Now you have moved from giving a pitch to having a conversation about a movie idea. Guess what, that's further than most people get. Of course, they still may not buy your story, but see how it works in your favor?

10 *Practice, practice, practice.*

Seriously, do this. Talk to yourself in a mirror. Bore the family dog. Record yourself and play it back more than once (so you get over the cringe factor of hearing your own voice). Not only will it give you confidence when you actually have to make a pitch, but it will also make it much easier to hear and correct problems or just awkwardness or long-windedness in your pitch statements. Remember that a pitch meeting—even giving a pitch in class—can be a traumatic experience at the best of times. Alvin Sargent (*Paper Moon* 1973; *Ordinary People* 1980) once described it as like being on camera with your fly down, so the more you practice, the higher your zip!

All of these rules lead to this simple conclusion: at the end of your opening pitch statement nobody should be reacting like Tom Hanks when presented with a rubbish transforming skyscraper toy in *Big* (1988): 'I don't get it.' Doubtless they will have many valid questions pertaining to the substance, detail and practicality of your movie idea, but they should already understand how we get from A to B and what both A and B represent in human and story terms.

If they don't, your pitch sucked.

End of story. No arguments. It's not their fault. They may be stupid producers—and most producers are very far from stupid, by the way. They just live in a different part of the creative world that has some different priorities. But it is your job to explain it to them professionally, in other words in terms they can understand and work with. These rules—and the minor variants you may find in other manuals—make you do this. Follow them properly and your pitch will be at least OK. If you can't do this, you are not going to go anywhere as a screenwriter. Sorry.

## What is a screenplay and how do I get there?

Let's recap.

In order to make the process of screenwriting as straightforward and painless as possible you can undertake a bunch of writing tasks before you actually start to write scene one. This is helpful because:

1 You need to fully understand *at the very least* the premise, theme and (thus) basic structure of your story before you start writing it. If you don't, you will almost certainly get muddled, stuck and generally frustrated. Your draft will not work and you will have to go back through it and unpick all the missteps and mistakes your lack of forethought created. There will be enough problems with your first draft (see Chapter 9) even if you have your structure nailed before you

begin, so to willingly add the probability of more for no reason is just silly.

2 If you are pitching an idea, not a spec script, you may be asked to jump through all the pre-writing hoops to be allowed to get anywhere near a first draft. This is just the way the development process works. You may have heard it called 'development hell.' That's when it all goes wrong, you and your producing partners are not seeing eye to eye, or the eccentricities of the movie business just walk up and slap you down for no particular reason. Sometimes it seems to happen just because it can. Thankfully, there is a way you can make an impact on keeping 'development' as far away from 'hell' as possible (although in my experience there is always a whiff of brimstone somewhere in the process). What you can do is be prepared and be clear about your ideas and your structure from the beginning.

The good news is that we are well on our way through the process. There is one more major and a couple of minor steps that we need to talk about before we get to page one of your actual screenplay. These constitute stage two of the pre-writing process.

The first and most important of the stage two documents is the *treatment*. In fact it is so important that, in order to really nail your pitch, you probably need to have written at least a short treatment beforehand. We will also have to spend a little time talking about, or at least, to go all Wiki on you, disambiguating the following: 'synopsis,' 'beat sheet,' 'outline' and 'scene breakdown.'

## The treatment

This is where you find out whether your story is going to work or not.

The treatment expands the premise and fills in the gaps so you can see the story clearly from beginning to end. Not all writers do treatments and, in the interests of full disclosure, I hate writing them and try and avoid them whenever possible. It is a great safety net, however, especially for inexperienced writers. If you have written ten good scripts, well, maybe you can do without one, but if you pitch an idea, if you go into development nowadays, you are almost certainly going to have to work with them.

There are a number of variations on a theme here, but what they all have in common is that a treatment is a prose telling of your story. It is not in screenplay format. It is not separated into formal scenes in the way a screenplay is. A treatment is basically a work through of all the important stages in your story, told as dramatically and evocatively and yet economically as possible.

In other words a good treatment should be a pleasure to read. It should flow and have the pace and tension your story does; only it is not a short story in the traditional literary sense. You are still writing for a visual medium and your treatment should reflect that. Rather, a treatment is a set of narrative encapsulations that gets you from beginning to end efficiently but with class.

Where the feast is at its most moveable is in terms of length. This is because different people involved in the development process may want different versions, from a page on upwards. When playing with others one just has to ask what length they want. When playing with … When working on your own, you probably want to write as full a treatment as you can. This may be up to 20 pages or so. Some writers go even longer, but I think there is a law of diminishing returns after about 20 pages where the document becomes unwieldy and less fit for purpose. Certainly in 20 pages you should be able to include every important story moment and plot incident.

What I usually do is work up to it. I start by telling my story in four pages, one per act but two for act two. We will talk about acts when we come to the 'W' structure in the next chapter. I then step back and look at how the story flows and how it is balanced and start working up each act as I go. Unless somebody is telling me to produce x pages, I don't really worry about how long it will be at the end. When it's done it's done.

The great thing about treatments is that they allow a reader to get a handle on the story fast. That way they can contribute to development discussions without plowing through endless screenplay pages. It is much easier to swap around, insert and remove short prose paragraphs than it is whole scenes with all their dialogue. Also it saves you wasting your time with all that dialogue writing if the story is going to go another way.

Having said that, it is acceptable to include some indicative dialogue in a treatment, indeed it can be very helpful in terms of getting a handle on character. Don't write whole scenes of it, just examples of a character's 'voice' and a few key speeches or exchanges.

## The top ten ground rules for a good movie treatment

1 *Make it dramatic.*
   It may not look like a screenplay yet, but this is still the story you

love, have committed your time and effort to developing and want others to become enthusiastic about. So tell it with some verve. Seriously, you wouldn't believe how many treatments I have read which plod along, mired in the most banal language as if the writer was resenting every minute of it. Of course, that's because the writer was resenting every minute of it. Yes, it's a chore, but it's important because it will make the final process easier. Now go write it properly.

2  *Hook us in early.*
This is a good check on your storytelling skills. Give the reader a reason to want to read on, something that speaks the uniqueness of your story, right up near the start. This is good screenwriting practice anyway. A hook doesn't have to be a moment of dramatic hyperbole or excess. It can be a subtle character moment that speaks volumes and makes the reader want to read on.

Here's an example of a very undemonstrative, yet telling character hook that I greatly admire from *The Verdict* (scr. David Mamet; 1982). The film casts Paul Newman as an alcoholic lawyer who starts the movie cruising for clients at funeral homes. In an early scene, played in one almost thrown away long shot by the way, Newman's character, Frank Galvin, is telling a joke in his regular bar. This is a serious drinkers' haunt. We know this because of the boxes of free raw eggs at one end of the bar, one of which, in another scene, we see Galvin break into his breakfast beer to set himself up with protein for the day.

Anyway, this little 'throw away' hook scene tells us everything we need to know about Galvin past, present and possibly future. Galvin tells his dumb joke but, in doing so, proves he still has the vestiges of presence and charisma to hold an audience and organize his thoughts efficiently: shades of Galvin Past; hopes for Galvin Future. He also repeatedly calls for rounds of drinks for everyone in the bar, but the barman makes no move to serve. Everyone clearly knows this is a pathetic, empty gesture: this is Galvin Present. The whole scene lasts about 30 seconds, but we learn everything we need to know about where this man is, what he once was and what he might be again. His whole story challenge is encapsulated in that moment and, if we have any heart at all, we want to see how it plays out. It's great writing, its apparent simplicity hiding complexity, and there isn't a giant space robot in sight.

3  *It should be no longer than it needs to be.*
Whatever length that is, either by instruction or your own development. Remember that the primary purpose of the treatment is to be easy to use and to refer to. Fifty pages are not your friends here.

4 *Always use the present tense.*
Your screenplay will be written in the present tense so you might as well get familiar with the style. Movies are written as if everything is just happening for the first time right now, in front of our eyes. This is convenient because, when we watch them, that's what it will feel like. Even a flashback unfolds in real time, so write it in the present tense.

5 *Show, don't tell.*
Here we are again. Remember, you are writing for a visual medium, so use your words to make us see it.

6 *Highlight and encapsulate.*
When you are writing each event, pick out the most important aspects in terms of story structure and character development and tell us those. Try and sum up the story meaning of the scene this way.

7 *Don't drown us in detail.*
We don't need every detail. We certainly don't need every part of your location descriptions. Work out what we need to know to fit this moment to what just happened and what is happening next. This is narrative economy again, but in treatment terms. Make sure we get it. Move on.

8 *Hit your key beats hard.*
We will talk more about beats in the structure chapter, but this instruction is about making clear the moments when major changes or developments occur in your story. Think back to our discussion of the theme. Remember, the theme doesn't change, but your hero/ine's attitude to the theme will. When that happens, make it abundantly clear, because that moment is a major hinge in your mechanism and you want your reader to get it. The same applies to major moments where your hero/ine is either knocked back or drives forward on their path to the ultimate goal. These kinds of hinge moments will come up a number of times (how many hangers on the rail?) so be ready to speak them loud and clear when they do.

9 *Don't hide your cards.*
Remember the surprise Bakery Planet of Brioche 9? Well the treatment is where you need to show us what's in your hand. No nasty budget or story surprises held until the screenplay, please. Play fair and let us know it all right here and now.

10 *Make it dramatic.*
Just testing …

So now we know how to work our idea into a treatment, we can go on very quickly to deal with a few other pesky terms you might come across. Because some of these terms have been known to bleed into one another and different people tend to call the same thing by different names, I am just going to give my version and move on. If you want further disambiguation, well we have already discussed a number of resources for you to go to.

A *synopsis* is really a short outline of the story. It is not a treatment in the sense we have been discussing, but is more like the account of 'what happens in the movie' you might find in a film review. Where your treatment is designed to enthrall the reader and help you sell your idea, the synopsis is a more dispassionate account that provides information but doesn't hook them in through the telling.

A *beat sheet* is a very useful development tool, both for a writer working alone (or in a partnership) and for keeping the discussions with development executives on track. Basically a beat sheet usually emerges after your treatment is already in decent shape and is a much shorter document than a treatment. I always try to work it down to a single page, or at most two pages. Its job is to flag the major story and plot developments and turning points in your story so that, by reading it, we understand the articulation of the dramatic skeleton that the detail of your story and plot will embellish.

Actually the image of a skeleton isn't a bad one to work with. The human skeleton has a whole bunch of bones. Temperance Brennan could name them all and, if I was writing an episode of *Bones* I would care more, but for now 'a whole bunch' is close enough for government work. The human skeleton also has a few major joints: elbows, knees, hips, shoulders and so forth. Your beat sheet shows you how the story equivalents of all those major joints work, not the difference between the frontal squama and the supraorbital margin.

Once again we are in piece of string measuring or bite size chunk weighing territory with this, but you probably have at least a dozen and no more than 20 *key* beats in your story. We will go on to talk about beats in detail in the next chapter in a section with the deeply witty title: '*Beating it up,*' but when something significant happens after which your hero/ine's situation will never be the same again you have probably hit a major story beat. Remember the reject, accept, sacrifice structure we ripped screaming from… well pretty much every other screenwriting book only in different language? Well those shifts in your hero/ine's relationship to your theme will be beats for your beat sheet for a start.

An *outline*, in screenwriting terms is kind of a treatment after it has been put through Dr. Brennan's flesh removal tank. It is all the bones—and now we do care about them all—with none of the flesh remaining. So an outline would give you every scene but in a sentence or so, just informing you of its function: 'x does y' or 'x realizes y' or 'x decides y' or 'x discovers y' and so forth.

A *scene breakdown* can mean different things. In screenwriting terms I have seen it used as a direct alternative to outline or to refer to an even more pared down version of an outline, with just a location indication, or perhaps just a slug line (see below) for each scene. It also has specific meanings in production scheduling and script supervision that I won't go into here.

## The screenplay

Woo and/or hoo! Sound hosannas, because we finally made it. This is what all of the pre-writing schlep has been leading up to. Yes it has been a chore to get here but, if you have applied yourselves to the principles and examples that have gone before, you should now have a workable screenplay idea.

As we have already mentioned, a screenplay is a document designed to be used by many people for just as many different reasons. In other words it is not simply a literary document; it is also a set of specific instructions for a diverse set of professionals from actors and directors to cinematographers, editors, location scouts, caterers and production assistants, all of whom need different nuggets of information from it in order to do their jobs efficiently and well.

So far we have focused on the beginnings of the *literary* journey you will be making in writing your script. Now we have to remind ourselves that the script will be displayed in screenplay format and that format has a bunch of rules. These rules make its secondary function as a set of instructions—a *blueprint*, if you will—as efficient and helpful as possible to the myriad professionals who will use it for their own discreet purposes as it moves towards and through production.

Also remember my earlier warning about format nerds.

One reason for including our little chats between Implied You and Friendly Me has been to establish a few of the ground rules of screenplay formatting. Hopefully you have picked these up and internalized them as we have been going along. I'm not going to give you a full exposition of screenplay format in this book. It would take ages and there are a couple of very useful texts that do the job better than I could and give it the space and focus I can't.

To this end, I recommend that you get hold of the second edition (at time of writing) of Christopher Riley's *The Hollywood Standard: The Complete and Authoritative Guide to Script Format and Style*, published by Michael Wiese Productions in Studio City, CA. This is not the most exciting book in the world but, as you might expect from its title, it is the place to go for the standard answer to any of your formatting questions. Of course, as we have already discussed, there are always exceptions to some of these rules. These exceptions play best when you have *already proven yourself* to be exceptional in the eyes of your readers. Until then there is Riley's useful book.

The second book is by William M. Akers and has the wonderful title *Your Screenplay Sucks: 100 ways to make it great*, also published by Michael Wiese Productions—with whom I have no commercial relationship, other than as a satisfied consumer, just in case you are now wondering. Akers is chirpy and fun and pulls apart most of the common mistakes in both format and content which writers tend to make. Here's number 4 of Akers's 100, a common film student problem, just for an illustration: 'Your story is only interesting to you!' To misquote Judge Reinhold in *Fast Times at Ridgemont High*: 'Read him. Learn him. Live him.'

What I will do is illustrate basic format with a few examples, and suggest why format is important and why you need to learn it and adhere to it as part of your screenwriting education.

## Basic spec screenplay format: it looks like this for a reason

In the American film industry, screenplays have certain elements that are standard. These standard elements should be followed *exactly*. As we have already discussed, if you don't do this it will be assumed that you are an amateur and *nobody* will want to read your script, however good it may be.

These are the bits you don't argue about but just do.

*[NOTE: All the examples of format in this book are only approximate. This is due to the size of the book's page and other publishing require-ments. They will show you the relationship between elements, however, and you will be able to pick up formatting with any standard screenwriting software program very quickly by following their example. Also I am not using 'more' and 'cont'd' when dialogue crosses onto another page.]*

## Spec script vs shooting script

Almost all of you will be writing spec scripts. These rules apply to specs and not to scripts that are going into production. A shooting script—one being prepared for production (and usually the kind of document you can buy in book form as a 'screenplay')—has slightly different rules and formats for things like scene numbering and transitions. I am not going to cover this here.

You must *always* use a courier font, such as *courier new* or *courier final draft* if you use that software.

Your screenplay will be divided into scenes. Each scene starts with a *slug line* followed by scene description (or *action*).

**The slug line** tells us—in this order—whether the scene takes place inside or outside: INT. or EXT. written exactly like this, *not* INTERIOR or EXTERIOR. It then specifies the location and whether it takes place in the DAY or at NIGHT. Occasionally you specify times of day, but for now just use DAY or NIGHT. If your scene takes place in two locations (we follow somebody as they walk outside from an interior location for example), you can use: INT./EXT.

IMPORTANT: This slug line is always written the same way because it is designed to provide very important information for the craft departments. The DP, for example, will have to plan what equipment and power to bring for an interior or exterior shoot, as they will for day or night. A scene which moves from one to the other will mean she has to plan how to match the interior and exterior lighting setups with filters, gels, HMI lights and other instruments.

In a slug line, the *only* period comes after INT. or EXT. *and nowhere else*. The complete slug line looks like this:

```
INT. CLASSROOM - DAY
```

As a rule you should never leave a slug line 'naked'. It should always be followed by description of some kind—even a few words. Don't go straight from slug line to dialogue, for example.

**Description** or action should be kept to an eloquent minimum—narrative economy again. *As with your treatment, write all description in the present tense.* You are telling us what we are seeing happen right at that moment.

Write only what we need to understand the action. When describing a location or a character, try and encapsulate them in a sentence or two at the most.

*Never* call shots or camera angles in your description. You should be able to speak what is important by describing what we see without this, and it *really* annoys directors.

Use short paragraphs encapsulating concepts split by white space rather than long dense paragraphs. It makes for an easier read and is a good way of testing out whether you are over-writing your descriptions. Don't over-use *italics*, as they don't show up well in courier fonts and it feels like you don't have confidence in your dramatic writing. Here's an example of description:

```
PROFESSOR KERNER, brilliant, bald and scary, gives a
lecture.
```

Note that the first time—and *only* the first time—we meet a character in your screenplay, their name is capitalized. This is so that cast information can be located easily for list creation and for the assistant directors to make up their call sheets and so forth.

**Dialogue:** Assuming someone is going to speak in your scene, we format it like so (character names before dialogue are *always* capitalized):

```
                PROFESSOR KERNER
     Welcome to CINE301, you lucky people.
     This semester I will be initiating
     you into the deepest and darkest
     secrets of the movies.

A PESKY STUDENT raises a hand.

                PESKY STUDENT
     Will this be on the midterm?
```

And so on. Some useful additions to the character line (before dialogue):

(O.S.) = off screen: PROFESSOR KERNER (O.S.) Use this when the character is in the space of the scene and speaking, but not currently in shot.
(V.O.) = voice over: PESKY STUDENT (V.O.) Use this for narration recorded after the shoot to be placed over a scene in the edit.

You will sometimes see a **parenthetical** inserted between a character's name and their dialogue thus:

```
                PROFESSOR KERNER
             (impatiently)
     No, and you are being pesky.
```

Try to *avoid* using parentheticals whenever possible. You should use them only when there is a real chance of the meaning of a speech not being clear. Don't use them—like in the example above—to give direction to the actor. The delivery should be obvious from the line itself and from the context. Actors and directors absolutely *hate* unnecessary direction in screenplays.

One good use of parentheticals is to indicate if the speaker is using a different language. You still write their lines in English but can indicate that they will speak the lines (in Spanish). Another can be to indicate when a character shifts their dialogue to address a different person (to Bob). Don't overdo that one; just use it when there is a possibility of confusion. Here's an example from Christopher Nolan's screenplay for *Inception*:

```
                    ATTENDANT
              (in Japanese)
         He was delirious. But asked for
         you by name. And...
              (to the Security
              Guard)
         Show him.
```

**Transitions:** Usually you don't write transitions—cuts, dissolves, wipes etc.—into a spec script, apart from FADE IN at the start and FADE OUT at the end. They waste space and are really the province of the director and the editor in post-production. This is especially the case with CUT TO: after all this is the default for any transition. If you don't tell us otherwise, of course we are going to cut. If you must put a transition in, for the sake of clarity or to signal a flashback or perceptual change of some kind, it goes on the right of the page, like this:

```
Professor Kerner picks up his remote control and calls
up his first slide.
                                            DISSOLVE TO:
```

Or WIPE TO: or whatever is appropriate. And then we move into the next scene:

```
INT, PROFESSOR HOXTER'S OFFICE — DAY
PROFESSOR HOXTER, a major hottie, slacks on the Internet
at his cluttered desk.
```

There is much more to it than this, but if you follow these simple rules you will be able to do most of the things you need to. Now all you need to do before you start writing is make sure your story structure is in proper shape; and that's the subject of the next chapter.

# 5

# 'Taming Wild Words': It's All About the Structure

INT. MANUSCRIPT — DAY
Implied You holds up a hand for silence.

> IMPLIED YOU
> Right, I'm starting this one. It's
> time to get serious. I understand
> creativity. I get the 'write what
> you don't know' thing. I am
> inspired, open minded, thinking
> laterally and consider myself
> officially warned about all the
> pitfalls that lead to becoming a
> movie doofus.

> FRIENDLY ME
> And now you want to know how to turn
> your new creative story ideas into
> screenplays?

> IMPLIED YOU
> No, I want you to teach me basic
> conversational Serbo Croat.

> FRIENDLY ME
> Point taken.

> IMPLIED YOU
> OK, so I know that a screenplay has
> three acts …

> FRIENDLY ME
> In fact there can be four acts. Or
> even five. It depends who you ask.

> IMPLIED YOU
> Well, I'm asking you.

> FRIENDLY ME
> Or eight segments.

```
                IMPLIED YOU
Segments.

                FRIENDLY ME
Or fifteen beats. Or nine essential
elements. Or seven key steps.
Strictly speaking they could be
seven rungs.

                IMPLIED YOU
You are having a laugh now, aren't
you?

                FRIENDLY ME
Or eleven steps.

                IMPLIED YOU
This stopped being funny a few lines
ago.

                FRIENDLY ME
Really? I'm just getting warmed up;
there are in fact sixteen steps.

                IMPLIED YOU
What, are they breeding?

                FRIENDLY ME
Unless you mean heroic steps? Then
there are seventeen.

                IMPLIED YOU
I may have to kill you.

                FRIENDLY ME
Before you reach for your
boomstick, let me see if I can
clarify things a little.
```

One of the most obvious ways your friendly neighborhood screenplay guru sells his or her last/best/only/one true method for screenwriting success is by announcing a miraculous new structural model that breaks story down to its simplest components. Yes, I know, you have already had my 'trinity,' so I'm implicated in this game of 'think of a number.' I'm also giving you my two linked—but certainly not miraculous—structural models.

So the bad news is that there are so many approaches to screenwriting competing for your attention. They all offer their version of truth, justice and the screenwriting way. But how do we navigate our way through them all? Well let's start the countdown with a few likely suspects:

*Seventeen heroic steps:* this is from Christopher Vogler's *The Writer's Journey: Mythic Structure for Writers*. It adapts the monomyth theory of Joseph Campbell to the world of creative writing. Campbell's work influenced Lucas and Spielberg and those who admire their work and attempt to follow in their footsteps. Basically Vogler suggests that all stories share certain mythic tropes, especially around the figure and fate of the hero. Myths have power. Write a screenplay using mythic structure and your story will also have power. It's great fun for *Star Wars* and the like; not so sure it's as helpful universally.

*Sixteen steps:* is from Keith Cunningham's own Campbell-inspired 478-page monster of a manual, *The Soul of Screenwriting: On Writing, Dramatic Truth, and Knowing Yourself*. Screenwriting 'by the numbers,' he argues, gets you nowhere without integrity and understanding the writing process. And by the way, skip forward to page 377 because here are my sixteen steps … hehe.

Oh, and in the interests of full disclosure, my 'W' model has an optional version with sixteen story beats!

*Fifteen beats:* this is from Blake Snyder's *Save The Cat: The Last Book on Screenwriting You'll Ever Need*. We talked about it in Chapter 1.

*Eleven steps:* this is from Jule Selbo's practical and down-to-earth manual, *Screenplay: From Idea to Successful Script*. Not much in the way of personal philosophy, but lots of sensible, mainstream 'how to' information and advice.

*Nine essential elements:* is from Donna Michelle Anderson's *The 1-3-5 Story Structure Made Simple System*. A puritanical and domineering little manual, this one, for naughty writers who need a little correction. Mmmm, correction …

*Eight segments:* is from Paul Joseph Gulino's *Screenwriting: The Sequence Approach, The Hidden Structure of Successful Screenplays*: 'A screenplay can be understood as being built of sequences of about fifteen pages each, and by focusing on solving the dramatic aspects of each of these sequences in detail, a writer can more easily conquer the challenges posed by the script as a whole.' We'll come back to the relationship between the part and the whole in a minute, but he's onto something with the recognition that what this is all about is 'bite size chunks.'

*Seven key steps:* is from John Truby's encyclopedic *The Anatomy of Story: 22 Steps to Becoming a Master Storyteller*. Wait, that can't be right … Ah ok, got it—there are seven key steps to story structure *within* the 22 overall steps to becoming a master storyteller. Actually I use Truby's book and find him very enjoyable as a tasty dipping sauce.

*Seven rungs:* this is from Amnon Buchbinder's somewhat eccentric *The Way of the Screenwriter*. It breaks story structure down according to the rungs on the 'Mithraic ladder' used in ancient Greek initiation rites and associated with what Buchbinder suggests become 'alchemical' transmutations: 'Story is about this mystical transformation of lead into gold.'

*Five acts:* is a classic stage play structure—hey, Shakespeare (or at least his future editors) can't be wrong, right? It's also used or implied in some movies. People usually cite *Goodfellas* (1990) as a key filmic example.

*Four acts:* is basically three acts with act two split at the midpoint.

There are many more like these, but the good news is that, even though they all have useful things to offer in their own ways, we can start culling the herd based on one simple proposition. Any and all books which deal with structural models of four acts or more, or which don't deal in acts at all, are optional. Of course, many of those listed above are really three-act models split into a number of smaller sections, so the culling is harder than it looks ... Still, all you absolutely *need* to know something about is:

*Three acts:* introduces us to the radical notion of a beginning, a middle and an end. All stories have these in some form or other, however disguised and whatever order they turn up in. We can't really get around this one in its most basic definition, even though not all screenwriters acknowledge three acts fully—Charlie Kaufman (*Eternal Sunshine of the Spotless Mind* 2004, *Synecdoche New York* 2008, etc) for one.

I'm sticking with three acts for one very important reason: most of the movie world—and especially the development world—thinks and speaks the language of 'Three Act Structure.' However you conceive of your own method of story making, if you can't also speak your pitch or your story in terms of three acts, you are just giving everyone another free pass to think: 'pfft, noob,' and ignore you.

Three act structure is an important part of your professional education as a screenwriter. As for the other beats and rungs and segments and steps, well, by all means go read those books. They are mostly proposing fairly sensible ways of pulling apart a big thing and laying out its components in different patterns in the hope that you will better understand the nature of the big thing by doing so. This is often a very good principle in teaching.

If, by now, you are wondering about the significance of the number of sections into which you can chop those three acts, roll some dice and I'll split and combine story elements to make them fit the number you rolled. The result might not be as elegant as some of the published models (including my own) when I do it off the cuff, but I'd be willing to bet my usual Really Small Amount Of Money that in each case the key purpose of the exercise would be functionally identical.

And what is the key purpose of the exercise? In my terms: to find a comfortable size of bite size morsel to chew on.

Some writers love working with their minds focused primarily on the great sweep and thrust of an entire story, while others naturally think their way up from the part towards the whole. What makes you comfortable? Whose tone do you respond to? How big a bite are you prepared to take right now? There's no absolute right and wrong here, there's just you and the way your own creative mind likes to work.

## What structure is for and where it comes from

Of course, stories have always had structure. In fact, stories *are* structure. They are clever ways of organizing and ordering information to communicate feelings, ideas, aesthetics, lessons, histories and much else besides. It feels great when your story is working, doesn't it? *How do you know it is working? Your structure tells you so.*

Many writers find 'doing structure' one of the hardest parts of their job. They resist it, especially what they think of as 'Hollywood structure,' as a heavy handed, cookie-cutter, industrial imposition that gets in the way of the purity of their ideas and characters. In my experience, many more writers resist the notion that there is any kind of learnable and—nightmare of nightmares—repeatable structural model for a screenplay than they do any other aspect of the writing process. What this attitude too often reveals is a lack of understanding of what structure really is.

Usually writers back away and claim that, yes, your theme must be consistent or, sure, characters should be true to themselves. Of course, they say, that is a very different proposition from being bound by a reductive structural model. We are free thinkers, we writers like to say, and we won't conform to such limiting devices. Well yes *but*, I would reply, if x, then also y …

If your theme is consistent, if your characters are true to their nature (but they also do something other than sit on their bums and watch the world go by in slab faced, gnomic silence), then already you are using most of my *wardrobe*:

*Character activity means a plot of some kind.*
*Character activity played faithfully to theme means a story.*
*As such, it needs control and organization.*

Guess what, that's really all that's behind screenplay structure.

The 'beats' examples that follow in this chapter only serve to help you articulate and highlight the control and organization you have already acknowledged your story needs. They are just a mechanism designed to help you check your progress at every stage based on the logic with which you designed your story premise. In other words, if you accept the fundamentals of storytelling we have been discussing in this book then you accept the intent of the structural models I am suggesting for you.

Actually, as an occasionally whiny writer, I kind of sympathize with this whiny writer's whine. But only kind of. I certainly don't subscribe to the idea that there is one absolute template for a successful screenplay. In this book I offer detailed models for you to try, and illustrations and examples to show how things can be done, but I don't try to force a complete structural blueprint on you as 'the law.'

I do, however, believe strongly that, whatever way you conceive of your structure, you must take it very seriously indeed, because structure is right at the heart of the contract you are making with your readers and your potential audience. Even when writers veer away from 'accepted ways of doing things' they often do so in order to make their story fit right. Another way of saying this is that writers are often tactically unconventional in order to be strategically conventional.

Here's an example of what appears to be an unusual structural choice at a tactical level but is really quite conventional strategically. It's a movie opening which goes against the grain of typical Hollywood screenplay structure for a with-the-grain kind of reason. The first scenes of *Greenberg* (scr. Noah Baumbach; 2010) introduce us not to the eponymous protagonist but to his soon-to-be romantic interest, Florence. She's a nice, mid-twenties hipstery doormat of a girl who is kind of lost and lacking any discernable ambition. She goes to a thing with a friend and hooks up with an age-appropriate hipstery guy and they go back to his place.

Florence stops outside the door and asks what 'this' is, because she's just got out of a long relationship (this is kind of a mantra with her). The guy smiles, in a rather unpleasantly disengaged hipstery kind of way, and replies that she shouldn't worry because '… this isn't a relationship.' Cut to them in bed in the dark, his back turned to Florence as he sleeps. She is awake, clearly thinking confused thoughts. She reaches out a hand and touches his back. Then she leaves. Yeah, sure, Florence isn't a lost soul. No, she isn't desperate for an emotional connection at all, poor dear. Why is this important? OK, well, mainly because we are about to meet Greenberg, who is a complete nightmare of a forty-something, narcissistic, sociopathic, recovering screw-up. He's also a lost soul, just a very different kind. For us to even get close to believing that Florence might be (kinda sorta) interested in somebody like that, we need to see her exposed in a moment of emotional vulnerability and truth. Sharing that moment with her before we have our minds clouded by the problem of Greenberg clarifies things for us.

Noah Baumbach sums it up like this, in an interview with Bob Verini:

In earlier drafts, I started the movie with him and it never quite worked ... I thought there was something particularly satisfying in putting you in a car with her; it's almost a short film about Florence at the beginning of the movie. I just liked the feeling of exploring in a simple, straightforward way a night in the life of this 24-year-old in Los Angeles. And after a disappointing evening during which she doesn't feel very good about herself, she gets a call from this person who needs help. At that point, the movie hands over to him, and it felt right to me.

The point is that this is an unconventional structural choice designed to contain an excessive character within the bounds of an otherwise pretty conventional story. Greenberg needs help to become less ... Greenberg. That means he needs a reason to be happy. Florence might just be that reason. It is all about establishing a story world in which a relationship between Florence and Greenberg is plausible.

That means it is basically primary exposition (of which more anon). The size of the challenge in making us believe in that connection is expressed through a structural reaction on the part of the writer. Its purpose is still to organize information in the story in the best way to bring us on board with what happens next.

This may seem like an odd comparison, but the opening of *Greenberg* plays like an inverse of the opening of *Star Wars*. Both films delay introducing us to their heroes. In the latter we are only introduced to Luke Skywalker after we have been given a lesson in context. Here's the universe. Here's the Empire. Here's Vader. Here's the princess and the droids. Here's the message to the lost general. Here's the desert planet. Now here's Luke—and we realize he's a tiny cog waiting to be fit into a galaxy-spanning story machine: that's what you are up against mate; good luck.

*Greenberg* does the same but flips the awe. Here's the world and here's

Florence. She is waiting for the world to offer her love, comfort and meaning. She seems tiny in comparison to the awesome mess that is the 'hero' Greenberg. Greenberg needs to find a way to reduce himself to the scale of a normal person: that's what you are up against mate; good luck.

Let's cut to the chase:

*Structure is communication.*
*Structure is control.*
*Structure is pleasure.*

When I talk about pleasure, I mean both yours and your readers'. Structure is all about you enjoying the process of crafting the enjoyment of those for whom you are writing. Of course we can experience the pleasure of a well-told story in many forms. These would include what we might call the 'unpleasure' of being frightened and disgusted by a cracking horror movie and of the overwhelming sadness we feel watching a good weepy.

Stories are powerful things. Well-told stories are persuasive. They convince us of the value of their content and they do this in large part through the clever organization—structuring—of their material. Of course, this is not universally a 'good' or 'progressive' thing. Traditional fairy stories, for example, are often carefully designed traps that encourage us to enjoy absorbing the principles of our own oppression. Generations of little kids learn about 'correct' behaviors—about what it means to be good boys and (especially) girls—by hearing what happens to bad children who don't listen to their parents, eat gingerbread from the roofs of implausibly weatherproofed forest cottages, reject the restrictive gender roles their societies have laid out for them and generally screw around.

Let's start by joining up with most of the other screenwriting books in reminding you that movies are just one link in a very old chain leading back through the history of drama to the Greeks and especially to a terrifyingly brilliant chap called Aristotle. Aristotle was, amongst other things, the first recorded Western literary theorist. His most famous work, *The Poetics*, is a lucid and comprehensive study of Greek drama and the principles of dramatic writing. Its influence on Western drama has been enormous, for good or ill, and many of the terms, principles and assumptions that underlie contemporary screenwriting practice come to us directly from *The Poetics*.

From Aristotle we get the first accounts of plot (*mythos*); character (*ethos*, sort of); dramatic reversal (*peripeteia*); spectacle (*opsis*); the tragic flaw (*hamartia*, sort of); and what Hollywood now thinks of as the 'redemptive ending' (*catharsis*, very sort of) to name but a few. In other words, if you haven't read *The Poetics*, you need to catch up. I'm not going to write about Aristotle directly in this book because he's been done to death and it's easy for you to find out about him. I am more interested in discussing what happened before the Greeks. Besides, *The Poetics* is very short, it is part of your general education as a thinking person, let alone as a screenwriter. Go read it. I can wait.

For those of you sad enough to be tracking the writing process of this book in historical real time (and enjoying the consequent temporal anomalies that emerge while reading it), the first screening of the first episode of the HBO series *The Pacific* is on in a few minutes and I wouldn't mind giving it a look. It won't take you much longer than that to read Aristotle.

Is everybody back? Well, I watched *The Pacific* and was distinctly underwhelmed. Hopefully it will go on to do more than spin the same wheels as *Band of Brothers* with a less interesting cast of characters and storyline. Ah well, I know how hard it is to write your way into a story—**exposition** makes all first episodes tricky—so I'll give it a chance.

NOTE: A little redraft after watching the whole series (it is now May 2010, time travelers) and yes, *The Pacific* did improve. I think it would have worked better as a unified piece of drama if it had run six or so episodes rather than ten and lost the Leckie book and the Basilone story. I may be way off of course, but it felt like they gave themselves a fundamental problem by valorizing a narrow definition of authenticity at the expense of the needs of dramatic structure. Anyway, I guess ten episodes were easier to sell to HBO—especially in the wake of *Band of Brothers*. Still, that proves the importance of giving works a proper chance before making snap judgments, a moral lesson for all writers (and television executives) there.

I mention the first episode of *The Pacific* only to reinforce the ubiquity of Aristotle's influence through a random 'at time of writing' example. The fact that it disappointed and annoyed me in terms of its dramatic intention and historical ambition is just an accident. More importantly for our purposes, I noticed a whole bunch of *mythos*, *ethos*, *peripeteia*, *opsis* and an overwhelming and, frankly, problematic yearning for *catharsis*.

Anyway, you have now read Aristotle, haven't you? You can find a whole bunch of material on his ideas online or in other screenwriting books, so I am going to move on to think about the story structure that comes *before* Aristotle. This is story structure of the kind the Greeks inherited rather than created. I hope you will find this little introductory lesson illuminating. We will play with some of these concepts again when we explore the 'W' model later in this chapter.

[NOTE: Whatever your view of *The Pacific*, if you want to see how to make a great movie about war watch Andrzej Wajda's *Kanal* (1957), Miklós Jancsó's *Csillagosok, Katonák/The Red and the White* (1967) or Elem Klimov's *Idi I Smotri/Come and See* (1985).]

## Ring compositions and the 'origin' of structure

Of course, story structure goes back much further than Aristotle. We find it in the myths, sagas and earliest written literature of cultures around the world. It goes further back still, into the oral traditions of bards, skalds, priests, shamans and law speakers from which those written traditions emerge. Indeed, structure is present in some form from the first time a thinking person tried to educate or entertain her companions with ideas.

Story structure emerges in similar forms in cultures across the ancient world, even when there is no direct contact between them. In other words *story structure develops because it is needed in all cultures*, not because one culture copies what another culture is doing. It is also apparent that certain principles of storytelling, such as the use of *parallelism*, are especially valuable to peoples the world over. Again, we can make such an assumption because they started telling their stories independently, yet in the same kind of way.

What we are going to do now is spend a little time with the earliest known story forms. We will then hike our way back to movie land but with our backpacks full of important lessons about how to understand the way our stories actually work. We may not use the exact structures our ancestors did, but we are still influenced and inspired by the same principles, even if we do not always recognize them as such.

Scholars have identified what they call *ring compositions* in many early works, from Homer to the Torah. Ring compositions come in different scales, but they share certain principles. A ring composition splits its story in half and bends it around a defined **midpoint**. This gives two sections of story that are linked by formal correspondences between incidents in each section. The story 'turns back on itself' as it establishes and then resolves its narrative.

Here's a simple blank diagram of a story ring with an arbitrary number of events or 'beats'. In reality there may be any number of these beats. To follow the narrative we follow the arrows, reading down the left, round the **midpoint** and back up the right. To appreciate the full meaning of the ring, we also read across between the corresponding pairs of underlined parallel beats (1 and 10 for example):

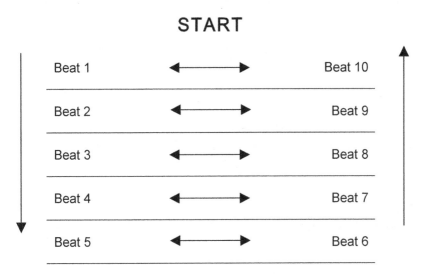

## START

| | | |
|---|---|---|
| Beat 1 | ◄———► | Beat 10 |
| Beat 2 | ◄———► | Beat 9 |
| Beat 3 | ◄———► | Beat 8 |
| Beat 4 | ◄———► | Beat 7 |
| Beat 5 | ◄———► | Beat 6 |

## MIDPOINT

In this way the tale acknowledges formal patterns of meaning. Ideas and incidents in both halves are linked through the repetition of vocabulary, symbolism and incident as the story turns back on itself from the midpoint towards the resolution. Something happens in the first half that resonates with its pair in the second half.

Here's a simple example of story parallelism in a movie we are already familiar with. In *This is England* the gang has fun playing football in the play area. Later the racists stop the Asian kids from playing football in the same area—a different event, but linked by the location and by a transformation in its meaning. Between these events, the story world has changed for the worse. The change resonates for the audience because we see it demonstrated in an already familiar situation.

*Ring compositions establish a pattern in the first half of the story which is interrogated, inverted, reinforced, overcome or otherwise transformed by parallel 'beats' in the second half in order for the meaning of the story to resonate.*

In her fascinating book *Thinking in Circles: An Essay on Ring Composition*, the great anthropologist Mary Douglas compared the cultural work of a ring composition to that of syntax: '[I]t *tames wild words* and firmly binds them to its frame. Another function is greatly to deepen the range of reference by playing on the double meanings of words. Another of its benefits is that it is a form of play; it gives the pleasure of a game to the composer and the reader' (my italics). *Structure is pleasure.*

Some ring-like compositions are straightforward and merely involve a simple patterning in a few lines of poetry or prose. Typically this takes the form of *chiasmus* in which elements cross over, are repeated with variation or otherwise correspond or rhyme in two halves A/B/B'/A' or A/B/C/B'/A' and so forth. The term 'chiasm' references the shape of the Greek letter *chi* that is written X. The X symbolizes how ideas and vocabulary cross over and back. Here's a well-known example from the book of Isaiah (King James Version, my italics):

A Make the *heart* of this people fat,
B and make their *ears* heavy,
C and shut their *eyes*:
C' lest they see with their *eyes*,
B' and hear with their *ears*,
A' and understand with their *heart*, and convert, and be healed.

| A heart | heart A' |
| B ears | ears B' |
| C eyes | eyes C' |

We can easily see how this kind of structure turns around the central C lines and returns, not to the start exactly, but to the start *transformed* as the ending. *Do these things*, the first three lines admonish us, or *this might happen*, predict the second three lines. This talk of transformation and correspondence in storytelling should already sound familiar to you from our discussion of the **'V'** model and the **wardrobe**.

Of course, like screenplays, ring compositions are often far more complex and subtle than the simple structure above. They work themselves out over much longer texts, epic stories, poems, or books of the Torah, for example, and they often contain other, smaller ring compositions within them. Unlike your average Hollywood screenplay, however, the underlying structure of many of these more complex ring compositions is very hard to discern without careful study.

Here's a brief example of the way language links story elements in a ring composition from an analysis of the story of Abraham and Isaac by Mary Douglas. You no doubt remember the story in which Abraham is instructed by his God to sacrifice his son Isaac to prove his obedience, only to be stopped at the last minute. This is one of the earliest literary examples of what later generations have come to call a 'dick move.' Douglas points out the organization of linked pairs of beats in the story. They are linked by using a common vocabulary to reference one another. Having established a language for the story in the first half, we notice its repetition in describing events in the second. When beats follow one another closely in 'story time' the connections are easy to see. At one point the story tells us that Abraham '*raised his hand*' to slay Isaac, and almost immediately in another verse the Angel tells him: 'Do not *raise your hand* against the lad.' Isaac is spared; the language echoes the action and the immediate reaction.

This is pretty straightforward, but sometimes ring compositions establish correspondences between beats that take place at very different points in the story. The 'raise your hand' example compares beats in the approximate positions of 5 and 6 in the blank diagram above, only separated by the **midpoint**. Douglas shows how each beat in one half of the story corresponds with one in the other, even those separated by most of its length (like 2 and 9 or 3 and 8 in our blank diagram).

On their way to the place of sacrifice near the start of the story, Abraham and Isaac pick up wood to carry with them 'for the *burnt offering*.' Much later, after Isaac has been spared, a ram appears in the thicket and Abraham takes it and offers it as a '*burnt offering* instead of his son.' The repeated vocabulary establishes an emotional resonance between these two moments. The words portend threat in the early beat—Isaac will be killed and his body burned—and relief in the later one—Isaac is saved and the ram will be burned in his place. Here's a simplified, abstracted illustration:

START

| | |
|---|---|
| Beat | Beat |
| 'burnt offering' | 'burnt offering' |
| Beat | Beat |
| Beat | Beat |
| 'raise your hand' | 'do not raise your hand' |

MIDPOINT

What I am trying to show is simply that ring compositions establish a pattern of correspondence throughout a story. They are examples of the power of parallelism in narrative. They link events in each story half and flag developments and transformations. When we are able to conceptualize our stories as a kind of ring *as well as* a linear tale, we start to anticipate, notice and appreciate matched pairs of story beats. That means we are looking to all parts of our structure for specific evidence of progression in our stories.

Don't get me wrong, our primary model for story structure will still be linear, if for no other reason than that you need to be able to talk about your script that way. It will work through our three acts one after the other. However, our model will turn on a powerful **midpoint** and it will expect us to understand the developing relationship between its two halves. Hollywood movies are doing this anyway, even if many writers have no knowledge of ring composition and its historical context.

I am not imposing an alien form onto screenplay structure. I'm just drawing your attention to one of the reasons why it has been such a successful model for storytelling. Later in this chapter I will show how understanding this play of correspondence across parallel beats gives you a helpful way of testing out your story's progression.

> IMPLIED YOU
> So you are arguing that screenplay
> structure is pretty much the same
> thing as these ring compositions?

> FRIENDLY ME
> Well no, I certainly wouldn't go that
> far.

> IMPLIED YOU
> But you are saying they both work
> because they key into a human
> affinity for a certain kind of
> structure?

> FRIENDLY ME
> It's not that we still try to write
> in rings; rather, that the lessons
> of parallelism still resonate in
> our writing. Hollywood's brand of
> storytelling is successful for a
> reason.

> IMPLIED YOU
> Your 'V' isn't a ring, though, is it?

```
FRIENDLY ME
No, but it is still an articulation
of structure as two related halves
which transform as they resolve.
We'll see clearer examples when we
look at the 'W' model later in this
chapter.

IMPLIED YOU
I was wondering when that was
going to appear.

FRIENDLY ME
We'll get there very soon. For now,
I think the most basic lesson from
the early history of storytelling
must be: doing structure is never
an option, even if there are always
options as to how we do structure.
```

Literary scholars and anthropologists have suggested several explanations for the presence of ring compositions in early written literature. The one I find most persuasive is that they are in part a continuation or remnant of memory and recitation techniques from oral storytelling. In this way the structural correspondences of oral poetry worked as a sort of mnemonic or aide memoire for both the bard and the audience. Think of it like a much more complicated version of a child's finger rhyme: 'I have ten fingers and they all belong to me. I can make them do things—would you like to see?' Remember that, unlike novels, even though we write our movie stories as screenplays, they are designed to be delivered and received visually and aurally, if not exactly 'orally.'

And yes, we haven't come so very far, because we still take pleasure in just this kind of structural correspondence in our storytelling today. Many screenwriting teachers suggest we still articulate our stories around a dramatic **midpoint**. We still expect beginnings and endings to correspond eloquently. We still imbue our stories with heightened kinds of verbal—and now also visual—language. We draw attention to its repetition and patterning as motifs, catch phrases and other forms of discourse. We still use echoing sequences and scenes and we still mirror action.

What's truly great about thinking in terms of parallelism is that it reminds us of how we really understand stories as readers or members of a movie audience. Even though we *tell* stories in a linear fashion we *receive* them both as a process of ongoing revelation—the linear part unfolds: this happens, then that and so on—*and* through anticipation and comparison—the 'ring' part. To make sense of the linear story we are always cross referencing new information with what we already know. We are also thinking about what that new information might lead to.

As David Bordwell reminds us, movie storytelling has largely avoided following the post-modern path towards ambiguity and what some critics call 'anti-closure.' It is still pretty ancient in its core instincts, even if those ancient ideas are disguised in giant robot costumes much of the time. Many of the principles I have been offering you in this book are just hints towards parallelism disguised in different forms. **Narrative economy** expects its payoffs. **Narrative excess** usually has to earn its moments of release from those structures. The **wardrobe** locks us into the transformation of a character's attitude to theme: she was this, now she's that. The **'V'** invites comparison between its two halves. Change of any kind can only be discerned by comparison. Parallelism is implied or inscribed in almost everything we do in screenwriting. *Structure is pleasure.*

No, of course this is not ring composition in the strictly anthropological or literary sense, but it is the offspring of thinking in parallels. Here's a very 'old hat' screenwriting example to show how planned parallelism is already inscribed into modern screenplay structure. You have probably heard the term '**inciting incident**' that refers to a moment or event in the first act of a film which sets the main action going. The **inciting incident** changes (*breaks* in my terms) the world, provokes the hero/ine into action and sets up the *expectation* in the audience's mind that a resolution will emerge to answer, repair, solve or otherwise provide closure to that incident: *A implies a future A'.*

Commonly, that resolving event or scene is called the **obligatory moment**. In other words, when you give us an **inciting incident** we already expect a scene or scenes to appear later to do the resolving. If we don't get an *A'*—an **obligatory moment**—we will feel disappointed, cheated out of part of the contract you established by giving us *A* in the first act of the story.

The **inciting incident** and its implied pair is just a well-known example of parallelism. Another works the impact of the **B Story** (your key subplot, of which more below) on your main story at the start and end of your second act. Yet another sandwiches the **midpoint**. Here we need to anticipate and then see immediate evidence of the consequences of your character's decision to fully commit to the resolution of their story. In fact, well-structured screenplays are full of implied or explicit parallels. A good writer does not make them all reductively obvious. Indeed, some of them may be written without the writer being fully conscious of what they are doing. This is also part of *narration*, which we will discuss in the next section.

Human beings are sense-making machines. Mary Douglas again, following Roman Jakobson: 'The brain works by building correspondences and recognizing them.' We are always searching for meanings and connections between ideas and images. It comes from a simple animal survival mechanism after all: bush moves + scary growl = lurking predator = back away slowly. Literary forms that play into this primary mental functioning are especially powerful, as Douglas argues: 'We can go on from the verbal medium to consider creation of parallels between and across the senses. Making divisions and seeing similarities, matching parts, like to like—this is the essence of creativity.' Audiences are looking to screenwriters for entertaining and fascinating correspondences between story beats and expecting our screenplays to provide them. The lessons we are taught by ancient ring compositions about the pleasures to be found in parallelism are vitally important for a screenwriter who is thinking her way towards her own story structure.

It seems counterintuitive to imply that structural restrictions can be liberating—what about **writing what you don't know**? But literary history is full of examples of prosaic, dramatic and poetic forms designed to enhance intellectual and creative excitement in this way, the iambic pentameter and the sonnet to name but two. Remember, literary forms like these give us pleasure because they allow us to see structure working beautifully to communicate meaning. The ludic, pleasure-giving function of structure is something we will return to again and again.

**Writing what you don't know** is all about the joy of discovery. We learn new things, make new connections and play new games with our storytelling. Structure is the mechanism we use to channel and discipline that creative joy so our readers and our audience can share it. Some of the terms and the medium may have changed since we first told the story of how Abraham took his son out for a pleasant stroll in the countryside equipped only with a big knife and an innocent expression, but many of the techniques still apply.

*Structure is pleasure.*

It always has been and always will be pleasure. Ignore it at your peril.

## Narration: positioning your audience

If structure is all about the audience's pleasure, then narration gives you one of the most important sets of tools that let you influence and even direct that pleasure.

Narration is not exactly structure itself; rather it is a way of transmitting structure. It sits on top of, underneath and twined around your structure and, even in the simplest stories, it has a very important role to play.

## Narrators

Narration really refers to the process of communicating your story to your audience.

We encounter narration in movies in numerous forms, from the overt and familiar to the more subtle and discreet. To take the first of those conditions, we all know what a narrator is: in the simplest terms it just means a storyteller. We know that, in stories of all kinds, narration—story*telling*—takes place in different forms depending, most obviously, on whether the narrator is personified in the story and whether or not they 'speak' in the first person or the third.

A first person narrator is like my voice in this book: 'I do this.' 'I think this.' We have a specific, personal connection to a first person narrator through a kind of direct address. In movies we are certainly familiar with first person narration. We know it from a range of films and genres, and some story types are even defined in part by their use of first person narration. The confident lad about town in *Alfie* (1966), his demonic counterpart, Alex in *A Clockwork Orange* (1971) and the equally self-confident eponymous American detective, hardboiled or otherwise, is often allowed to keep his first person voiceover in the transition to motion pictures. Well, are you going to argue with Mike Hammer? I thought not.

Here's the detective, Philip Marlowe, narrating the opening of Raymond Chandler's novel *The Big Sleep* (1939), just in case you had forgotten the style:

> It was about eleven o'clock in the morning, mid October, with the sun not shining and a look of hard wet rain in the clearness of the foothills. I was wearing my powder blue suit with dark blue shirt, tie and display handkerchief, black brogues, black socks with dark blue clocks on them. I was neat, clean shaved and sober, and I didn't care who knew it. I was everything the well-dressed private detective ought to be. I was calling on four million dollars.

Third person narration is the default in prose fiction: 'She does this.' 'He thinks this.' It is no less present and controlling than first person narration, it's just usually more modest about how it does the job. Just to prove that not all American detective stories are told in the first person, here's the opening of Dashiell Hammett's *The Maltese Falcon* (1929):

Samuel Spade's jaw was long and bony, his chin a jutting v under the more flexible v of his mouth. His nostrils curved back to make another, smaller, v. His yellow-grey eyes were horizontal. The v *motif* was picked up again by thickish brows rising outward from twin creases above a hooked nose, and his pale brown hair grew down—from high flat temples—in a point on his forehead. He looked rather pleasantly like a blond satan.

There is so much one could write about these two opening paragraphs, but for now let's focus on a few things that we can take to our discussion of writing movies.

The first person narrator is a character in the story, or with the knowledge to comment on it. First person narration tells us how the character chooses to introduce 'herself' and to tell 'his' story. What does Philip Marlowe consider important about his appearance and attitude? This kind of narrator can take positions, make judgments and generally interpolate their character between the 'truth' of the story and the reader. This immediately begs the question: *Can we take him at face value?* All we have to go on, in this example, are Marlowe's words, and we don't yet know whether or not we can trust those words—can trust Marlowe himself. This is a critical issue for understanding the function of narration, and we will come back to it in a minute.

Third person narration can appear neutral but is always in some way foregrounding the attitude of the author or, perhaps more accurately, the author as they choose to present their voice in this particular story. It can also be used for characters telling their own tale in the third person, such as the knowing, prosy bookending narration in *The Brothers Bloom*. However, because we are not necessarily limited to the knowledge and attitudes of one character in a story, third person narration is usually the most flexible mode of storytelling. This is the main reason why it is the most common, both in prose fiction and in screenplays. Third person narration can tend towards the omnipotent. We don't always know who the narrator is, other than the author's default voice, so it can present itself as the all-knowing God of the story.

When we read the third person description of Sam Spade we have no reason to assume it is anything other than accurate. Of course, third person narration is very much also a voice; it isn't simply neutral and objective. Right from the start, Hammett's narration has attitude and wry humor—remember the quip about resembling a '… blond satan'? At least we are usually one step removed from asking about trust and truth right from the start, although those questions may well come up later.

Second person narration is much less common and is more usually encountered in songs. We do find it in the occasional novel, such as Italo Calvino's *If on a Winter's Night a Traveler* (1979) or Jay McInerney's *Bright Lights, Big City* (1984). The usual function of second person narration is to try and speak directly to the reader, even though the 'you' is in fact the s/he of the story, pulling them into identifying with the events and characters in the story: 'You do this.' 'You think this.' It is a hard mode to sustain and one against which readers have a tendency to rebel: 'You think this.' 'No I don't.' Indeed, I may be running into this trouble with some of you with my little Implied You/Friendly Me interludes myself.

Some stories are also told with multiple narrators, or layers of narration of various kinds, such as we are given in Conrad's *Heart of Darkness* (1899). The one thing that unifies all of these types and their various subtypes is that they have been chosen because their authors are trying to establish a particular relationship with their readers which, they hope, will best suit the needs of their story.

The style of narration, including the voice of the narrator, is designed specifically to maneuver the reader, or in film terms the audience, into a particular position in relation to the story. In cinema, narration tends to have less to do with the voice of an upfront narrator than it does with a range of techniques designed to achieve that positioning of the audience. Some of these techniques are part of the screenwriter's storytelling toolkit, and some, while influenced by the written story, are technical and aesthetic choices ultimately in the control of directors, cinematographers, editors and composers and so forth.

In mainstream Hollywood films, narration tends to work 'invisibly' to give the audience the illusion that they are witnessing events in a coherent and believable fictional world. Other styles of filmmaking bring different priorities, and some are intentionally self-conscious, speaking directly to the audience as a way of reminding us that we are watching a work of fiction. Here we might think of Brecht in the theater and Godard in the cinema.

### The control of story information

Whatever the politics of the filmmakers, narration is about the control of story information. Whenever you are watching a film, if you want to know what job the narration is doing ask yourself the following simple questions:

- *Who knows what and when?*
- *How much are we being told?*
- *How reliable is our information?*

Then ask yourself: How much fun am I having because of the answers to those three questions?

Take the beginning of *Yojimbo* (scr. Akira Kurosawa; 1961), a movie about a ronin (a lordless samurai) who destroys the two bandit gangs running a small town by playing them off against one another. The film opens with the wandering ronin, played by the great Toshiro Mifune, coming to a fork in the road. We haven't seen his face yet. We follow him from behind, a lonely figure in a landscape. At the fork Toshiro pauses, with no reason to go either one way or the other. He picks up a stick and throws it into the air. The stick lands, pointing down one of the paths and Toshiro follows its lead towards—who knows what?

In this example, we know very little and so does our hero. The film is offering us a story based on a chance decision. The ronin might have gone one way, but fate draws him and us along with him, to the little town with the warring gangs. The narration is telling us: 'Let's find out what happens together.'

Here's an opposite kind of example, this time from television. Hopefully you all still remember the classic detective show *Columbo*, with Peter Falk as the bumblingly brilliant schlub who solves murders in high society. It was one of my favorite programs as a kid and it told its stories in a very particular way. In each episode of the show we would see a murder committed at the start and we would also see who committed it. The murderer would inevitably be rich and arrogant and they would underestimate the deductive powers of the unassuming and distinctly lower class detective who turned up to investigate the crime.

For the audience, the principle pleasure of watching *Columbo* lay in knowing whodunit and watching the detective start from nowhere and catch up. Because the villain was inevitably a patronizing, smarmy bastard, we really wanted him caught and we hated him for putting down our hero.

In these two examples, therefore, the writer puts the audience in opposite positions in terms of knowledge, but in each example *we are where we want to be* to get the most enjoyment from the story.

- In *Yojimbo* we know nothing and the ronin knows nothing.
- In *Columbo* we know everything and Columbo knows nothing.
- In *(500) Days of Summer* we know nothing and Tom knows every-thing—he's been through the (500) days after all—and yet he doesn't

know what it really means. The film has us join him on his search for that meaning from different ends of the knowledge spectrum.

• In *Rashomon* 1950, another Kurosawa film, we see the same events told from the perspectives of different participants. Here we learn that we cannot necessarily trust the information we are being given and we become invested in seeking the truth through the fog of motivations.

In all of these cases the story maneuvers us into position in such a way that we are quickly engaged with the central problem of the story and its world. Many films change the starting contract over time. Typically the audience starts with little information and gradually increases what Bordwell would call the 'range' and 'depth' of its knowledge, just as it increases its commitment to the hero/ine's story. John Truby would talk about narration in terms of planning your 'reveals,' for example. The control of revelations, both to characters in the narrative and to the audience—and these may be different and come at different times for each—is another way to conceptualize the work of narration in screenwriting.

All genres, but especially thrillers, mysteries, detective stories and horror films, will often include their audience in a complex game with knowledge and ignorance. The narration shifts us back and forth from superiority to inferiority in relation to the characters and events on screen. When it works well and key plotting isn't completely obvious to the audience well in advance, revelation can be a very powerful tool. An example of a well planned and mostly unexpected revelation I enjoyed recently was the sequence that establishes that Sam is a clone in the science fiction mystery *Moon* (scr. Nathan Parker; 2009). Perhaps I should have paid more attention to the tagline: 'The last place you'd ever expect to find yourself.'

M. Night Shyamalan's career has been built around the high concept revelation. Typically he takes the narration 'knowledge game' and makes it into the central thesis of his movie. In *The Sixth Sense* (1999), we spend the movie alongside the lad Bruce Willis, trying to work out why Haley Joel Osment sees dead people, only to find out that Bruce is … well, what did you think he was going to be? In *The Village* (2004), we spend the whole movie trying to work out whether there are really monsters in the woods, only to find out the movie is set in the present day and the village elders are scaring people away from finding this out. In *Signs* (2002), we spend most of the movie hiding in Mel Gibson's basement and really don't care a damn what is going on because surely even being slaughtered by invading aliens is better than that.

Cinematic narration offers many more combinations than these, but hopefully you can begin to see how decisions about positioning the audience and your hero/ine in a particular relationship with knowledge, truth and trust have a great deal to do with our enjoyment of your film. A case in point is how we introduce our audience to all of the key story and story world information they need to catch onto at the start of your movie. We call that process 'exposition', and it is one of the hardest things to write well because it is all about telling us stuff and we know that's breaking one of the rules of our trinity. Good expositional writing shows what you are telling without the audience feeling they are in the classroom looking at the dramatic equivalent of Powerpoint slides.

Exposition happens in many forms but, as a special treat, I'm going to take us through one of my favorite examples, from one of my favorite films, featuring the great Michael Caine. His performances as Len Deighton's working class cold war spy Harry Palmer are one of the great joys of 1960s cinema and amongst my all-time-favorite movie performances.

Harry is asleep in his little London flat right now. Let's go say hello ...

## Exposition

The alarm clock just woke up Harry Palmer. While he was sleeping, he missed the short pre-title sequence of his own spy movie, *The Ipcress File* (scr. Bill Canaway & James Doran; 1965), so let's fill him in fast so we can get on with talking about the main storyline.

```
                FRIENDLY ME
Morning Sunshine.

                SLEEPY PALMER
Oi, what are you doing in my flat?

                FRIENDLY ME
Just letting you know that while
you were sleeping we saw a scientist
kidnapped and his bodyguard shot.
Clearly somebody was expecting foul
play.

                SLEEPY PALMER
I suppose Colonel Ross sent you?

                FRIENDLY ME
You'll find out soon enough.
```

```
               SLEEPY PALMER
        Who are you anyway? My name is ...

               FRIENDLY ME
        Yes, we know. Now go back to sleep
        so we can start the title sequence.
```

The alarm clock just woke up Harry Palmer.

As John Barry's wonderful, lugubrious, jazzy and distinctly un-James Bondy theme plays over, we follow Harry as he goes through his morning routine. Let's see how much we learn about him in the title sequence alone:

Harry switches on the bedside lamp, revealing a pack of Gauloises Disque Bleu cigarettes. No working class Woodbines for well traveled Harry Palmer.

Harry reaches behind him to check whether last night's 'bird' is still there. She isn't. A bit of a lady's man is our Harry.

Harry looks around—a blurry P.O.V. He puts on his heavy, dark-framed glasses. Hmm, James Bond doesn't have bad eyesight. But now that's much better, Harry can see properly. He checks out his modest flat. Still no 'bird,' sadly.

The glasses were a very important part of the characterization, as Michael Caine recalls in an interview with uncut.co.uk: 'Well, we decided we wanted him to be the antithesis of Bond. Obviously there wasn't any competition with Bond because Harry wasn't another great, suave spy. He was more like a real spy, an ordinary guy who you wouldn't look at twice in the street. So we gave him some glasses. I wore glasses naturally, so I knew how to use glasses; I took them off and put them on very easily. But what worked for me is the minute I took the glasses off, I wasn't Harry Palmer. I saw Sean [Connery] having difficulty trying to get away from James Bond and I thought, "Well the minute I take these off, I'm not Harry Palmer." Which proved correct.'

Harry gets up and draws his curtains, revealing grimy London rooftops and chimney pots. This isn't James Bond's flat and it certainly isn't his neighborhood.

He walks over to the alarm clock, which is on the other side of the room. Nice little character moment there. Clearly Harry needs rituals to help him get out of bed in the morning.

Harry opens his front door and grabs the morning paper and a pint of milk. He starts to make coffee, grinding his own beans and using a cafetière. He's a man of some sophistication and not just 'an ordinary guy' then, our Harry.

But wait, what's this? He's opening his tabloid paper to the racing page and marking today's runners for a potential flutter. He's a man who is moving between classes, aspiring and modern yet also comfortable in his working class cultural origins. He is also a gambler not a plodder, a major character clue that will be played out by the investigation plot later on.

Harry puts on his jacket and then searches for something under the pillows. He finds a woman's bracelet, but clearly he wasn't looking for that. Harry pulls back the covers—ah, there is his little automatic pistol. He checks the safety catch and slips it into the waistband of his trousers. So Harry is a man who takes a gun to work. In our minds we run that by the pre-title sequence and get ready to position him in relation to the kidnapped scientist affair.

Now the titles have finished and, if we have been paying close attention, we already know a good deal about him. Most importantly, we know something of the complexity of the man. We see his contradictions and we are given hints at his talents and possible weaknesses. Hint: both have a lot to do with him being cocky (expects a lady to be in his bed, pushing at the cultural boundaries of his class origins like many of his generation in the early 1960s).

Anyway, now Harry is out on the streets. Let's follow him and see what he gets up to.

The next scene sees Harry arrive at work in a seedy attic flat where a surveillance operation is taking place. This is the unglamorous end of the spy game, and Harry brings his cheeky, irreverent personality to bear. He is late; he doesn't care. We learn he is still in the army, but he doesn't act as if discipline is the first thing on his mind.

Later, he reads his report of mundane activities into a tape recorder, combining humor and a cynical detachment from the boring minutiae of his current operation with sound deductive reasoning: a larger delivery of milk might mean there are more people inside the target house, or just that they are drinking more tea. He can do his job well, then, even when it is reduced to the most mundane of tasks, and even if he doesn't seem to care much about it.

Now a colleague turns up early to relieve Harry. Ah, Harry's the one the boss wants to see immediately when something serious comes up. He heads out with a final practical joke at the expense of his replacement.

Cut to the Ministry of Defence. Harry shows his pass and is called 'Sir' by the guard. He's important to somebody then.

Cut to Harry's boss, Colonel Ross, feeding the pigeons on his windowsill. Ross is old-school British army, but by no means the foolish stuffed shirt we may want him to be, based on his attitude to our Harry—see, we like him already. 'Sergeant Palmer reporting as ordered, Sir.' He keeps Harry waiting, talks to him without turning round—'Close the door, Palmer'—and treats him like an unruly child. The big news? Harry is to be transferred to another department where his unique talents might get more of a workout than in counting milk bottles. What is Harry's first question? Is it a promotion and will he be getting a pay rise? Bond wouldn't ask that because it just isn't done—oh, and of course Commander Bond (Royal Navy) doesn't need the money.

There might be a pay rise and Harry responds that now he can get the grill he has been wanting for his kitchen. It is no surprise that we find out later Harry is a good cook, but right now this response is just to signal his difference from Ross and to needle him.

We also get an introduction to the bureaucratic world of the British intelligence services. There is much talk of forms and records (and of course Palmer's insubordination on record); of departmental loyalties and protocols: 'Harry Palmer doesn't play by the book in a world where "ooh look, lots of books we have to play by".'

Now we move straight to the world of Harry's new department, spread across a number of front companies sharing buildings elsewhere in London. There is an employment agency, a film distributor and a firework company, which all link up in a maze of drab stairways and cramped hallways. We start in the employment agency, which is specializing in domestic servants—Colonel Ross is ostensibly here to interview a butler. This takes us back to the old Britain Harry's generation is breaking free from. In part this is a movie about the end of class deference, about the changing of the old guard and the danger of being left behind.

That danger brings us directly to Harry's new boss and the villain of the piece. Major Dalby is Colonel Ross's less successful double. A passed over major, he is told he should be grateful for his job and gets the full patronizing treatment from Ross, which he, in turn, unloads on Harry in a telling interview which almost duplicates the previous scene in Ross's office: 'Shut the door.' There are a few minor differences in the shooting which subtly set up Dalby as the villain but, on the surface, the scene plays the duplication for humor before Harry follows Dalby through the maze of offices to his new department.

On the way, Harry is told to exchange his automatic for a Colt .32 revolver. In a subtle and nicely judged bit of character work we see Harry sign for the new gun and then say he would prefer to keep his automatic. He is told to use the revolver and takes it, but the choice to have him complain after signing for the gun speaks volumes in terms of Harry's attitude. He knows the bureaucracy will win, but he can't resist kicking against the pricks anyway. This is a major character note because it keeps him on the trail despite being smacked on the nose with a rolled-up newspaper by the system long after a normal man would have given up.

And so we go on, with more introductions to new colleagues and with the start of the main investigative plot and the minor romantic subplot, but in these first 20 minutes of the film we are given all the information we need to understand who Harry is, what he does, where his talents lie, to see why Ross puts him into Dalby's outfit as a plant and to understand his actions throughout the film which get him into very bad trouble and also get him out of it. The main events are waiting to occur, and we are now ready to understand and enjoy them through our hero.

That's **exposition**. It happens by turns subtly: Harry turns on the lamp and we 'happen to see' French cigarettes (slightly out of focus, no tedious pan over coyly revelatory mementos of childhood here); and obviously: Dalby reads him his personnel record (insubordinate with criminal tendencies). The various techniques we can infer from this short account of the opening act of *The Ipcress File* combine to make sure we are prepared for the unfolding of the movie's story along with our hero/ine. Let's outline a few of the best ones:

1 *Show, don't tell—yes I know: 'yawn.'* But there is a reason it is part of the trinity: it always turns up to help you. Example: Harry grinds coffee beans (modern/aspiring middle class) vs. Harry's tabloid racing section (traditional/working class). Don't do this:

```
Redundant Boy is reading the SPORT SECTION. Snideman
enters.

                 SNIDEMAN
        What are you reading, Redundant
        Boy? It seems I have just gone
        temporarily blind and can't see for
        myself.

              REDUNDANT BOY
        Oh, hello there, Snideman. I'm
        reading the Sport Section, because
        I like sport. I wonder what crazy
        pranks I'll get involved with as
        a direct consequence of my
        fascination with athletic pursuits…
```

*[1. Writer's Chat] Writers' Failbot: 'Redundant Boy fails at exposition.'*

2 *When you do tell, make us want to hear it.* Example: Dalby reading the negative litany of Harry's officially reported personality traits to him from the personnel form, so that Harry can smirk and agree. Dalby then goes on to prove he's no fool either, when he remarks that he can use someone with Harry's criminal tendencies.

In screenwriting we refer to statements that speak their literal meaning as being *on the nose* and generally try to avoid them where possible. Of course, sometimes the simple eloquence of being on the nose is exactly what is required. We just try and save the literal for special occasions, so it plays strong rather than dull. Remember Bob telling Jenny he loves her, from Chapter 1? Here, however, we don't resent this kind of literal **exposition**. It comes from character: Dalby asserting his rank and class superiority and plays to character; Harry unashamedly agreeing with the assessment. He's proud of himself, unimpressed by Dalby's pretentions and knows perfectly well these talents make him useful. It's a little bit of on the nose **exposition** that works hard. It goes on to enable two entertaining and revelatory character moments and makes us excited to see Harry use his dodgy talents in action.

This is a great key to character development: use your **exposition** to whet the audience's appetite. Make them want to see our hero/ines use their unique talents and personalities. Think of Tracy Flick in *Election*, for example.

3 *Always work towards narrative economy.* Example: the whole title sequence is just somebody getting up and ready for work, but look how much we learned from it. This is a world away from the typical film student's flat, **exposition**-free 'getting ready to go out' montage that tells us nothing other than what brand of toothpaste their friend who let them shoot in the location uses and that the director doesn't know what their film is about and has no problem wasting the audience's time until they figure it out. In film school we make jokes about how every student film begins with a hand reaching out to turn off an alarm clock. Well this is how to do it right.

4 *Sell your hero/ine's uniqueness early and often.* Example: Harry tricks his colleague at the surveillance operation into saying something rude about Colonel Ross, only to reveal: 'You've got some wiping to do. That tape's still running.' He's something of a prankster, and we learn this by seeing it happen, not through someone leaning over to a colleague and remarking: 'I say old chap, do you know that Harry Palmer fellow?' 'Why yes, I seem to recall having met him. Why do you ask?' 'Well, I have it on good authority that he is something of a prankster.' 'You don't say? I believe I also have been informed of his

jocular proclivities. Indeed your assertion calls to mind a long and involved example of his character recounted to me by Forbes-Ffitch from Special Projects the other day. Allow me to recount it in all its detail.' 'By all means, old chap. By all means.'

5   Use duplication as **expositional** reinforcement. Example: There are so many in this example, notably the two interviews with Ross and Dalby. Also, remember those two little moments in the title sequence introducing us to Harry's interest in the ladies? He reaches over in the bed at the start, and then later he finds a bracelet while searching for his gun, just in case we hadn't registered the first clue. The point is that we are much more likely to register important information if we get more than one instance of it. Ideally you would find ways of giving the same information in different forms. We learn Harry is something of a gourmet from watching him grind coffee beans and from his comment later that he wants to buy a new grill. Don't overdo this, because then it becomes boring and obvious, but using humor or disguising that you are repeating—he is looking for his gun, he finds the bracelet—will take you far.

**Exposition** doesn't end with the first act, by the way. We enjoy learning about our characters and their world. Good writers keep allowing that process to happen all the way through the script. In *The Ipcress File* the theme of Harry's culinary interests plays out again later when he cooks dinner for Sue Lloyd, and again in a scene in a supermarket with Colonel Ross. Normally people don't reveal everything about themselves to strangers on first acquaintance, and that includes to the audience. We have to work at them to get them to open up. So it should be with screenplays. **Exposition** should work on a need-to-know basis. What do we need to know to get us to the next thing we need to know? Think of it like an emotional onion skin. We peel away layers to reveal truth.

## The 'W' model of screenplay structure: acts and angles

As we have seen, narration is about making a storytelling contract with your audience. However, that contract is founded upon a shared assumption that the story being told is worth the telling. One way many screenwriters try to make sure stories live up to their promise is by working them out as the logical sum of a number of parts. If this happens, then this other thing needs to happen as a result or response and so on. In this way of thinking, each of these parts has a specific function in and of itself but also contributes vitally to the success of the whole.

I never went to the British equivalent of Shop Class, so I know nothing about cars and engines. Despite this handicap—and stop me if I'm way off here—I am fairly certain that cars (and even some Toyotas) have important stuff in them like gears and brakes and engines and fuel tanks and cables and axles and wheels and cup holders. All of these parts are designed to do something specific. I'm pretty confident that a brake is designed to slow the car down, a wheel is designed to go round and that a cup holder is designed to hold spare change, donut crumbs and random iPod connectors, for example. But the individual parts also connect to other parts and make up systems, and without all of them, the car would not run. Well ok, maybe your car will work without a cup holder, but just you try driving to work without coffee on a Monday morning. So it is with a screenplay.

Or so it can be if it helps you to think about it that way.

Yeah, I know that car metaphor was reductive, but many people in movie land talk about stories in a mechanistic kind of a way. Sometimes they do this for the simple reason that it makes sure both parties know what they are talking about. Remember that film is a collaborative medium, and a common 'language' enables that collaboration. One thing most writers will agree on is the need to talk about *acts*. To condense our previous discussion, we need to talk about them precisely because everyone else does. Frankly there is not much point in offering you a structural model, even just as a piñata, which asks you to embrace a system that doesn't at least work with the three acts.

Acts have a long tradition in drama and have been used for dramatic as well as pragmatic reasons. Different forms of drama typically use different act structures. Most plays, up to and beyond Shakespeare but before the advent of modern drama, used a five-act structure with each act having a different role within the story. Gustav Freytag would call them exposition, rising action, climax, falling action and dénouement, for example. Sitcoms and episodic TV drama series have their own multiple act structures (terrifyingly, sometimes as many as seven acts for an hour-long show) defined in large part by the insertion of more and more commercial breaks. Webisodic drama often appears irregularly, in story blips or beats, sketches or gags of varying length.

The movie-standard three acts give you a beginning, a middle and an end for your story. The assumption is that you will use them to do appropriate kinds of work in each: establish, develop and resolve your story. Not all films follow the Hollywood three-act structure and we have talked and will continue to talk about some of them as we go. However, the focus of this book is to get you confident with the basic geography before going too far off the path into the jungle, so forgive me if I focus much of our attention on the contents of that handy three-act map.

Of course some ensemble stories work slightly differently and we'll discuss ensembles soon. Also some movies have been known to disguise their relatively conventional stories with tricks like telling them in parallel forwards and backwards, like *Memento* (scr. Christopher Nolan; 2000), or out of sequence, like *Pulp Fiction* (scr. Quentin Tarantino & Roger Avary; 1994). They still have to do the same kind of work, only presented in a different way.

In other words, needing to work with the three-act structure doesn't mean we can't be creative in how we think about those three acts. This is where my little '**W**' model of screenplay structure comes in.

You remember I promised to give you the '**VW Wardrobe**' approach to screenwriting back near the start of the book? We slid down the steep slopes of the '**V**' when we were talking all about world building and little cartoon birds. We opened the '**Wardrobe**' when we were talking about the importance of your theme and how it helps you link in every aspect of your storytelling. By my calculations, that means I still owe you the '**W**'.

## Acting it all out

The '**V**' was a simple little guy with its two *angles* giving us a very basic dramatic movement from negative to positive (– +). We took a world designed to test out our hero/ine and broke it so they would have to get their act together to fix it. In the process of breaking and fixing, our characters learned something and, thus, *changed*. In doing so, however, they also *changed the story world*. It wasn't the same at the end as it was at the beginning. Better hopefully, worse maybe, but always different. You remember all this though, right?

With the '**W**', all the '**V**' stuff still applies, only we give it a lot more attention to detail and most of that detail sits in between the break and the fix. With the '**W**' we have a second diagram-in-a-letter which tells us a number of useful things by its shape alone. Kick the '**V**' in the nuts and you get the '**W**'. It looks something like this:

Firstly the '**W**' has four *angles*. We are going to use the angles as our first deviation from the simplicity of the three-act model. The first angle corresponds to act one. The last angle corresponds to act three and the two middle angles make up act two. In this way we could say that the '**W**' is four acts disguised as three. We are still going to talk about three acts so that you can talk to all the three-act people and not confuse

## THE 'W' BASIC MODEL

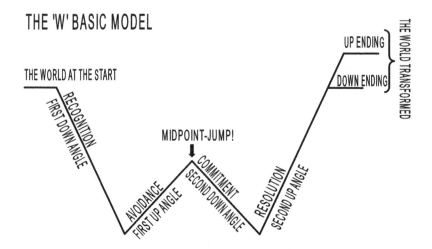

them, but we are also going to follow the four angles *within* the three acts because they guide us in an important way towards anticipating what our stories are probably going to be doing at the time.

So the second important lesson to be taken from the shape of the **'W'** is that it gives us a sequence of angles that illustrate the emotional and dramatic shape of most movie stories. They go down, up, down and up again in that order (or, in emotional terms, negative/positive/negative/positive: –+–+).

Once again, is this the answer to all structural questions? I don't think so. Is this your new god? I certainly hope not. Will it help to keep you on the right track if you get stuck? I believe so. Act logic is based on story logic. If you are instinctively resisting all this because you are worried that it is too formulaic, think about the logic of our basic story models. A problem implies a negative move. A solution implies something of a positive move. Playing the story out to feature length, keeping the hero/ine honest and making them work for their supper just gives you a second positive and negative move in the middle. It's pretty straightforward and it is just one model to play with amongst many. As an old university friend of mine used to say, in Franglais for some reason: 'ce n'est pas le surgery de brain.'

Let's start our thinking by expanding the model of the **'V'** into the **'W'**. The **'V'** broke a world and fixed it for our viewing pleasure. The **'W'** breaks the world, cobbles together a quick fix or an easy false victory that doesn't hold or satisfy, breaks it again, and then finally fixes it at the end—or at least tries to.

Imagine a sailing ship in a storm. The powerful winds break the mast, so the crew jury-rigs it quickly to keep some canvas up and thus control the ship. This only holds for so long, because it was never going to be as strong as a real mast. When, inevitably, the jury rig also breaks, the sailors are in a true life-and-death situation and have to find a way of making a lasting fix that will let them ride out the storm.

Another way of thinking this is: the hero/ine gets what they think they want without trying too hard and realizes it isn't all it's cracked up to be. Now they want the hard thing that was hiding underneath the easy thing.

Now think about this in character terms. The **'W'** works because people—and thus also our movie characters—usually take the path of least resistance.

If change were easy, stories would be dull. If the fix to a problem could always be locked in by a simple act of will, we storytellers would not have much to write about. Jenny Craig makes money not because losing weight is easy but because for most people it is hard. If everyone who was overweight just woke up one morning and said to themselves: 'OK, time to eat right and exercise more,' and then went on and did it, there would be no obesity problem, the healthcare systems of Western countries would be in much better shape, and I'd be so hot I'd burn myself.

In reality, when we are faced with a problem in our lives our usual instinct is to find a way of addressing it that takes the least amount of time, effort and emotional, physical and intellectual commitment possible. It is only when whatever jury-rigged fix we put in place doesn't work that maybe we will put some real effort in. Tell me I'm wrong. I thought so.

## Act one: first down angle

That's the way most movie characters work. The first act—and in our new **'W'** language, the first *angle*—is about showing your protagonist/s what's wrong and getting them to decide to do something about it or to understand what they face and must attempt to survive (*Kanal*) or even just bear witness to (*Idi I Smotri*):

'Luke, Empire bad. You come free princess and spank Empire.'
'No, I must farm moisture ... for some reason.'
'But look, stormtroopers kill family.'
'Hmm, Empire bad. I go free princess and spank Empire.'

Notice that the first angle is a *down angle*. This part of the story is about being faced with a problem or challenge. Your hero/ine hasn't started the solving or resolving or witnessing or surviving part of the story yet, so in emotional terms we go from positive to negative with a turn towards the positive again at the end of the act when they decide they will try and solve it.

Sometimes the positive to negative move is obvious. In the first angle of the romantic comedy *The Holiday* (scr. Nancy Meyers; 2006), Cameron Diaz and Kate Winslet have major bloketastrophies which bust open the emotional status quo. Cameron catches her guy cheating and the object of Kate's affection gets engaged to someone else. Although both women are seriously messed up in different ways, it takes those disasters to focus their minds and let them do the big impulsive thing that will set them on the path to happiness: they swap houses for a holiday. Who knew it was that simple?

Of course, in lots of films we begin in a world with not a whole lot of positive elements to hand. It will take more than a house swap and a hot Jude Law injection to save or redeem the protagonists of *Brazil* (scr. Terry Gilliam & Tom Stoppard; 1985) or *Gran Torino* (scr. Nick Schenk; 2008) for example.

At the start of *Brazil*, Sam Lowry is hardly thrilled with his life as a small cog in the engine of a nightmarish bureaucracy, but things are going to get a whole lot worse. At the start of *Gran Torino*, Walt Kowalski's wife just died, he hates his family and his neighborhood is being taken over by Asian immigrants who just remind him of his experiences in the Korean War. He's not a happy bunny to start with, but then things get worse.

In other words, the move of this angle is not necessarily from a world where everything was positive and now it is negative. Rather, it is about educating the audience into the problem of the world and of the protagonist so that we understand what is broken, what needs fixing and why our hero/ine is the person we want to spend time with as they try to do it.

Our emotional move as the audience of the first down angle echoes the anxiety of this problematic: 'Oh noes,' we are thinking, 'those poor people. Now if only they could just have a nice hot Jude Law injection.'

## Act two

Ask any screenwriter and they are likely to tell you that second acts are the hardest to write. Once you have your story idea and your theme, you know pretty much what you need to tell us to set things up, and that set up leads logically to a pay-off at the end: afraid of bunnies in a world where 'ooh look, bunnies' leads to either 'learns to live with bunnies' or 'kills all the bunnies with special bunny eating acid,' remember? The hard part is what comes in between.

Second acts need to take your hero/ine from 'decides to do something, but is basically winging it' to 'finally ready to try and sort it all out.' Frequently, by the end of the first angle characters have decided to change something in the world (external), or a surface symptom of what is a deeper problem in themselves, but have not yet understood that real change means addressing some fundamental part of their personality (internal).

Cue significant pause and plaintive murmur of 'What now?'

The answer to 'What now?' in its simplest terms is *change*. I know, who'd have thought? Your second act encompasses the change in your hero/ine that lets them go from incompetent, inexperienced, blinkered, self-deluding and generally rubbish (pick one or more) to 'the man or woman with the plan.'

In a typical Hollywood movie, everything in your second act serves the process of character change or, in a heavily plot-driven movie, getting your character the tools and information needed to win in the end. Here's an imperfect example of the former and a better example of the latter to sell the process, in part by omission. Think of the plot-heavy *Clash of the Titans* (scr. Travis Beacham and Phil Hay & Matt Manfredi; 2010). Our hero Perseus is an angry ancient Greek, and yet somehow also Australian demigod fisherman (aren't they always?) who needs to kill a huge great sea beast, the Kraken. Everybody tells him he can't do it and even the gods (well, at least his dad, Zeus) keep offering him help in the form of gifts. 'No, cobber,' says Perseus. 'Strewth, the gods are a bunch of hoons and drongos, so I'm going to give it a burl as a bloke. Er, man.'

So off he goes and gets most of his companions killed to test out the cool monsters, which is all as it should be in this kind of movie. Nevertheless, Perseus eventually realizes he needs more help (this is a common and often dramatically poignant moment, even in less 'stuff happens and we get to watch' movies, so pay close attention) and starts down the path to making a grudging accommodation with his old man, although the motivations for this shift are still somewhat opaque. He eventually ends up with a magic sword, a reflecting shield, Pegasus the flying pony and the recently severed head of the gorgon Medusa to turn the Kraken to stone. As you do of a morning.

Cue the very short third act and an unlikely race against time to save Alexa Davalos from being eaten.

Start of act two: Perseus hates the gods and has no clue how to kill the Kraken.

End of act two: Perseus still hates the gods (this is something of a story problem, I fear), but finally has come round to accepting their help and now has the knowledge and the tools for the job.

Of course, *Clash of the Titans*, bless its little 3D heart, is not the most complex of stories. Usually the change or preparation needed in your second act has much more to do with your hero/ine's internal, emotional change, but the job is basically the same no matter how complicated and nuanced your movie.

```
             IMPLIED YOU
     Yeah, I get that, but I am still
     suffering from a major case of the
     'what nows?'

             FRIENDLY ME
     Right. That's why the 'W' model is
     going to break the second act into two
     sections—two angles—for easier use.
```

### A note about subplots

I want to talk about this here because the start of your second act is where a **B Story** typically gets going. Your story may have a number of threads that involve different characters interacting in your story world. It is important to make sure that they all have a direct impact on the unfolding and the resolution of your primary story. They should address the theme your hero/ine is struggling with, otherwise they are simply a **narrative economy** fail.

In movie land these threads or subplots are given letters to distinguish them: **B Story**, **C Story** and so forth. There is no rule about how many subplots your story can generate, but the more you have the harder your story will be to control. There is also no hard and fast rule about what kinds of subplots come under what letter. The titles are just a matter of convenience. However, it is common usage to call the main friendship or romantic subplot the **B Story**. Other significant threads get their own letter as they emerge. That's the system I will be using in this book. Remember that there is a difference between a romantic plot and a romantic subplot. The former drives the whole story, as in a romcom. The latter is a secondary story line in a different genre.

Having said there is no rule about naming subplots, I would draw your attention to Dara Marks's alternative approach in *Inside Story*. She offers a very persuasive model using **A**, **B** and **C Stories** as a way of understanding how your hero/ine learns and demonstrates growth and change in your story. I am going to introduce it here, but direct you to her excellent book for a fuller account. She thinks of the core relationships as a triad designed to resolve the problem of the story. Thus the **A Story** is the *external* problem that can only be solved if the hero/ine makes an *internal* change in the **B Story** that is expressed in a *relationship* in the **C Story**. This change is then manifested through that relationship to resolve the problem in the **A Story**. It's a very useful way of thinking about character relationships, but I won't steal any more of her thunder here.

## First up angle

At the start of the second angle (the beginning of act two) therefore, your hero/ine has most likely decided to get off their ass and grow up/ do the right thing/get the girl/be less of a douchebag/right the wrong/ survive the attack of the rabid weasels/resolve the unspoken conflicts at the heart of their family/make sure their shirts no longer match the wallpaper, or whatever. But they have only *decided* to do something; they haven't actually done it yet. That means they haven't yet learned, changed or earned their survival or redemption in any way through their actions. They are basically the same person they were at the start with the same personality, instincts, talents, skills and flaws. That means they will do exactly what you or I would most likely do: use the skills they already have to try for a quick fix. It will work for a while, but it will only take them so far before they are out of their comfort zone and need to think again.

My friend Tony Moon uses the example of holes in the road to help his students in Southampton to understand the way this angle often works, and I've also heard it in slightly different form from other writers. Imagine your hero/ine walking down the road. They come to a small pothole and step over it. Another, wider pothole appears in front of them and this one they jump with ease. A third hole appears and this one takes a running jump to clear. And so we go on, with the holes—the challenges to character and obstacles to progress in story terms—getting progressively wider, deeper and harder to overcome.

For a while—for the length of the first up angle indeed—your hero/ine can overcome the obstacles on their own or without adding appreciably to the talents, equipment and support they started out with. A point will come, however, just before the end of this angle, when they can't jump the pothole without some major assistance. This is where the relationships established or rekindled in your **B story** might help (change), new skills might be needed (change), bigger risks taken (change), or a combination of all of these (major change).

In fish-out-of-water stories, this angle has fun with the juxtaposition, so in *Big* this is when Tom Hanks is really enjoying the 'being big' part of the story, after the initial shock and before it gets weird with Elizabeth Perkins and before he realizes he has to find a way to get back to his family. In *Legally Blonde* (scr. Karen McCullah Lutz & Kirsten Smith; 2001), Reece Witherspoon started the movie *merely* blonde, but after a terrible bloketastrophe she goes to Harvard Law School to win him back and thus becomes *legally* blonde just in time to have plenty of fish-out-of-watery fun in this angle. Things will get harder all too soon, but Hollywood movies let their hero/ines have a bit of fun without pushing them too hard just yet.

Blake Snyder, in one of his smartest, center-of-the-bullseye moments, refers to this part of the movie as 'the promise of the premise.' In other words, it's what the poster, the trailers and the pitch statement of the movie told us we were going to get. It's what made you want to go see the movie. Now, in this angle, that debt is being paid.

In *Aliens*, for example, we are promised the plural in spades and, sure enough, in this angle we let those crazy xenomorphs loose on our cocky but totally unprepared space marines for fun and frolics: 'They're coming outta the walls!' It is not yet 'Game over, man. Game over …' and the final extended struggle for survival is yet to come. Right now, however, we're 'in the pipe, five by five' and it's all great fun, before we submit to the unforgiving mathematics of: 'They mostly come at night. Mostly.'

It is also an angle that is all about enjoying the interface between genre and character. In *Brick*, Brendan has decided to find out who killed his ex girlfriend Emily, and why. Now *Brick* is a smart mix of high school and hardboiled detective movie, and Brendan, who has operated as something of a detective once before, launches himself mind and body into his investigation. He knows Emily had become involved with the cool, druggie crowd at school and so he starts by putting pressure on the connections between that crowd and the local drug dealers.

His first target is Brad Bramish, a jock hooked into the drug network. Brendan winds Brad up—which is not hard to do—and fights him in the school parking lot. Not only does Brendan win but, through his victory, he gets a step closer to finding the local gang leader, The Pin. Here Brendan is being written true to genre. He is not a country house detective in the Miss Marple line, winning by brains alone. He is a true hardboiled detective, putting his body on the line as an investigative tool.

Brendan is in control at this point. He knows what he is doing and he is able to manipulate personalities and groups he already understands. All of this is leading up to the moment where his easy leads dry up. He finds he can't go any further without taking a big risk, without putting his life on the line. He uses his innate skills, personality and knowledge to take himself to the brink, but then he has to jump into the unknown and the potentially uncontrollable world outside of his high school comfort zone. We'll come back to *Brick* as a full case study in the next chapter, but Brendan's hardboiled pranks have taken us to the **midpoint** of the story. Thanks, Brendan—he doesn't get much encouragement, poor thing. It's the thought that counts.

## Midpoint

The **midpoint** is the fulcrum of the second act.

In Hollywood screenplays the **midpoint** is typically the second moment where the hero/ine has to make a commitment. The first choice in the first down angle of act one was easy by contrast. This time there is nowhere left to go without instigating real change and often encountering real danger (emotional and/or physical). Your hero/ine's starting skill set has led them here and we all had some fun watching the journey. Now they are standing at the crease like a nervous Australian tail-end batsman about to face Harold Larwood at the top of his game. That's a cricket reference by the way. I could have gone with baseball, but I decided to pick an actual sport instead. Google it, because the 'bodyline' controversy is one of sport's great stories and is worth at least another TV movie.

Here's an example from *Up in the Air* (scr. Jason Reitman and Sheldon Turner; 2009). By the **midpoint**, the **C Story** involving Natalie's project to fire people by teleconference and the **B Story** of Ryan's developing relationship with fellow business traveler Alex intersect in Miami. Ryan has told Natalie he doesn't believe in love. She hears him give a motivational speech: 'Your relationships are the heaviest components in your life. Set that bag down. The slower we move, the faster we die … we are sharks.' Natalie's boyfriend has dumped her (by text = poetic justice + ouch) and Ryan and Alex take her out for drinks. The conversation turns on how as we grow older our expectations for relationships change. Natalie is kind of appalled by how little both Ryan and Alex are willing to settle for. She moved to Omaha for her ex, so she knows from dedication.

They go on to crash a convention party. Natalie gets drunk and hooks up. Alex and Ryan also have a night. Before she leaves, Ryan tells her: 'I really like you.' She replies: 'I like you too.' For Ryan this is a major statement. He is jumping into emotions that come as close to love as he is capable of feeling. That's his **midpoint** crisis. After this his commitment to no commitments is severely tested. He invests more and more in Alex and less and less in his professional life. Natalie—the Ryan in training—also has her crisis, and the manner of her dumping brings her to understand the pitfalls in her teleconferencing project. The veneer of icy professionalism cracks and she is on the slide towards quitting.

Natalie also lashes out at Ryan and calls him on his 'bullshit philosophy.' She tells him he's a twelve-year-old living in a 'cocoon of self-banishment.' We've wanted to say that to him for the entire movie, so we like her for her honesty. Remember, after the **midpoint** nothing can be the same. Feelings and circumstances have changed so much that our characters are now committed to a journey they resisted, couldn't understand or were unable to access previously. Ryan is now filling up his backpack with the heaviest thing—a relationship—and, in doing so, breaking rule one of his Tony Robbinsesque 'philosophy.'

Natalie's confidence in herself and her work has been undermined and her experiences in the second down angle will only reinforce this. Of course, this is the job of the second down angle. We know things will get harder after the crisis or commitment of the **midpoint**; this angle is all about making it so.

## Second down angle

After the **midpoint**, the second half of act two is a down angle which takes our hero/ine from a second moment of commitment, through their ultimate trial, to revelation and the formation of a plan to resolve the story in the next act. This is usually the most serious and emotionally fraught part of the story—even in comedies—because only through this process of testing does your hero/ine *earn* the right to succeed or at least resolve the story.

Remember, Hollywood screenplays are typically locked into the American Dream via the shackles of the Protestant Work Ethic or, as they say in Yorkshire, 'you don't get owt for nowt.'

In *Up in the Air* we follow Ryan and Natalie as their business trip takes them to Detroit. Here Natalie's online firing protocol is tested, and now she finds the going very tough emotionally. If she hadn't been dumped by her boyfriend, if she hadn't had the Miami experience, she wouldn't have had the unfeeling nature of her work brought home to her in such a stark fashion, and her empathy for the man she has to fire would have been less overwhelming. The **midpoint** makes everything harder.

After the test of Natalie's program, she and Ryan are brought back to Omaha. Ryan decides to detour for his sister's wedding in Wisconsin. He's never home and had been avoiding the event, but now he invites Alex to be his date. The wedding sees Ryan having a great time with Alex and simultaneously learning to be a better brother. He is humanized and offered a glimpse of 'real life' in this terrific sequence. This is great writing; it may seem counter-intuitive for the end of the second act to feel so positive and life affirming, but of course poor Ryan is being set up for a fall.

The better things are going with Alex right now, the worse it will be when it all falls apart. The down angle still applies, only we understand its full meaning after the fact. We do see Ryan learning to change as a brother after he is exposed to his family's contempt. That story thread is classic down angle material. The good times with Alex fool Ryan into throwing the rest of his life away on the hope that the relationship is real. The **midpoint** makes everything harder.

Things go so well that, at the end of the angle, Ryan blows off his biggest and most prestigious motivational speaking gig in Vegas to travel to Chicago and see Alex. He thinks he no longer believes in his philosophy of life because now he's a smitten kitten. Remember, Natalie was right; emotionally Ryan is basically a twelve-year-old acting on a big crush. So Ryan turns up at Alex's home to find—surprise—she has a husband and family. He leaves to the sound of Alex telling her husband he is 'just somebody who was lost.' That's so true.

In this moment the **B Story** pays off and, in doing so, enables the resolution of the **A Story**. Remember that **B Stories** have an important supporting function. They should always be more than just an excuse for romantic interludes or moments of abstract friendship. Narrative economy requires the integration of the action of the **B Story** into the story proper. Otherwise we are just wasting time and money once again.

In *Up in the Air*, the **B Story** derails Ryan from his work, his philosophy of life, and all of his certainties. That's a big task, and it reminds us how important subplots are. We'll see another example of this in the case study of *Brick* in the next chapter. Here the resolution—the consummation in this case—of the **B Story** provides the vital clue to solving the mystery of Emily's death.

## Act three: second up angle

Third acts are almost always the shortest of the three acts, often no more than fifteen or twenty pages and sometimes even shorter. By now, your hero/ine should have learned what the story needs them to learn to put the 'W' fix in, both externally in the story world and internally as a person. If you have worked your structure well, all that now remains is for you to enact the resolution we know is coming and that your hero/ine is now ready to undertake (or at the very least influence). This is where all of your attention to parallelism speaks loudest. You've set things up, now pay them off.

The pleasure for the audience in this second up angle is all about experiencing your hero/ine's personal renewal, even if you then pull the rug away with an ambivalent or even down ending. It is also about appreciating the elegance with which you have tied up the threads of your story and the satisfaction of seeing the world made new again. We'll examine in more detail how films do this in the section on beats, later.

In Hollywood, the up ending has always been king. Leave the audience smiling, is the assumption, and they'll come back for more of the same. Most movies end on a happy note, so we'll take that as read and focus our examples on the alternatives. Firstly, an up ending does not necessarily mean that all will be well for the hero/ine themselves. Remember that it is also the job of the story to fix the *story world*. Characters may fail, die or be left in decidedly ambivalent circumstances, but a well written ending makes sure we understand that their personal journey has come to a dramatically—and thus thematically— satisfying conclusion.

Ryan has what he always wanted in the final angle of *Up in the Air*. Ten million miles on his loyalty card and he gets to go back out traveling. He has been given the ingredients for perfect 'lightness,' but of course it's no longer the answer he's seeking. Now it will be forever tainted by his experience with Alex. The irony is that he has caught up with the audience in understanding the emptiness of his lifestyle, just when he gets the opportunity to live it permanently.

In terms of parallelism, all the set-ups for Ryan pay off. What has changed in the interim is Ryan himself. His personal development means those pay-offs have very different meanings than we expected they would in the first angle. His discovery of real feelings for Alex has changed him. We know that his experiences have made him a better person because, despite their differences, he writes a glowing reference for Natalie after—perhaps because—she quits her job.

Anyone who has seen *The Searchers* (scr. Frank S. Nugent; 1956) will be left in no doubt by the iconic final shot that Ethan is an outsider, unable to be part of a family or a home. His job is done, however, and his long search has mended the family he can now be no part of. In *The Searchers* the story world is mended thanks to Ethan's actions; but he is damaged goods, excluded from that mending. The ambivalence of its ending—of how the ending resolves the themes of the story world and the individual—is what makes *The Searchers* a great movie. The famous final shot of *The Graduate* (scr. Calder Willingham and Buck Henry; 1967) leaves us with a similarly ambivalent feeling. The eloping couple sit in the back of a bus, their expressions betraying the uncertainty that lies in their future: what do we do now?

Uncounted war and adventure movies kill off their heroes, who die to ensure the success of the mission. 'Dulce et decorum est,' and so forth. Even the lad Bruce Willis has his moment of heroic sacrifice in *Armageddon* (scr. Jonathan Hensleigh and J. J. Abrams et al.; 1998). Stranded on a giant dirty ice cube in space, he has to push a button to detonate the explosives that will break up the asteroid and save the world, killing himself in the process. Of course these moments of pathos don't always play as intended. I remember sitting in the cinema for this one with multiple members of a British audience yelling out 'push the button!' just so this overlong and overblown movie could finally end. Perhaps it's just a cultural thing. Perhaps it's just a Michael Bay thing.

The further we travel from the Hollywood mainstream, the more acceptable a 'down ending' becomes. One of the truly great down endings comes in *El Gran Silencio/The Great Silence* (scr. Mario Amendola, Bruno Corbucci, Sergio Corbucci & Vittoriano Petrilli; 1968), a kind of Marxist spaghetti western. The movie pits Jean Louis Trintignant's mute gunfighter 'Silence' against corrupt bounty hunters led by Klaus Kinski—I mean, who else? By the climax of the movie, the townspeople have been captured and are being held in the local saloon. Silence has an injured hand and is outnumbered many to one. Bravely he struggles to the saloon and we are all set for what promises to be a great heroic final gunfight.

This isn't *Rio Bravo* (scr. Jules Furthman and Leigh Brackett; 1959), however, nor even *Per Un Pugno Di Dollari/A Fistful of Dollars* (scr. Victor Andrés Catena, Jaime Comas Gil & Sergio Leone et al.; 1964). First, someone shoots Silence's good hand, which is just not cricket. Then Klaus Kinski shoots Silence down when he tries to draw his gun with his crippled hand. Klaus then kills Silence's girlfriend, murders all the hostages and the villains ride away to collect their bounties. Goodbye. The end. Pick the bones out of that one. Of course the film is making a very European 1970s-style leftie statement about the nature of heroism and of history. We learn in a text crawl that the massacre is the catalyst for better laws and thus has a value in historical terms even if all the good guys die at the time. It is a cheat in its way, but also a chance to stick a defiant finger up at John Wayne and all who sail in him.

## Spanking your hero/ine

Now that we have skimmed through the basic act structure of my little 'W' model, there is one more task to impress upon you before we look at the structure of the acts in more detail: *always spank your hero/ine.*

Then ask yourself: 'Have I spanked them hard enough?' If in doubt, do it again only harder. There's no law against using corporal punishment on imaginary people. They don't even need a safety word, so go for it.

```
          IMPLIED YOU
Can I use my hand, or did you have a
particular instrument in mind?

          FRIENDLY ME
Use your pen or your keyboard, but
lay it on either way.

          IMPLIED YOU
You clearly didn't understand my oh
so subtle code for 'what the hell
are you talking about?'

          FRIENDLY ME
One of the greatest crimes against
storytelling I see in many, if not
most first draft screenplays is a
lack of serious and sustained
threat. There is nothing worse than
a story that doesn't have major
consequences for its characters if
they fail.

          IMPLIED YOU
Oh, you mean there isn't enough at
stake?

          FRIENDLY ME
Exactly. It doesn't matter whether
you are writing a comedy or a
tragedy, if you don't test your
```

characters properly your audience
won't care about them. Whatever is
at stake needs to be really felt.
It needs to be life and death in
the terms of the movie.

                    IMPLIED YOU
So that doesn't always mean actual life
and death?


                    FRIENDLY ME
It means that failure should be the
nightmare scenario, not just a minor
annoyance. So: 'I owe the landlord
$50. Oh noes, what to do? That's
really going to cut into my latte
budget for the next few weeks' isn't
enough to make a good story.


                    IMPLIED YOU
But if you live in Bangladesh and $50
is your income for several months,
that's a very big deal.


                    FRIENDLY ME
And a very different story.
Exactly.


                    IMPLIED YOU
But what about those mumblecore or
indie movies that are really
character studies and not
plot-led?


                    FRIENDLY ME
Mumblecore movies are all about
real emotions. That's their whole
point. For example, Hannah is
really worried about her pattern of
'crush' relationships that leave
destruction in their wake in Hannah
Takes The Stairs. She is very
dissatisfied with her emotional life
and that's a very big deal for her.


                    IMPLIED YOU
But they don't all follow your 'W'
model, do they?


                    FRIENDLY ME
That's right. Remember the 'W' is
just a model to help you understand
how many, but not all, movies
work. Mumblecore characters still
have problems, still need to work
through them and still deal with

```
the issue of change, even if for
them change is learning to take
the day off work to play trumpet
naked in the bath with their new
boyfriend.
```

If your hero/ine can win through using their starting skill set there isn't much of a story. Work them hard. Test them hard. The same applies to major supporting characters. I mean even the Terminator learns enough to realize it has to sacrifice itself for the greater good at the end of *Terminator 2: Judgment Day*, and it's just made up of bits of welded Arnold.


## Beating it up

OK, so what's really going on here is a little bit like a matryoshka, one of those sets of Russian nesting dolls where each doll looks the same only small enough to fit inside the previous one. We are asking similar questions of all our levels of storytelling. What's at stake changes in terms of the size of the immediate target, but the relationship between the part and the whole must be consistent in thematic terms.

*Stories* enact a dramatic function—character bends to the will of the theme and resolves it.
*Acts* (and 'W' *angles*) enact a dramatic function—they take a character from one attitude to the theme or key position in the story to another.
*Story beats* enact a dramatic function—they encompass a significant development in the dramatic function of their act or angle.

And so on down through *sequences* and *scenes* to *scene beats*.


## Bite size morsels

We are going to play around with this model and divide each of the four angles of the **'W'** first into two and then finally into four beats. This will help us think about the work each of the four angles needs to do in reasonably standard Hollywood terms. We'll also give the beats silly names designed to make quick sense of them. As usual I am making no great claims of personal genius in parts of this. On the contrary, I am borrowing from a variety of sources historical, mythical and screenwriting guru-ical. For example, you can certainly see traces of Snyder and Vogler in the functions of some of the beats, and I acknowledge it fully. As always, I recommend you read their books if you want additional 'beat models' to work with.

What makes mine different is the way the 'W' is linked developmentally to the work of the 'V' and the **wardrobe**. Then there's the way I use angles to articulate dramatic function; the focus on corresponding parallel beats by using a 'ring' as well as a linear model (of which more later) and the flexibility the model gets from the matryoshka effect. My purpose is to provide you with a flexible and integrated learning model, *drawing on good practice*, not my own set of arbitrary absolutes.

To that end, the 'W' offers a series of linked models from which you pick the one which best fits your creative needs. Depending on the amount of detailed direction you want, there is a 'W' version that is likely to be useful to you. My own favorite is the **Half Angle** version (see below), but sometimes I like to step back and see the story in greater or lesser detail depending on what kind of problem I am working on at a given moment. We have 'W' versions to let you do this easily.

As usual, if it gets in the way of you having fun as a writer, or gets in the way of you feeling free to **write what you don't know**, then junk it, or just use it as a brain check later on.

## The 'W' beat sheets

There is an approach to digesting story structure that takes the whole story as a single bite. My '**Wardrobe**' is one way of visualizing that, and we have already thought about it in Chapter 4.

This time, however, we are going to have fun with a range of smaller bite size chunks. The next smallest still requires a very large appetite and is what we might call the **Full Angle** version. It thinks in terms of the four angles of the 'W'. We just spent some time on this above, so I'll move straight on to the next smallest bite, the **Half Angle** version. This one splits each angle in two and gives each half-angle a specific job to do. Here's the whole thing at a glance:

## The 'W' in half angles

FIRST DOWN ANGLE—RECOGNITION
    A. Primary exposition.
    B. From rejection to acceptance.

FIRST UP ANGLE—AVOIDANCE
  C. Doing just fine on my own.
  D. Pushed to your (opening) limits.

MIDPOINT—JUMP!

SECOND DOWN ANGLE—COMMITMENT
  E. From leap to crisis.
  F. Through crisis to revelation.

SECOND UP ANGLE—RESOLUTION
  G. The plan and the pushback.
  H. The resolution and its meaning.

Let's take the beats as they come:

### FIRST DOWN ANGLE—RECOGNITION

The angle is all about giving everyone enough information to get the story going. At its simplest, it is about your hero/ine traveling far enough to *recognize* the story challenge and then deciding to try and overcome it.

### A. Primary exposition

The first half angle is all about introductions: to our hero/ine; to their world; to the problem or challenge they are going to face; and to the link between plot challenge and story challenge. Usually we can think about this also in terms of internal and external character challenges if we want to. So, in *2012* I must de-flake myself (internal) to save my family and the world (external).

The first half of the angle has to get us through as much **exposition** as we need in order for the next beat to work. In other words, if the **from rejection to acceptance** beat is all about deciding what to do, the **primary exposition** beat needs to help us understand enough about the situation to help the viewer appreciate that decision making process in the context of character and goals.

At the end of this half angle, Robert McKee and others point out that Hollywood movies typically need one of those **inciting incidents** we mentioned a few pages back. We talked about this in relation to ring compositions and audiences anticipating and searching for correspondences between story beats across the movie. The idea is to kick the plot into gear while locking the anticipation of a second story moment near the end of act three into the mind of the viewer. That future moment

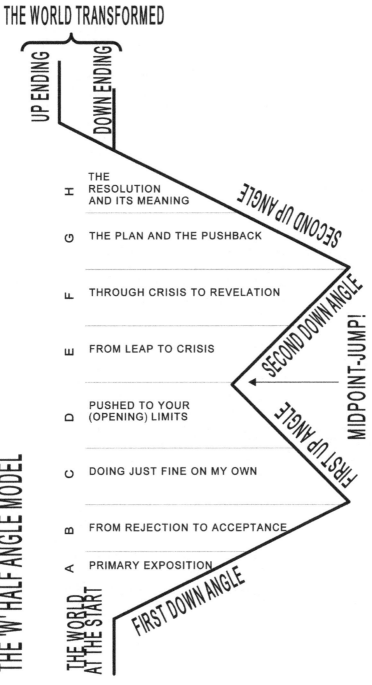

resolves, or at the very least addresses the resolution of our opening challenge *as expressed by the inciting incident*: 'Hmm, Empire bad …' in the first angle of *Star Wars* implies the **obligatory moment** where Luke will spank the Empire in the last angle. We don't know exactly what form that spanking will take, whether it will be delivered by an X Wing Fighter to the Death Star or Luke's bare hand to Grand Moff Tarkin's skinny old bottom, but we know it is coming and we are already looking forward to the moment.

Not all films are this literal minded, but if yours has a conventional conflict between a hero/ine and a villain/ess you need to have established the terms of that conflict—specifically the entertainingly evil nature and intent of the antagonist—so we already want to see its resolution.

### B. From rejection to acceptance

We know the issue at stake, now we need to see the first significant character move in the second half angle. Usually the hero/ine has a moment of revelation where they understand 'things cannot continue as they are.' Romantic comedies, for example, offer us catalysts with either or both the negative revelation of a bloketastrophe or girlamity or the positive revelation of a potentially romantic encounter—or both.

What follows is helping them make their initial decision to do something. As we have seen, most Hollywood hero/ines are reluctant at the start and take some convincing, and many movies only allow a limited understanding by their protagonists of the true, personal implications of the story problem in the first act or angle. Sometimes they are just not ready to understand and accept its true import yet. Sometimes they will have to work hard to uncover the full truth.

This almost always necessitates an early expansion of the character stock in your story. See how the logic of story is already getting you to make simple structural decisions?

We will deal with supporting characters more fully in another chapter, but, for now, your hero/ine needs an opponent of some kind to articulate the story problem. They are usually, but not always, introduced early on. *This Is England*, for example, saves the main antagonist for later. It opens with minor enemies to set up Sean's 'father problem' at school during primary exposition and adds resistance from his mother in this beat.

Of course the opponent can be the hero/ine themselves at this point if the story is about coming to self awareness or addressing an internal problem that gets in the way of normal social functioning (*Greenberg*), but we need the opposition articulated so we understand what is at stake.

Remember to spank hard: *Star Wars* blows up a whole planet to 'demonstrate the power' of the Death Star, and murders Luke's family. The fact that your protagonists are going to debate their proper actions usually means they need one or more friends, associates, mentors, lovers or similar sounding boards. Perhaps one of the most unlikely of these can be found in *Die Hard*, where the young limo driver bullies the lad Bruce (yeah, right) into fessing up about his marital problems on the drive from LAX to his wife's office building. He even speaks Bruce's ideal story outcome to him (involving Bruce and Mrs. Bruce running into each other's arms) just in case the audience doesn't get it. Of course, Bruce needs all the help he can get if he is going to evolve from dinosaur to mammal in the next 90 minutes, but still ...

Indeed, this is a common Hollywood trick. Get someone else to tell your hero/ine what they want or what they need to do in order to resolve their plot and story problems early on. Then add a diagram with arrows and boxes and large print titles in case we missed it.

Of course, just because you introduce character sounding boards in this angle doesn't mean the sounds they reflect need to be accurate or even especially helpful. Every character has their own motivations, opinions, prejudices and so forth, and part of the fun of writing is to establish a series of corresponding characters who help get the story done between them but also influence the route we take to get there. More of this in Chapter 7, but remember, that route doesn't need to be direct.

Here's a straightforward romantic comedy example. Let's Aniston it up again by bringing our old friend back in a third Jennifer story. Changing gear this time, our movie is called *Sunspots*, because Jennifer is in love with her very best friend. We'll call her friend Copey, just because now I can see them together in my mind and it is making me giggle. Now Copey is in love with perky Jean, not mopey old Jennifer. First angle, what happens? 'Oh Jennifer,' says wistful, lovelorn Copey one day at the Neolithic burial mound—did I mention they are both archeologists and that a shared love of the antiquarian, the esoteric and old Neu and Faust albums will eventually bring them together? 'Oh Jennifer, how am I ever going to get perky Jean to notice boring old archeologist me?' Jennifer now has a choice. She knows how to help him, but she doesn't want to lose him. And so the lying and the comedy begin ...

By the way, in romantic and buddy comedies your lovers or buddies are often your protagonist/antagonist pair. The character who leads the romantic story, or the straight man in a buddy comedy, is typically the protagonist. Think *When Harry Met Sally*—Billy Crystal leads the story and gets protagonist status while Meg Ryan pushes his buttons and memorably fakes having hers pushed—or *Planes, Trains and Automobiles*—Steve Martin is the straight man struggling to get home despite the disruption caused by John Candy's infuriating but well meaning buddy antagonist.

### FIRST UP ANGLE—AVOIDANCE

The angle is full of action and fun but this is really a smokescreen for your hero/ine trying to *avoid* the need for real change or commitment. They travel to the point at which this won't work anymore.

### C. Doing just fine on my own

This half angle lets your hero/ine run with the ball using their innate skills and instincts. This is the start of the jury rig fix when it seems to be holding—although your hero/ine need not be succeeding with every step—and the wind isn't yet strong enough to break it. This half angle lets you have loads of fun with the substance of what made you fall in love with your leading character in the first place.

Here's a silly example from the enjoyably zany if flawed comedy *You Don't Mess with the Zohan*. We like the Zohan because he is both the ultimate Israeli counter terrorism agent and a peaceful, creative, hummus loving, wannabe hairdresser who fakes his own death to escape the never-ending cycle of violence in his homeland. He moves to New York and just wants to cut hair, get along with everyone and have sex with anything that moves.

In **doing just fine on my own** the Zohan fails at finding a hairdressing job in part because his style is 20 years out of date, but mainly because his military training keeps getting him into trouble. He is still convinced of his own genius, however (in other words, doing just fine is still holding *in his mind*), and believes all he needs is a real chance to prove himself.

In one entertaining scene he terrifies a salon full of children by describing in gory detail what happens if you don't keep your head still when scissors are cutting hair near your jugular vein. One thing leads to another, and soon he has all the children in the salon shrieking and has rendered one child unconscious with a commando style nerve pinch. Needless to say, he doesn't get the job.

We still like the Zohan, however, because we know he meant well. He just needs to get the two aspects of his character working in harmony to be able to get and hold his dream job. Amusingly failing towards initial success is a comedy alternative to the easy success of this beat and angle. Either way there is not much at stake yet. Anyway, this is the relatively simple task of the movie's second angle jury rig solution, uncovering the plot of an unscrupulous property developer and attempting to bring harmony between the local Arab and Israeli small business communities will come in the third, and hardest angle.

The **doing just fine on my own** beat also links the **B Story** directly into the **A Story**. The **B Story** often develops into a romance plot, even if your hero/ine doesn't realize it yet. For example, the Zohan meets the beautiful Palestinian owner of the hair salon and eventually persuades her to give him a chance. He is not thinking about love at this point, just proving his talent at cutting hair. Needless to say, this will change. Soon afterwards he is also recognized by a Palestinian taxi driver who starts a subplot about inept would-be terrorists which will play out through the rest of the movie.

### D. Pushed to your (opening) limits

This half angle just moves the action of **doing just fine on my own** into more dangerous territory. What changes is that your hero/ine's opening skill set is running out of skills. The holes in the road are wider and your hero/ine is getting to the point at which they no longer have the equipment to fill them in or bridge them. We are still having fun with our hero/ines but we are also pushing them towards the **midpoint**, at which the level of commitment and endangerment required of them (however defined) is going to increase dramatically.

Another way of working **pushed to your (opening) limits** is to use it to complete your hero/ine's simple opening goal. Just when they think they have the thing or the person they have always wanted, they find that it was a false dream, revealing a deeper, more meaningful and certainly harder to achieve dream beneath it, or their happiness comes under the kind of threat they have to go 'all in' to resist.

The Zohan … Wow. I can't believe I'm still writing about the Zohan. I must have a soft spot for the guy. Perhaps it's our shared love of hummus. Anyway, the Zohan achieves his opening goal by the **midpoint**. He is in New York, making his living cutting hair. Now, of course, he realizes he is in love with the Palestinian salon owner who is not only his boss but also the sister of his nemesis. All bets are off.

In romantic comedies, the C and D beats frequently involve some initial version of 'getting' the boy or girl. Our hero/ine will go on to lose them again in the E and F beats, just in time to win them back in the final angle.

A fifth variation is to think of this half angle setting up the **midpoint** as a second crisis. Your hero/ine has tried to put things right in the first up angle, but has been beaten back, prevented, or lacks the strength or the will to take things forward. Something happens in **pushed to your (opening) limits** that forces their hand. That's the way it works in a wonderful independent movie that won the Grand Jury Prize at Sundance, *Winter's Bone* (scr. Debra Granik & Annie Rosellini; 2010).

Seventeen-year-old Ree has tried her best to find her bail jumping, drug dealing dad. She has worked her way around her secretive outlaw relatives and Ozarks neighbors in so doing. She is now pretty certain that her father has been killed, but has no evidence to prove it. To ask more questions would put her life in real danger. That's when the bail bondsman turns up. He tells her she'll lose the property in a week unless she can prove her dad is dead. Now Ree has a stark choice, give it up and lose the house and land or keep searching where she has been warned by dangerous people not to go. The stakes are raised for her as she has to decide whether or not to jump.

Remember, spank your hero/ine hard—although in this angle it may be your hero/ine who does much of the early spanking. Remember how much fun we have watching Brendan do his hardboiled detective shtick beating up jocks and intimidating stoners in *Brick*? If nothing else, make sure that if you play the false victory midpoint version, the falseness of that victory exposes a whole bunch of spanking yet to come.

### *MIDPOINT—JUMP!*

We talked about this before, but the **midpoint** is usually where your hero/ine has to reassess their situation, or is forced into escalation or decision by a ramping up of the threat in the plot. They have most likely come to an impasse. Perhaps new goals have been revealed, although they must still serve the theme. Either way, your hero/ine now begins to understand the true nature of the commitment they will have to make in order to sort everything out in the end. It is unlikely that they know *how* to solve their problem at the micro level yet; this usually happens in **through crisis to revelation**, but they know that things are about to get much more serious.

Think about the midpoint of *(500) Days of Summer*. Tom, desperately insecure in his relationship with Summer, asserts his masculinity and his claim to be an actual, real, stand-up boyfriend by punching a yuppie douchebag who comes on to Summer in a bar. Summer is horrified, not just by the violence but by the assumption it implies about the status of their relationship. Tom has jumped from needing to know where he stands to telling her where he thinks he stands. He has forced the issue and, although things don't all fall apart right away, he is not going to like where he lands.

In *Winter's Bone*, the midpoint comes on a cut from the scene with the bail bondsman to the one with Ree in a cattle auction. She is searching for Blond Milton, the leader of the local outlaw clan. She tried to see him before, but was warned off by Merab, his woman. We know

Blond is a bad man, but now Ree feels she has no alternative. She jumps into very dangerous waters.

## SECOND DOWN ANGLE—COMMITMENT

This angle is where your hero/ine earns the map to their success. Real character change happens here because the story forces your hero/ine to *commit* or get off the pot. By the end of this angle they should have traveled far enough to be prepared to face their ultimate challenge.

### E. From leap to crisis

Ramp up the pressure now. This is where your hero/ine should be feeling out of their depth, struggling to find a way forward. Enemies pile in, self-doubt increases, everything should be pushing your hero/ine towards a crisis. Lives should be at stake here, literally or metaphorically. I know I always ask you if you have spanked your hero/ine, but this is the beat where you need to get a bigger paddle, as you are now a slightly less psychopathic version of Ben Affleck in *Dazed and Confused*. **Through crisis to revelation** will only work if your audience believes the crisis. **From leap to crisis** is where you earn that belief.

In *Kick Ass*, Dave freaks out as he is drawn ever further into the all-too-real and all-too-violent world of 'superheroes' and gangsters. His need to extricate himself leads him into making rash decisions (he instinctively trusts Red Mist and takes him at face—or rather mask—value) that bring about the crisis in the next beat. If he hadn't trusted Red Mist he wouldn't have exposed Big Baddy's safe house to attack from the bad guys.

### F. Through crisis to revelation

By now it should be clear that, in Hollywood movies, hero/ines earn their redemption, success and general woohooness at the end of the story by paying their dues along the way. Remember: Protestant work ethic? If ever there was a beat in which to spank your hero/ine, you are now the *full* Ben Affleck and **through crisis to revelation** is that beat.

As other screenwriting books have noted, there is frequently a close brush with death in this beat. Of course, just as with the tarot card 'Death', we are not always speaking literally. Death can mean the death of hope or the transformation (and thus a kind of death through obsolescence and rebirth) of the character. It can mean the breaking down of the very last internal barrier or defense mechanism that prevents your hero/ine from understanding or acting in a thematically 'correct' fashion.

Sometimes 'death' can be a narrow escape, the death of a friend, or simply witnessing the death of another. In *Kick Ass*, Dave and Big Daddy have been captured by the bad guys and held in a warehouse. It looks like all is lost as the villains start to stream video of their upcoming execution as a lesson to the public not to be a hero. They are both beaten badly and have been doused in petrol when Hit Girl attempts a rescue. She succeeds in killing all the henchmen, but can't save Big Daddy, whose burns are too severe.

Now Dave feels incredibly guilty for leading Big Daddy to his destruction and that pushes him to man up to help Hit Girl take down the big boss in the fourth angle. He will also take on a brotherly role as Hit Girl is integrated into school and 'normal life' at the end. There is no way she would accept his friendship and help if he hadn't fought the final battle with her, and there's no way he would have fought that battle if Big Daddy hadn't died at the end of this angle. See how it works?

## SECOND UP ANGLE—RESOLUTION

No great surprise, this is Act Three. This is where we draw our threads together for the purposes of resolving the theme and closing our **wardrobe** on the changed story world implied by our exposition and made inevitable by our hero/ine's journey along the clothes rail of story.

### G. The plan and the pushback

If you have played your Act Two right, your hero/ine should know what has to be done and have the skills, insight and opportunity to take action to resolve themselves and, thus, the movie. This half angle is about making the plan and acting on it. There should be last minute reversals, maybe even shock revelations (possibly involving a bloke in black power armor telling you he's not actually *uncle* Vader), and you still need your well-worn hero/ine spanking paddle to hand. After all, where's the fun of a final battle if it isn't a real challenge?

That leads us to the *pushback*. Strong resistance to your hero/ine's plan is as important to the success of your angle and your story as a good plan itself. We may know in our hearts that our hero/ine will win out in the end (well, probably), but that is exactly why we need to make their victory entertaining. In *Kick-Ass*, Mindy (as Hit Girl) invades Frank's building and kills 2345364654.6 hoodlums in entertaining ways. However, she ends up getting herself trapped in the kitchen, weaponless and facing a guy about to shoot her with a bazooka.

She will need Dave's help to get out of this one. How his help manifests (it involves a jetpack and Gatling guns, which go together like pizza and … me) is also all part of the plan. After all, *a really good plan is prepared to push back at the pushback* and it comes in the next half angle.

This beat is also a good moment to restate the thematic or story function of your resolution, just so we remember what all the plot pyrotechnics are serving. In *Kick-Ass*, Mindy lays out her need for resolution to the theme of broken families and revenge for the death of her mother that has been driving her and Big Daddy all through the movie. She tells Dave: 'My mom already died for nothing so I'm sure as hell not going to let my dad die for nothing too.' Now Dave has to get on board for the final battle, but also to help construct a 'normal' future life for Mindy after all the derring-do has been daringly done.

This is the angle where we want to feel the full value of your hero/ine's transformation. They (and you) have worked really hard to get to this point, so don't undersell that struggle, that personal transformation, by making the resolution a cake walk. If your script is the kind of story in which you have taken the trouble to teach your hero/ine mad skills, now is the time for you to have them use all of those skills in the coolest way possible.

> FRIENDLY ME
> You know that with great power comes great responsibility, Spidey?
>
> IMPLIED SPIDEY
> Yeah, yeah, I suffered through all that. I accept who I am. I'm ready.
>
> FRIENDLY ME
> Hmm, I don't know. Are you strong?
>
> IMPLIED SPIDEY
> Listen, bud, I've got radioactive blood.
>
> FRIENDLY ME
> That sounds like it should make you weak as a kitten. Well, let's see. Can you swing from a thread?
>
> THWIP.
>
> IMPLIED SPIDEY
> Take a look overhead.
>
> FRIENDLY ME
> Wow. That was pretty cool.
>
> IMPLIED SPIDEY
> Are we really going to do the whole song?

```
                    FRIENDLY ME
OK, go get 'em! But remember to use
all your powers in really cool ways.
We have saved a whole bunch of the
budget for this, so make sure it's …

                    IMPLIED SPIDEY
Don't say 'Spectacular.' I've moved
on and so should you.

THWIP.
```

## H. The resolution and its meaning

The action of **the plan and the pushback** should have got you to the point at which your hero/ine *can* succeed if they make a proper second effort. Whether they *do* or not is up to you and how you are playing your theme, but if they have no chance at all and the audience knows it, or, conversely, if everything is all over bar the shouting and the victory is a foregone conclusion, you are missing the dramatic tension of this angle.

So this half angle resolves the theme and the story through the plot. Its primary purpose is to demonstrate in the figure and fate of your hero/ine the truth of whatever you set out to tell us about life.

To check if you have done your job, ask yourself only one question: *did your hero/ine's transformation enable your resolution?*

If so, big joy; if not, go back and fix it right away. *Nothing else matters in story terms.*

*Remember, success in your story does not always mean victory in your plot.* Your hero/ine can fail gloriously and still enact valid closure on your theme, on their 'transformational arc' if you will. If your **wardrobe** is as strong at the end as it was at the beginning and the clothes rail of your hero/ine's journey is still fixed firmly to the stout walls of theme, you are in good shape. The only question that remains is how, if at all, you want to dwell on the resolution of your story. Does its conclusion resonate fully or do we need to see its impact on your transformed story world in more detail?

At the end of *Star Wars* (yes, yes, Episode IV) we don't need to hang about because we all saw the Death Star get spanked, and that is the **obligatory moment** that pays off the **inciting incident** back on Tatooine in a big way. Give us everyone grinning sheepishly as they get their medals, and a Wookie grunting, and go straight to the credits. At the other end of the spectrum are the 412 endings of *The Lord of the Rings: The Return of the King*, which, as most people agree, did go on too long. Strictly speaking, all those scenes were meaningful in terms of the adaptation from the literary source, but that's the difference between the pleasures of reading and viewing.

To round off our example from *Kick-Ass*, after they have killed Frank, Mindy and Dave fly off on the jet pack and land on a rooftop at dawn. They reveal their identities to one another—a big superhero moment, of course, even though Mindy already knows Dave's identity. Cut to high school, and bullies attempt to bully Mindy on her first day. They'll learn. Kick-Ass has retired happy because Dave is no longer invisible to girls, at least until he returns in *Kick-Ass 2: Balls to the Wall*, which is apparently on its way. The only person still committed to a secret identity is Chris, who is determined to be a super villain: 'Wait till they get a load of me.'

All this information is communicated in about a minute of screen time, and that is possible because all the threads have been set up beforehand and we know what we need to know. This is how things should be; the last thing you want to be doing before you roll credits is explaining stuff. Revealing, yes: it's a great end reveal when we discover that 'Verbal' is Keyser Soze in *The Usual Suspects* (1995), but that is just answering the question that had been hanging over the whole movie. Tying up loose ends or showing that the truth of a mystery defaulted to option A rather than B is fine, but again this is not entirely new material. At least it shouldn't be.

Well, that's a brisk tour through the **Half Angle** version of the '**W**'. The next is the **Sixteen Beat** version, but I'm going to save that for the case study in the next chapter. As a beat sheet, however, it looks like this. Feast your eyes on all the fun yet to come:

### The 'W' in sixteen beats

FIRST DOWN ANGLE—RECOGNITION
   A. Primary exposition.
   *1. '... in a world where "ooh look, stuff."'*
   *2. 'If only ...'*
   B. From rejection to acceptance.
   *3. 'Shan't.'*
   *4. 'Oh, all right then.'*
   *Did you spank your hero/ine today?*

FIRST UP ANGLE—AVOIDANCE
   C. Doing just fine on my own.
   *5. 'You may not realize this yet, but ...'*
   *6. 'What, me broken?'*
   D. Pushed to your (opening) limits.
   *7. 'Meh, this is harder than I thought.'*

8. *'Leap? But it's dark?'*
*Did you spank your hero/ine today?*

MIDPOINT—JUMP!

SECOND DOWN ANGLE—COMMITMENT
  E. From leap to crisis.
  9. *'Bigger kids came.'*
  10. *'Er ... little help?'*
  F. Through crisis to revelation.
  11. *'It sucks to be me.'*
  12. *'Oh, riiight ...'*
  *Did you spank your hero/ine today?*

SECOND UP ANGLE—RESOLUTION
  G. The plan and the pushback.
  13. *'I have a cunning plan.'*
  14. *'Bandits, three o'clock high.'*
  H. The resolution and its meaning.
  15. *'Eat judge boot, creep.'*
  16. *'Oh brave new world ...'*
  *Did you spank your hero/ine today?*

## The 'W' as a ring

Now let's flip the **'W'** around and look at it as a kind of ring. We have been talking about parallelism and the pleasures of correspondence in storytelling. Thinking about the structure of your story not only as a linear progression but also as a 'game of two halves' in which the parallel sets of beats 'talk' to one another in the language of story development helps us keep our structure on track.

The 'ring' reminds us that whenever we advance our narrative in the first half of our screenplay, we give ourselves the opportunity to pay off that advance in the second. Sometimes this is required, expected and obvious to the reader and viewer: **Exposition** demands **Resolution**, for example. Sometimes, however, the relationship between story elements is a matter of constructing a subtle and elegant geometry with your story which may not always be transparent to your audience but which will certainly help in their enjoyment of your hero/ine's struggles.

Let's start by laying out a couple of levels of ring structure so we have a reference. Read down the left to the **midpoint** and then back up the right. Then read across the underlined pairings:

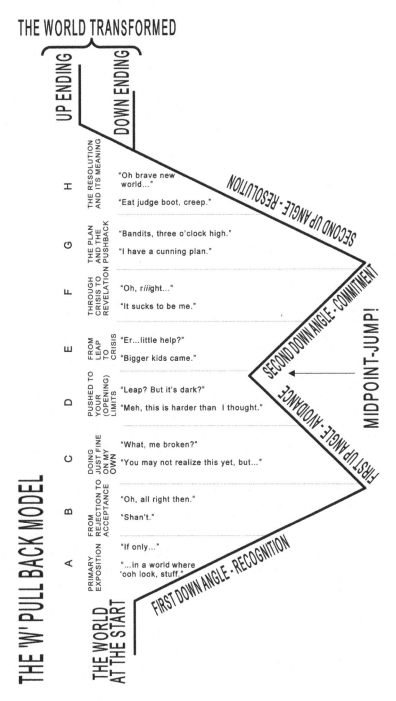

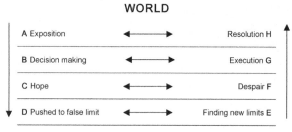

**WORLD**

| A Exposition | ←→ | Resolution H |
| B Decision making | ←→ | Execution G |
| C Hope | ←→ | Despair F |
| D Pushed to false limit | ←→ | Finding new limits E |

**MIDPOINT—leap!**

Or in more detail:

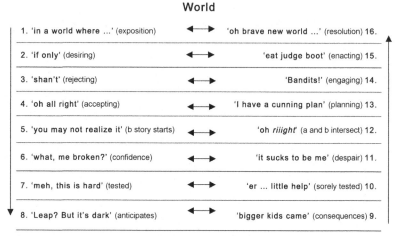

**World**

| 1. 'in a world where ...' (exposition) | ←→ | 'oh brave new world ...' (resolution) 16. |
| 2. 'if only' (desiring) | ←→ | 'eat judge boot' (enacting) 15. |
| 3. 'shan't' (rejecting) | ←→ | 'Bandits!' (engaging) 14. |
| 4. 'oh all right' (accepting) | ←→ | 'I have a cunning plan' (planning) 13. |
| 5. 'you may not realize it' (b story starts) | ←→ | 'oh *riiight*' (a and b intersect) 12. |
| 6. 'what, me broken?' (confidence) | ←→ | 'it sucks to be me' (despair) 11. |
| 7. 'meh, this is hard' (tested) | ←→ | 'er ... little help' (sorely tested) 10. |
| 8. 'Leap? But it's dark' (anticipates) | ←→ | 'bigger kids came' (consequences) 9. |

**MIDPOINT—leap!**

What we notice in these diagrams is that each first-half beat is completed, advanced, undercut or otherwise reflected in its corresponding second-half beat. The second half of the first act is all about **decision making**, for example, while its pair at the start of the third act is all about the **execution** of the plan that is the eventual consequence of that decision making. This pairing reminds us that we need to help our hero/ine develop to the point where they can make such a plan by the start of act three.

Likewise, the first beat of the second act and angle is often about (misplaced) confidence, or at least **hope**. Its pair is the final beat of act two, which is all about the dark before the dawn: **despair**. This pairing reminds us that we have to spank our hero/ine from one to the next for them to have changed and learned enough to earn and enable their resolution. The hope is false, or misguided, or ignorant. The despair is the result of all of that being peeled away. Each beat gives you a writing task and a deadline by which to complete it—the arrival of its pair.

To recap, you don't have to keep signaling correspondence in some obvious way all the time. Rather, the ring is both a reminder and a license:

1 There are specific story tasks that need to be accomplished between paired beats.
2 There are opportunities to show character change and story progression by reflecting or twinning scenes, events, locations and dialogue in both beats.

*Remember what our old friend narrative economy teaches us: everything in a screenplay pays off. Looking at the script as a ring shows us how that happens.*

Let's take a quick look at the pairs laid out in our second diagram:

**1 & 16** We establish the story world at the start in our primary exposition and we reflect on its new, *changed* state at the end as the final breath of our resolution.

**2 & 15** This pair links your hero/ine's opening desire with their taking the final action necessary to achieve it. It is a move from unrealistic hope to realistic expectation: how far we have come.

**3 & 14** This reversal pairs your hero/ine's initial and probably under-standable reluctance to get a clue with their first action having got one. 'I can't do this' meets 'I can, even though I may still be very scared, and it starts now.'

**4 & 13** Your hero/ine decides to take action at the end of the first act and makes a realistic—if often unlikely—plan at the start of the third. What these pairs remind us of is the jobs you need to do in between them. This one is about developing your hero/ine's knowledge and understanding, now they are able to make that plan. The previous is about developing their confidence and self-belief.

**5 & 12** These beats typically bookend the *story function* of your **B Story**. The **B Story** doesn't necessarily begin and end here, but its primary points of intersection with the **A Story** happen here. The **B Story** does its main work between these and thus helps enable your hero/ine to enact the change they need to make before entering the final act and angle.

**6 & 11** Once again this is the hopey/despairy pairing. The first sees our hero/ine making progress with limited commitment and under-standing, working on their opening skill set. The second sees them broken down and finally open to true self-awareness and the transformation it brings. You can also work it as a meeting between 'I'm doing the wrong thing well' and 'I'm doing the right thing now.'

**7 & 10** This pair anticipates the major change enacted between the previous beats. It is really a question of degree and ramping up the spanking. Your hero/ine of beat 7 thinks things are getting tough, but they ain't seen nothin' yet. These beats also play to self-awareness, as by beat 10 your hero/ine should be learning some very painful home truths or facing up to the true nature of their challenge.

**8 & 9** This is about anticipating the consequences of commitment and encountering those first consequences. This pair gives your hero/ine real credit with the audience because it shows them taking the midpoint jump while knowing that means some form of pain and suffering to come. One follows hard on the other, so you need to be sure 8 pays off in 9, as that expectation will be fresh in our minds. 'I know it's going to get harder' meets 'Oh look, it just did.'

These pairs enact micro resolutions all the way through your story. You can flag them by using transformed visual motifs, paired scenes, reworked lines of dialogue or similar markers, or you can keep their correspondence implicit. Once again I am reminded of *(500) Days of Summer*, which pairs scenes in the same location (IKEA, Tom's favorite park, the record store, the diner) to emphasize the emotional distance between events and pairs of dialogue scenes (I love Summer's knees/I hate Summer's knees) or reflections in the same way.

Either way, they can be your fallback checklist to make sure you are doing a solid structuring job on your hero/ine's arc. I'll give an extended example of how this correspondence works in a movie in the next chapter.

## Making a scene

Let's start by asking the simplest and most obvious question. Why do we separate our screen stories into scenes? This is the first and best question to ask, because the answer underpins all of your important decisions when writing a scene.

*We write in scenes like we speak in sentences; each scene encapsulates a discreet 'story thought.'* This thought may advance the story or, at the very least, it may reveal something important about character, or it may do both. If it does none of the above it shouldn't be in your script.

This is worthy of repetition, so expect some déjà vu later on. In fact it's so important that I'm going to get somebody much more impressive than me to remind you right now. This is how David Mamet put it in a memo to his writers on the TV show *The Unit*. The memo was leaked after the show finally got cancelled, and has become pretty much required reading for movie land screenwriters:

ANY SCENE ... WHICH DOES NOT BOTH ADVANCE THE PLOT, AND STAND ALONE (THAT IS, DRAMATICALLY, BY ITSELF, ON ITS OWN MERITS) IS EITHER SUPERFLUOUS, OR INCORRECTLY WRITTEN. [Mamet's caps]

The basic mechanics of scene writing are pretty simple: in screenwriting we change scene whenever we change location or time. In other words, here I am in the coffee shop writing (establishes I am a writer) and arguing with my friend who tells me to get a real job. Then I go next door to the grocery store to buy some sugar from the cute girl who works there (I don't need sugar, I just want an excuse to chat up the girl, but, although I don't know it yet, I will get to pour the sugar into the fuel tank of a getaway car, thus thwarting a bank robbery later on)—deeply exciting plotting, this ...

So, in this example, we cut to a new scene because I am now somewhere different. INT. COFFEE SHOP – DAY becomes INT. GROCERY STORE – DAY.

Note that each of these scenes has a dramatic purpose beyond the simply informational. In the first I have the intention of defending myself against accusations of being unrealistic and wasting my professional life, and in the second I have the intention of getting to know the cute girl. The scenes also establish the character notes that I am an inquisitive writer and a hopeless romantic. That way, when I follow a strange and menacing guy I see hassling the cute grocery clerk and get mixed up in a bank robbery, nobody is altogether surprised. These scenes advance the story and inform the audience about character.

David Mamet once again:

QUESTION: WHAT IS DRAMA? DRAMA, AGAIN, IS THE QUEST OF THE HERO TO OVERCOME THOSE THINGS WHICH PREVENT HIM FROM ACHIEVING A SPECIFIC, ACUTE GOAL.

SO: WE, THE WRITERS, MUST ASK OURSELVES OF EVERY SCENE THESE THREE QUESTIONS.

1) WHO WANTS WHAT?
2) WHAT HAPPENS IF HER [sic] DON'T GET IT?
3) WHY NOW?

THE ANSWERS TO THESE QUESTIONS ARE LITMUS PAPER. APPLY THEM, AND THEIR ANSWER WILL TELL YOU IF THE SCENE IS DRAMATIC OR NOT.

IF THE SCENE IS NOT DRAMATICALLY WRITTEN, IT WILL NOT BE DRAMATICALLY ACTED.

THERE IS NO MAGIC FAIRY DUST WHICH WILL MAKE A BORING, USELESS, REDUNDANT, OR MERELY INFORMATIVE SCENE AFTER IT LEAVES YOUR TYPEWRITER. YOU, THE WRITERS, ARE IN CHARGE OF MAKING SURE EVERY SCENE IS DRAMATIC.

Similarly, but more simply for the sake of this example, here I am in the coffee bar with a bad case of writer's block. I'm staring at my blank screen and clearly I've lost my mojo and can't write anymore. Here I am three hours later, same place, same blank screen. The light has changed, as it is now evening. My frustration level has increased so that, when my friend turns up, I am already in a really bad mood. This causes a row that ends up in an important revelation about why I am such a mojoless loser. When we cut from the first to the second moment, we change scene: INT. COFFEE SHOP – DAY becomes INT. COFFEE SHOP – NIGHT. Same location; different time.

A scene communicates its intention/s and then we move to the next. It is distinct, but not isolated. A good writer understands not only the scene's place in the overall process of storytelling, but works its relationship to the scenes which come directly before and after it. In this way, scenes often work as part of a *sequence*. The sequence is a combination of several scenes that enact an event or a more extended idea. The individual scenes all advance the narrative, but the idea or situation is too complex for one of them adequately to express it on its own.

For example, the plot event of the bank robbery we just talked about might be told in a half dozen scenes, each in a different location in and around the bank: car drives up outside; robbers take over the bank; they force the manager to open the vault; they search the back offices for anyone not accounted for; they lock the hostages in a room; they escape with the loot. Each scene gives us a different part of the event and each moves the plot forward a nudge, but the robbery as a whole works at the level of the sequence.

We have already talked about story beats. A story beat is composed of one of more scenes which work out an important story move and take us further on our journey along the 'W' rollercoaster. A scene does this at a smaller scale of nesting doll, and has its own internal beats, as we shall see below.

## Writing to be acted and directed

So far, we have spent a good portion of the book thinking about your own creativity as a writer. Now we need to spend a little time thinking about the creative needs of some professional colleagues who will work with your screenplay during production. You may remember that we discussed the end use of your screenplay briefly, and thought about how format had a lot to do with making everyone else's job as easy as possible while maintaining the dramatic intent of your story. Well, two sets of people who rely on you to achieve this balance need some special attention.

Of course, actors and directors always need special attention, because they are such special people. Look at them over there behind the purple rope in the VIP area, all sparkly and enticing with their expensive dental work and freshly buffed egos—or is it expensive egos and freshly buffed dental work? I can never get that straight. Now, now, resist your cynical writerly instinct to go 'pfft' at this point, and remember that we writers love *all* the directorly and actorly peoples. Without them we wouldn't be paid less than they are. Without them our work wouldn't get ripped to shreds in development and destroyed on the screen. Why, some of our best friends are …

Wait, many of them are brilliant artists and technicians and bring dimension and depth to our work that we only dreamed of while sat in Starbucks typing away, all hopped up on lattes. Wait, some of us writers are also actors and directors. Wait, without actors and directors, films wouldn't even get made from our stories. Wait, without actors and directors we would never get paid at all, and pay means freshly buffed— if rather less expensive—dental egos …

Actors and directors need particular attention because they are amongst the most important *attractions* our scripts deploy. They will also be looking at our scenes for special kinds of hints as to how to do their jobs. Now, of course, not all actors and directors were trained or work in the same way, but all of them are looking to your work to guide them through the process of transformation from page to screen. I'm not going to go on at length about their professions because that is not the focus of this book. However, it is worth bearing in mind that directors work on the assumption that each significant scene you write will have its own *dramatic micro-structure* through which they can justify the emotional truth they will be working with their actors to achieve.

In other words, a director expects each of your scenes to provide the security of a 'mini wardrobe' in which to hang actors' performances. For their part, actors look to your scenes for evidence that will make them feel secure in hanging their best gear on the clothes rail their director offers them. Just like you, good actors and directors will certainly be lace-curtain peeking. They will be looking at a scene in the context of the rest of the story so as to judge how to pitch the intensity of the drama at that particular moment. They will also need to know how far and in what ways a given character relationship has developed by the time of any given scene. Remember that films are almost always shot out of sequence, so this curtain peeking and cross-referencing is vitally important.

## Scene beats and character tactics

When we talk about dramatic micro-structure we are really talking about scene beats. Scene beats are those moments in a scene in which the story takes a turn because something changes; usually because someone *responds* to an event or character in a particular way. A scene beat is a very popular little chap. Indeed, your actors and directors will be searching for him as soon as they start reading your scene. You use scene beats to change the dynamic of a scene (in Robert McKee's terms, from + to – or from – to +) and to shift the tactical stances of your characters.

Remember that a scene is only worth writing if it advances the story or at least provides new information for the audience. 'Advancing the story' means your characters interact in such a way that, by the end of the scene, they have moved another step or two down the path towards the resolution, even though *they* may not realize it at the time. Of course, moving down the path is sometimes a slow, painful and traumatic process; hence scenes often turn from positive to negative and yet are still productive and still move your story forward.

In other words, in conventional movie storytelling, characters have defined *goals* in scenes. If yours don't, then either you need to give them story goals fast or cut the scene, because right now it isn't helping you much. The pleasure of drama lies in large part in watching characters go about achieving those goals, and helping or resisting other characters achieving their own ends. To do this, characters use emotional, psychological and pragmatic tactics that we see play out across the scene beats.

These scene beat tactics are also very important to actors, because when they recognize a tactic, or the implication or 'ghost' of a tactic, in another character's reaction, they can also *play* it. For example, many actors and directors use a technique involving active verbs to work with scenes and scene beats. What they do is to articulate the character's tactic (their 'action', in Stanislavsky's term, to achieve an 'objective') as a verb. So, in this beat, the way I am going to get what I want is to, let's say, *praise* you—or taunt you, or tempt you, or plead with you, or seduce you, or order you, and so on.

This actorly decision doesn't change the words of your scene, only how they are played. For example, someone can say those three scariest words, 'I love you,' in so many different ways, from the obviously sarcastic to the absolutely sincere, depending on the circumstances. Remember our scene way back near the start of the book with Bob and Jenny on their big dinner date, when Bob tells her for the first time that he loves her? I hope so, because I distinctly remember telling you to make sure you have half your mind as Bob since then. Anyway, depending on how Bob and Jenny are doing in their relationship, and depending on Bob's personality and his reading of Jenny and of the whole situation, he might say those words in a range of different ways. He may have every intention of saying it seriously and then chicken out at the last moment and say it playfully. For her part, Jenny may read through that cop out or not as her character and the situation demands.

So the actor playing Bob in the movie of that scene will have to make a choice, along with his director, about which is appropriate. Indeed, they may try a number of different options in rehearsals, or even in takes, to see what feels most in character, what gets the most appropriate response from the actress playing Jenny, and just to give the director performance options she can work with in the edit. Your job is to write the kind of scenes that inform and direct that choice. It's not your fault if the actor is a lump of wood and the director has no sympathy for your material. It is your fault if you haven't given them the best chance possible to overcome their limitations, thanks to the dramatic clarity and intensity of your writing.

This kind of acting technique can come across as narrow and reductive when done badly, but a good actor can use verbs to be specific and directed and to respond to her colleagues in a very human way. The use of active verbs and applying tactics or actions to achieve the objectives of scenes and beats is all part of the much more complex world of actors' training. I am merely using it as an example of how and why actors and directors will always look for and work directly with your scene beats.

Characters are just like real people, in that they have personalities, strengths and weaknesses that lead to them being more likely to act in one way than another. They also have short- and long-term goals which further direct and constrain their actions. What does X want from this scene and from the other character/s that are in it? How does that immediate 'want' help her get where she ultimately needs to be in the story as a whole? Also, just like real people, they should be making judgments about the other characters in the scene. How well do they know each other? What is their opinion of this or that person's character, morality, strengths, weaknesses and likely behavior? How do they expect that character to react in a specific situation or to a particular kind of argument or method of persuasion?

If these also sound like the kinds of questions actors ask in preparing for a role, that's because they are. The answers to these and similar questions tell us that characters approach each encounter just like we do, with tactics both instinctive and unconscious and explicit and goal oriented. Actors and directors will be searching your writing for clues to answer these questions for themselves, so it is a very good idea to approach your writing with all of this in the back of your mind.

Here's a silly example. Let's say you are fourteen years old and you want to go with your friends to a rock club to see scary Finnish black metal outfit Impaled Nazarene without adult supervision. Yes, they really exist, bless their dark little hearts. Being neither Finnish nor a black metally type person, I became aware of them when I was back in England, playing for Southampton's university ice hockey team (go Spitfires!). We would use Impaled Nazarene's charming, wistful little ballad 'Goat Sodomy' as our skate out song. I blame the presence of too many mad Finns on the team, but we felt it gave us a psychological advantage. Hey, it beats 'Eye of the Tiger', right?

Now Impaled Nazarene seemed like a good band to pick in order to set up a real challenge in getting a mother to agree to let her kid go to that gig. I could have picked whatever the current incarnation of Hannah Beiber or Justin Montana might be, but where's the challenge in that? To start with, let's give her kid a suitably Finnish name and call him Pekka. So how would Pekka approach the parental problem? What tactics would he use to achieve his goal?

Pekka's tactics would, no doubt, be based in the first instance on weighing up the likelihood of his mum saying 'yes' under any circumstances. This would lead to a decision as to whether to tell her the truth or do something like arranging an innocuous fake event on the same night and just go without telling her. Let's assume, for the sake of the example, that we all live in Bizarro World and Pekka thinks mum is persuadable. The next question Pekka has to ask himself is: What kind of approach is his mum likely to respond to, from emotional blackmail through actual blackmail to a rational argument about the value of subcultural engagements in facilitating healthy adolescent socialization? Yeah, that last one will play.

See how this works? Now, imagine the scene between Pekka and his mother as he tries out each tactic in turn and she responds with *her own tactics* based on her personality, her view of the proposed event, her take on the tactic Pekka just used and her own understanding of her son and how he will react to certain kinds of argument. Of course, she has the option just to laugh in his face and say 'no,' but that's cutting out half the fun. Think of each tactical shift as a scene beat and you are already writing to be acted and directed.

Now, remember to write your scenes with half your brain as Pekka.

## Case study: scene beats in *Juno*

Let's try a real screenplay example, the lovely scene in *Juno* when she tells her father and stepmother, Mac and Bren, that she is pregnant. This is Scene 47, starting on page 25 of the excellent Newmarket Press copy for those of you who want to follow along with the text. The scene in the finished film is slightly different, with a few elements cut, but I'm going with the published version for this example.

Anyway, by my count this scene has six key beats and a kind of **midpoint** beat (of which more anon), although you can argue the toss over a couple. The key beats play out as follows. The name at the left of each beat refers to the character that turns the scene at each moment. We might call them the 'owners' of the beats:

1 Juno: 'I'm pregnant'
2 Mac: 'Who is the kid?' (The father)
3 Mac: 'Did you say you were thinking about adoption?'
4 Bren: 'Honey, had you considered, you know, the alternative?' (Abortion)
5 Mac: 'I thought you were the kind of girl who knew when to say when.'
6 Mac: 'Just tell it to me straight, Bren. Do you think this is my fault?'

It's pretty easy to follow the dramatic outline of the scene from the beat lines above, right? Juno, whose scene goal is *tell the folks and live*, drops the bombshell, and each subsequent beat explores a different aspect of Mac and Bren's response to the news and to Juno's arguments in favor of her continued survival. As the scene progresses, Juno is moved out of the false security of logic and surface maturity (the 'I made a mistake but, check it, I've already solved it neatly' ploy) and has to admit she is not completely in control (the 'ok, you got me, but I'm really trying here' ploy).

Note that, although she has prepared answers and solutions to most of Bren and Mac's questions, her revelation at the start of the scene takes the ball out of her hands and puts it in theirs. How do we know this? Well, simply because, as you can see from the list above, Mac and Bren own all the beats after the first. After that moment, the conversation turns because either Mac or Bren turns it. Juno is a smarty-pants to be sure, but the scene structure tells us she has had to cede control.

The only exception is the **midpoint** (see below), which is sort of an in-between beat. It is an admission of weakness from Juno that enables the satisfactory emotional resolution of the scene. Because the scene turns around that **midpoint**, we can even make a case for the beats to play as a kind of mini ring: A/B/C/MID/C'/B'/A.

I'm certainly not saying all scenes play this way, but look how this one works:

1/6 or A/A' = original sin.
2/5 or B/B' = sex and responsibility.
3/4 or C/C' = the pragmatic solutions.

OR:

| 1 / A I'm pregnant (I made a mistake) | 6 / A' Is it my fault? (I made a mistake?) |
|---|---|
| 2 / B Who is the father? (blame) | 5 / B' When to say when (shifts blame) |
| 3 / C Adoption? (solution) | 4 / C' Abortion? (solution) |

MIDPOINT: "I'm not ready to be a mom."

The scene works to a practical resolution at C/C', after which we know what is going to be done and that everyone is in agreement. It then turns back on itself to resolve the outstanding emotional issues that cannot simply be contained by that pragmatic solution. Mac and Bren need to finish processing their feelings about Juno's situation, and they start to do this in the second half of the scene.

The whole scene articulates off the **midpoint**. This is one of Juno's most honest statements in the scene and it is what allows and enables the resolution. Bren and Mac have to hear her mature pragmatism but also her human understanding, imperfect and immature as it is at this point in the story. It offers us a good lesson about how scenes can have multiple functions.

When we look at the scene as a ring, we can see how Mac, whose trajectory is all about ascribing and shifting blame, takes on board this incorporative familial function. His first instinct is to assume fault lies with the man—'who is the kid?' Then, when he realizes who the 'man' actually is, blame shifts towards Juno—'when to say when.' Finally, after he has had a little time to reflect, his fatherly instinct is to further shift responsibility onto himself as a parent. We can map his shifts very clearly as A/A' and B/B' when we lay the scene out like this.

So remember, the resolution of surface or immediate character goals should not *necessarily* dominate a scene. Therefore those goals are not necessarily resolved at the *end* of that scene: *they are not necessarily the climax.* The more important function of this example from *Juno* is not the pragmatic solution to the problem of Juno's pregnancy; it is the deeper function of bonding the family around that solution. Good scene structure, like good dialogue, moves us from surface to depth.

In some ways this scene works as a guide to the storytelling of the movie as a whole. Juno has a problem and tries to contain it logically and maturely. She manages to set the constituent elements of a satisfactory solution in place fairly quickly (false victory). She then realizes that things are never that simple. Juno spends the rest of the movie learning and maturing emotionally. She reassesses her understanding of the value of relationships, the nature of love and commitment and what adulthood means.

In Diablo Cody's story, the 'I'm pregnant' scene transforms expectations and turns the negative revelation of Juno's pregnancy into a potential positive as we come to understand that she has chosen her family well. I think it's the best scene in the film and does a number of important jobs in setting up the family dynamic that Juno is going to have to work with through the rest of the movie. Its charm comes from how it overturns the clichés by—I know, shock—having Mac and Bren act like real people who love Juno despite her situation and want only the best for her. Of course, it's all still excruciatingly embarrassing for Juno to have to go through, which makes for a lot of fun along the way.

For the sake of all the actors and directors, our scene beats need both individual and collective attention. Their task is to work with what is on the page to hit the right emotional note for each performed beat and to place that note correctly within the symphony that is a full character performance over the course of an entire movie. Each scene plays both within itself—how does each character feel *now*—and as part of an emotional process across all the scenes. They need to find immediate truths that also do not disturb the overall emotional balance of the piece. This is not an easy task, but understanding the value of beats and working with that understanding in your writing will help make that task easier.

Now, lets find an example of how all of this structure stuff works in practice.

# 6

## Case Study: *Brick* in the 'W'

What follows in this chapter is a detailed case study of *Brick* (scr. Rian Johnson; 2005), to show how the '**W**' can work in its linear as well as its 'ring' form. Remember, not every movie works exactly like this and I am not proposing this kind of structure as a 'one size fits all' solution for every structural challenge you will face. On the other hand, lots of movies are structured in this way, and the model is certainly flexible enough to accommodate a wide range of genres and story styles.

*Brick* is a low budget independent movie that combines the teen high school and hardboiled detective formulas in a fresh and imaginative way. It doesn't pander to its audience with a bland redemptive ending, and it takes risks with everything from its original teen-hardboiled *idiolect* (see Chapter 8) to the way in which that dialogue is inhabited—often intentionally undercut and 'thrown away'—by the performance style of a uniformly excellent cast.

While *Brick* is by no means avant garde, neither is it a standard piece of cookie cutter Hollywood fare. For all those reasons I felt it would be a good pick for our major case study in this book. I also happen to like and admire it, which made the analysis that follows a pleasure rather than a chore!

Note: I have taken dialogue examples from the film itself, not from the screenplay. Any errors in transcription are, therefore, my own. If you catch any, feel free, as always, to laugh and point. Annotated drafts of the screenplay are available online at IMSDB, the Screenplay Database and other sites.

### Theme

*Brick* is all about *control*. Everyone in the story is trying to control everyone else. The emotional manifestation of this is *possessiveness*. The intellectual manifestation is *manipulation*.

Before the start of the movie, Brendan initiates a sequence of events because of his possessiveness towards Emily (his desire to *control* her) that eventually results in her death. He investigates the circumstances of her death by manipulating (*controlling*) the people and groups who have a connection to those events. Meanwhile his *self-control* is continually tested by a range of adversaries who want to manipulate him for their own ends. The story follows him as he gradually *cedes control* in exchange for access and information. He finally learns the truth after a moment of emotional vulnerability. Once he fully understands what happened and why, he *re-establishes control* over himself and the story world to bring events to a just conclusion, even though he is damaged by the process.

### 'Ooh look, bunnies' version:

*Plot:* 'Brendan needs to uncover the truth in a world where "ooh look, everybody's corrupt" ...' See his problem?

*Story:* 'Brendan is possessive in a world where "ooh look, everybody's fighting for control" ...' See his problem?

### 'V' version:

Emily is Brendan's emotional world. This is unhealthy because it comes from Brendan's need to possess and control her.

The high school community is Brendan's story world. He begins outside it by choice and gradually works his way back in.

Emily is 'broken,' which also breaks Brendan emotionally. He is also culpable because he drove her towards a dangerous path.

The high school community is already broken because everyone is corrupt, deceitful and vying for dominance over each other.

Brendan knows he can't truly fix his world, because Emily is dead. He thinks he can make reparations by searching for the truth about her death and bringing some kind of justice to those responsible. In this way he will at least address the rupture in his internal, emotional world while repairing part of the story world.

This sets up something of a *down* ending because even though Brendan will succeed in bringing justice to those responsible, the process leads to him being badly damaged both emotionally and physically.

**'W' version:**

### *FIRST DOWN ANGLE—RECOGNITION*

At the start of the movie, high school kid Brendan finds the body of his ex-girlfriend, Emily, lying in shallow water outside a concrete storm drain.

Two days before, a sequence of events starts which will lead Brendan to this terrible, inevitable moment bookending the first act and angle.

**Recognition:** In this angle, Brendan has to recognize and come to terms with the painful consequences of his previous moral and emotional decisions. By driving her away, thanks to his possessive nature, he may even be indirectly responsible for Emily's death. He also recognizes that, due to his outsider status, knowledge of the high school social network and previous experience of a kind of detective work, he is the person with the best shot at solving the mystery of her death. He is also emotionally driven to do so. It quickly becomes apparent that Emily was linked into the drug scene and that Brendan's investigations have a good chance of disrupting the local dealing. This gives him linked internal and external (plot and story) motivations.

**Narration:** The audience knows what is coming right from the start and can read Brendan's present actions and past decisions against the certainty of Emily's death. This allows us to begin to make judgments about culpability and character, even though we have no idea as yet who actually killed her or why.

This narrational decision is important. The choice isn't as simple as just starting with a dramatic image—dead girl in drain; rather, it positions Brendan for the audience as *always already doomed*. One of the great strengths of *Brick* as a story is that it never allows Brendan to escape from the inevitability of his own disappointment, from his personal emotional down ending. It doesn't matter that all the while he is working for truth and justice according to his own lights.

*Warning:* Don't be fooled by this narrative strategy. This is *not* my way of saying it is now ok to go write the first draft of *Endless Spiral Of Depressing Crap My Protagonist Can't Escape From Because That's What Life Is Really Like Man And I Know Because I'm On Pills For My Nerves* (see Chapter 2). On the contrary, *Brick* is always entertaining, imaginative, frequently surprising and often very funny. The fact that it also happens to be about somebody who is in for a rough ride is balanced by our pleasure in the detective plot, by Brendan's mad hardboiled skills and by his success. It proves that well written down endings can be entertaining, not that relentless, unalleviated grimness is anything other than relentless, unalleviated and grim. For which read completely predictable and thus a narrative bore.

## A. Primary exposition

### 1. '... in a world where "ooh look, stuff"'

And we're off—hooray! We learn that this is a world in which almost everyone is corrupt—less hooray. We learn that Brendan, who is no angel himself, even if he is on the side of light, is an embittered high school kid. We learn that his ex-girlfriend Emily is in trouble and that he plans to find her.

OK, take a deep breath and get out your Junior Detective Notebooks because this expositional beat is a biggie. It all starts when Brendan gets a note in his locker from Emily giving a time and the location of a street corner. We match her bracelets to those seen on the corpse in the opening scene, so we are pretty sure she is going to die.

He goes. There is a public phone there. Emily calls him on it. She's scared: mentions the words 'Brick', 'Pin' and 'Tug'. He offers to help. She is scared off when a Mustang drives by—later we learn that the car belongs to local tough kid Tug.

A cigarette butt is flicked out of the car window. Brendan notices a distinctive blue arrow brand mark on the butt. Make a note in your notebooks, fellow junior detectives, because this will be very important in **ooh riiight** later on.

Brendan, clearly worried about Emily, sets out to find her. As a first step, he meets up with another kid, The Brain, who has played schoolyard detective with Brendan before.

Brain tells what he knows of Emily's life since breaking up with Brendan. It hasn't been a happy time for her as she has been gradually sinking down the social food chain, starting with the 'upper crust' and then passing down to associate with some of the drama geeks. Brain also tells Brendan Emily's current locker number.

On his way to high school drama world, Brendan breaks into Emily's locker and finds half a torn-up party invitation in her notebook. He checks in with the queen of drama, Kara, a vampy old flame who comes on to him. Brendan resists; she knows more than she is telling.

He sneaks into the drama green room and finds a complete copy of the party invite. He calls the number and speaks to upper-cruster and soon-to-be femme fatale Laura, who gives him the party details after he tells her he has Emily's invitation.

Brendan turns up at the exclusive McMansion party and is noticed by Laura and her sort-of boyfriend, dumb jock Brad Bramish. Laura clearly wants to pump Brendan for information about his search for Emily. Her motives are, as yet, unclear, but she is not afraid to use her sexuality to pursue them. She gives him his next clue, a location: 'Coffee & Pie.'

Once again, Brendan resists her advances and so gets to follow Laura as she meets Tug by his Mustang, which we recognize from before.

*And break:* see how the detective plot allows us to learn on parallel tracks so easily? As Brendan begins to follow the trail leading to Emily, we pick up important information about the social network in the school; the potential for personal corruption and manipulation at every level; Brendan's well developed detective instincts and the strength of his self-control in resisting Kara and Laura.

All of this can be shortened to: *how the story world works.* Remember that, for the writer, the story world is an external expression or consequence of the hero/ine's internal world: *investigating the world = investigating the self.*

*And we're back in:* next morning Brendan goes to stoner hang-out 'Coffee & Pie' and rousts stoner king Dode, who is now Emily's sort-of boyfriend. This is a funny scene where Brendan's hardboiled tough guy chops are put on display for the first time. Importantly, Brendan beats Dode without breaking a sweat. This isn't much of a challenge for him yet, and Dode takes a slapping and likes it. Well maybe he doesn't like it, but nobody cares.

Dode tells Brendan that Emily has changed her mind about needing help and wants to be left alone. Brendan tells him he wants to hear it from her in person.

Brendan follows Dode and sees him meet with Emily. Dode gives Emily a piece of paper that she slips into her notebook.

### Partnered with: 'Oh brave new world'

Remember, the main purpose of the 'ring' version of the **'W'** is to check progress through *parallelism.*

Remember also that we are *already* anticipating a comparison between 'before' and 'after' at many points in our story. As soon as we are introduced to Brendan's world, we look forward to the corresponding final beat because we know that, if this story is any good, change will have happened. This anticipation is happening for the audience *anyway*, no matter what you do, and drawing attention to it is just a check to make sure you understand and work to that comparison in your writing.

World A to World A', *exposition* to *resolution*, this partnership is pretty straightforward. We compare the story world at the beginning of the movie with how it is doing at the end. That comparison allows us to judge the overall *work* of the story and, by extension, of the hero/ine. In *Brick* we make a judgment through these two parallel beats based on the relative success Brendan has had in investigating the drugs and social corruption in his high school, as well as Emily's murder. On that basis, the world gets something of an up ending while Brendan gets a downer. He has done his detective work well, but has learned terrible truths and emerges with physical and emotional scars.

### 2. 'If only ...'

OK, now we get into more intimate personal territory. Our expositional quests and questions continue but now they come much closer to home as Brendan is confronted with his own boyfriendly inadequacies. Typically, as its name suggests, **if only** ... is the big yearning beat, a wishing that the hero/ine and their story world were set to rights. It bonds the audience with the hero/ine in willing that goal. In *Brick* the yearning is certainly there, but our experience of it is uncomfortable and our subsequent alliance with Brendan likewise.

Emily visits Brendan at the back of the school where he hangs out alone. She's a pallid stoner mess. She tells him to drop it and forget her. She scolds him for being possessive and isolated: 'What are you? Eating back here, hating everybody. I mean who are you judging anyone? I really loved you but I couldn't stand it. I had to get with people. I couldn't hack a life with you anymore.'

Brendan asks her to come back (**if only** ...). She refuses: 'I don't want to be put away and protected.' She won't tell him anything about her troubles, and says goodbye: 'Whatever you have to do to let me go, you gotta do it.'

She leaves. Brendan has stolen her notebook. Clearly he's nowhere nearly ready to let her go. He finds the note Dode gave her—a symbol like a letter A and one word: MIDNIGHT.

Back with The Brain, Brendan asks about the symbol. Brain tells him the upper crust kids have a code for places to meet when they are doing dodgy deeds. Maybe this is one.

At home that night, Brendan obsesses about the symbol. Eventually, long after midnight, he visualizes it as the entrance to the storm drain. He goes to check it out. Sure enough he finds Emily's body and we have our **inciting incident**. We have also caught up with the film's opening sequence. Someone (we find out later that it is Dode) is watching him from the darkness of the tunnel. In the darkness of the tunnel they knock Brendan down and run off.

### Partnered with: 'Eat judge boot, creep'

So this parallel links *desiring* something and *enacting*, doing what needs to be done to finally achieve it. It takes a long time, most of the story indeed, for that will, that yearning, to find suitable expression. This is because in a good story your hero/ine may not be ready to put on the judge boot in **if only …**, let alone connect it effectively with a perp's mouth. In Brendan's case he is always ready to do both; just he has a lot of investigating to do before he knows which perp gets to eat his final heel.

Once again this is about anticipation. Your audience will feel for the poor sap or sapette in the first angle, and will yearn with them for an **eat judge boot** moment. We expect it and will likely feel kind of cheated without it. Remember that **inciting incidents** have a pair with their **obligatory moments**. Typically it is in these two beats that we establish and resolve that link. Of course, the judge boot might be your hero/ine's lips and the eating might be kissing, but the same applies.

In *Brick*, Brendan can't achieve his deepest **if only …** because Emily won't take him back and then she dies. He has, however, been forced to begin to re-engage with the wider story world and this will lead to success in addressing causes if not results. This is the beat in which Brendan finds Emily's body. The **obligatory moment** comes when he lays out the terms of Laura's destruction to her on the sports field and we see the brick fall from her locker.

### B. From rejection to acceptance

### 3. 'Shan't'

**Shan't** is never a real option for Brendan, but he acknowledges that he 'should' walk away. Nevertheless, **shan't** is still an important beat for him because it's very evident impossibility does much to sum up his key problem in the story: he can't let go of Emily. If he could, the story might end here. Remember, our theme is all about possessiveness and self-control, so he can't let go. The very inadequacy of his internal debate is an eloquent summation of the driven focus that will sustain him to the resolution.

This beat has been building throughout the angle. Every time Brendan is called on his innate 'Brendan-ness' we are really setting up the impossibility of **shan't**. In some ways any debate over right action is for the audience more than it is for Brendan himself.

Onscreen, **shan't** happens in a flash in the library scene when Brendan asks Brain to tell him to walk away. Brain does so, clearly knowing Brendan won't. Sure enough, Brendan immediately dismisses it.

### Partnered with: 'Bandits, three o'clock high'

Again, this parallel is pretty straightforward. *Rejecting* transforms into *engaging*. The fears and weaknesses that prompted your hero/ine's initial uncertainty or unwillingness are manifested in the worst way in the 'bandits' resisting your hero/ine's plan. **Bandits ...** is about engaging, not enacting, because there is still a whole lot of struggle left to be struggled. This is the start of the final challenge, not the conclusion. That's why it makes a good pair with **shan't**. It enacts the transformation of will, not the **obligatory moment** of final confrontation.

By this point, if we have done our job right, our hero/ine can (probably) take them or at least fail gloriously in the attempt. In *Brick* we know that Brendan is driven from the start, but facing the real possibility of imminent death is still a tough challenge. Because of Brendan's innate 'thickness' when it comes to all things Emily (see below), this parallel plays a little weaker than it might in other movies, but at least he realizes the implications of his decision and knows a smarter man would walk away. This gives us something to work with when **shan't** looks across at future **bandits**.

### 4. 'Oh, all right then'

The Brain knows Brendan will investigate Emily because Brendan is 'thick.' This is a wonderfully fecund word to describe Brendan; it encompasses three key meanings:

1 Brendan is 'thick' with Emily, possessively tied and unable to separate his identity from her, despite her pleading.
2 This emotional thickness makes Brendan 'thick' in a second way: thick as a plank when it comes to making rational decisions about leaving well alone and not getting himself involved in dangerous situations while investigating Emily's death.
3 Brendan is also 'thick' in the way of a true hardboiled detective, thick skinned, able to take his punishment, to lead with his face when his brains and fists alone won't get him where he needs to be.

So now the detective plot starts for real, with the stakes raised: a simple missing persons case has become a homicide enquiry. Brain agrees to 'op' for Brendan and Brendan tells him to keep the cops out of it as they would only 'gum' things.

Next, Brendan goes back to the body. On the way he remembers a previous argument from when they broke up, which has him telling Emily: 'You're the only thing I love.' She replies: 'You can't keep me safe. I'm in a different world now.'

Brendan takes his first step into act two by hiding Emily's body in the dark drain tunnel so as to gain time for his investigation to play out. Character is action (thank you R. McKee). Although, we don't know how long it has to countdown, the movie now has a big clock running.

### Partnered with: 'I have a cunning plan'

This parallel links a beat which is all about *accepting* the need for jumping onboard with the story with one dealing with *planning* its final outcome. 'Somehow …' meets 'and this is how.' The one implies the future need for the other, and again we understand that the function of the **'W'** as 'ring' is to remind us of that anticipation. The hero/ine of **oh, all right then** is *not* ready to make the **cunning plan** that will lead to resolution. We want to see how they become ready, and **I have a cunning plan** is the story deadline for that to be achieved.

This is a good parallel, because your hero/ine may well make a plan of some kind in **oh, all right then**, but it will be flawed, defeated or just a jury rig unable to stand the stress of the story. It will have failed or need major modification by the **midpoint**. It all starts so well: 'We can pay you two thousand now, plus fifteen when we reach Alderaan.' However, all that leads to in act two is: 'Our position is correct except … no Alderaan. Suddenly I have a bad feeling about this because I felt a great disturbance in the force and, by the way, that's no moon.' And … cue tractor beam.

In **oh, all right then** Brendan wants nothing more than to have a plan to put things to rights. This is made explicit in his conversation with Brain. He just doesn't know enough to make one yet. Finding out is what the whole of act two is going to be about.

### Did you spank your hero/ine today?

Rian Johnson spanks Brendan pretty hard in this angle. He is brought face to face with his inability to be the kind of boyfriend Emily needed. He is forced back into a corrupt community (the high school social world) that he despises and has rejected. He even has to understand that that very rejection is one of the causal factors in the breakup of his relationship and in Emily's predicament. Finally, he finds her body and, with it, the end of all his hopes. Brendan has already worked hard to get this far, and the story has only just begun.

Yup, a pretty hard spanking, all things considered, but this is a down angle and things are going to get a whole lot worse.

### FIRST UP ANGLE—AVOIDANCE

In this angle Brendan pushes ahead with his investigation from *outside* the corrupt high school drug world. He makes early progress—this is an 'up' angle after all.

By the end of the angle—by the Midpoint of the script—he has found out all he can from the outside and realizes he will have to dive into those murky waters and get wet if he is to have any prospect of uncovering the truth about Emily's death.

**Avoidance:** In *Brick*, Brendan defines himself as an outsider. He has spent his high school life separating himself from what he sees as a poisonous social world, so much so that he drove Emily away in the process. She couldn't be a hermit and needed a broader social life. What she found when she dived back into that world was death.

For all these reasons and more, Brendan is very reluctant to put himself in any position that might compromise his outsider status. He knows he can't trust anyone other than Brain, and he works hard to tread the mean streets while keeping the trash off his shoes. Also Brendan is a control freak, and that doesn't play well with others. In this angle he will find he has no alternative. This is avoidance in the terms of the story, and we see it repeatedly expressed as an issue.

Being an outsider only gets you so far, however, and eventually Brendan has to decide whether to put his life in others' hands and jump into Emily's world. He cannot avoid full immersion forever. With it will come access to the knowledge he needs to solve the mystery, along with revelations that may destroy him emotionally.

Remember, *Brick* is in part a hardboiled detective movie and it needs to be taken seriously as such. The job of the detective in the American idiom is to do exactly what Brendan is doing, to walk the mean streets so we don't have to. To risk or even compromise his moral probity and get covered in the scum through which he wades for the greater good of solving the crime. The detective is best placed to accomplish this because he is neither criminal nor policeman. Rather, he is an insider's outsider, a man able to cross boundaries and work both sides of the street when he has to.

We already have the evidence that Brendan has this combination of talents, but it is in this angle that we see him play them to full effect. I defer to Blake Snyder's evocative term 'The Promise of the Premise' to account for the joy of seeing Brendan work. These scenes are what we were promised when we were told *Brick* is a hardboiled high school detective movie.

*C. Doing just fine on my own*

**5. 'You may not realize this yet, but …'**

OK, this beat is about setting the **B Story** in motion, but—take a note—that happens pretty much automatically when you take the **A Story** forward.

As with most beats in *Brick*, Brendan's actions have both expected and unexpected consequences. Right now, Brendan views the interest of femme fatale Laura as most definitely unwanted. It will turn out to be vitally important as things develop, however.

So Brendan starts by quizzing Brain on possible meanings of some key words that have come up in the investigation so far. Brain tells him 'Pin' could be short for 'Kingpin,' the semi-legendary drug dealer who supplies the high school kids. Brendan realizes he needs to find a way of connecting with this figure who lurks at the heart of the corrupt story world.

Brendan's plan for this angle is to cause a ruckus amongst the main social players, drug buyers and other possible links to The Pin. The object: to get noticed by him, to get a reaction and to work that to get closer to the truth. This is good hardboiled detective thinking: if in doubt, kick at the door of the mystery until someone opens it or kicks back. Whoever kicks back is probably the person you were looking for in the first place. Or at least they are going to be connected with that person.

Step one: Brendan starts to manipulate the players by leaving a simple message with drama queen Kara: 'Tell The Pin that Brad was my calling card and I need words.' He figures that trouble for one of The Pin's biggest customers will get his attention.

Step two: Brendan picks a fight with big dumb major drug customer Brad Bramish. We covered this briefly in the previous chapter. Annoying him isn't hard. Now skinny Brendan beats bulky Brad down. He does so by putting everything he has into his punches and never giving up. Brad underestimates him and loses, but Brendan has taken real physical damage in the process. It won't be the last.

First hooked fish: Brendan stumbles away from the scene of his victory and Laura follows. **You may not realize this yet, but …** you will need Laura's help to survive the movie. **You may not realize this yet, but …** Laura is also the key to solving the mystery. **You may not realize this yet, but …** Laura is the eventual sort-of semi-romantic subplot. **You may not realize this yet, but …** Laura is the **B Story**. **You may not realize this yet, but …** even though you kicked at The Pin's door, you already got the attention of the woman at the evil heart of the mystery, behind even The Pin.

Right now Brendan can't trust her: 'I can't trust you.' See? Even though (especially because) she tells him she wants to help.

## A quick aside: why we love femme fatales

The problem for femme fatales is that we usually know they are femme fatales from the outset. That's because they act all femme fataley— really, they should learn about this in femme fatale camp (now there's a concept for a movie ... well, maybe a very short sketch). The problem for our heroes who are in danger of being fataled by a femme is that, even though they can usually sense the danger, a good femme fatale is smoking hot and usually much more interesting than the bland alternatives available, despite—or perhaps because of—the poison in her soul. The femme fatale is simultaneously a joyous celebration of the power of smart women and a classic example of men punishing them for their very smartness.

In movie terms they make great characters because they are the intellectual equals or even superiors of the hero and make him earn his victory or take him down to hell with them. As we shall see, one of the best features of the final angle of *Brick* is that Brendan brings justice but nonetheless is left in his own little hell of Laura's design. Anyway, for Laura to do her story job we have to be thinking how, in happier circs and with 17% less soul poison, she and Brendan would make a great couple and could take on the world together. Fortunately Nora Zehetner has a full hand of talent to play as Laura.

Now we have met Laura before, but it is in this beat that the terms of her role are established for the rest of the movie. She asserts her interest in Brendan's world here, and offers herself as a partner. In story structure terms this is the **B Story** offering to help the **A Story**. This is typically a second act function and is separate from introducing her as a character.

Anyway, Brendan's a bright lad and he spots Laura as trouble a mile off. 'With you behind me I'd have to tie one eye up watching both of your hands. I can't spare it.' Remember the whole 'control' thing? He will need to be beaten down a whole lot more before he lets himself succumb to her charms. We have all that to look forward to. Rian Johnson knows it, the audience knows it and the actors know it. Genre tells us it is coming and narration reinforces it. When Laura emerges as the **B Story**, everyone is united in a wry smile of anticipation.

See, structure is pleasure!

## Partnered with: 'Ooh riiight ...'

Well of course it is. Look across the 'ring' as we see the *start* of the **B Story** in parallel with its crucial revelatory *intersection* with the **A**

**Story**. This parallel might actually resolve the **B Story**. More likely that will come later, but it is the moment at which the **B Story**'s key task in enabling the resolution of the **A Story** happens. Typically this pair enacts the primary relationship subplot. This is vitally important because it is your key test of whether your hero/ine can learn to play well with others. Remember how we talked about well-written story problems infecting your hero/ine's entire social world? Well, this pair asks whether they can find the penicillin.

*Brick*, of course, works it in a different way. Laura becomes Brendan's helpmate and then, in his moment of ultimate weakness, something more. Brendan gets the final clue from that moment, ties everything together and proceeds to make his plan. In *Brick* the intersection of the **B Story** in **oh** *riiight* ... finally reveals Laura as the antagonist, and so she becomes **A Story** material and is resolved as such in the fourth angle.

### 6. 'What, me broken?'

In this beat Brendan faces down the authorities. He is in full form, at the top of his game, confident, independent, morally self-righteous and very determined. Even taking a beating from Tug proves the effectiveness of his strategy. When we see him run the table like this we wonder what could possibly go wrong.

So Brendan phones Brain. Brain tailed Kara like he was told. He saw her make calls on a payphone—clearly she didn't want the numbers appearing on her phone bill. Brendan fills Brain in on the whole Brad deal: 'Now we've shaken the tree, let's wait and see what falls on our heads.'

Brendan turns round. As if by magic The Pin's goon, Tug, 'falls on his head.' Bam! This is narrative economy as comedy. The shake-the-tree plan is clearly working, but Brendan takes a beating to add to the punishment he took fighting Brad. Once again, it won't be the last.

Cut: we are in school VP Gary Trueman's office for a scene that plays like many a gumshoe/cop face-off from hardboiled stories of yore. Trueman wants him to play house informant: 'You've helped this office out before.' Brendan replies: 'No, I gave you Jerr to see him eaten, not to see you fed.' This was the outcome of the previous piece of schoolyard hardboiledness for which Brendan and Brain teamed up. Jerr, a minor drug dealer, was taken out of school.

It's more complicated and less savory than this, however. When Emily and Brendan were going out, she started hanging out with small time dealer Jerr. Brendan did not approve, so he got in with Jerr, partnered up as a dealer and then ratted him out to the VP. That's what the argument with Emily is about when we flash back as Brendan goes to move her body.

Back in Trueman's office, Brendan lays it on the line: 'You got a discipline issue with me, write me up. Suspend me. I'll see you at the parent conference.' **What, me broken?** They come to an agreement without Brendan telling the VP what's going on. Brendan gets a free pass as long as he doesn't force the authorities' hand. In return, Trueman expects him to sort things out. If he can't, and if the school needs a fall guy, Brendan's it.

### Partnered with: 'It sucks to be me'

This parallel plays between *hope* and *despair*. Certainly in many instances the hopefulness of **what, me broken?** may well be hesitant or contingent and will almost certainly prove to be premature or even false, and the despair of **it sucks to be me** is usually tempered because we know it is the darkness before some kind of dawn. For the audience, the anticipation of this parallel lies in expecting the former to be broken so that eventually the latter can be transcended. In other words, it's all about character development. I know, who'd have thought?

From being at the top of his game to a disillusioned, almost broken shell, Brendan's descent is all too obvious. In *Brick*, Brendan is never big on hope in its narrowest, most sparkly definition. Rather, he has an expectation of success on his own moral terms that becomes compromised as he is drawn further into the underworld. His transformation plays out as increasing vulnerability in the face of physical and emotional trauma. In **it sucks to be me**, Brendan learns some more terrible truths. He sees a man killed and realizes that it could very easily have been him. Of course, these terrible truths are essential for solving the mystery, but they also damn him to his down ending.

### D. Pushed to your (opening) limits

### 7. 'Meh, this is harder than I thought'

In this beat, easy leads have dried up. Brendan is feeling his bruises. Underneath his tough exterior we begin to see evidence of the physical toll being taken. Acting on opportunity, he finds he has more licks to take, however. Although this beat happens pretty fast, its difficulty is accounted in all the new bruises on Brendan's face.

So Dode and Kara are dead ends and Brendan needs to recuperate. He heads home, but on his way he sees Tug's Mustang in a parking lot. About to smash its window with a concrete block, Brendan stops when Tug returns. He takes another bad beating but keeps getting back up, asking to see The Pin. Eventually even Tug is impressed by his stoicism, although Tug wouldn't know the meaning of the word, and locks him in the trunk of the Mustang for the drive to The Pin's place.

Brendan forces the trunk during the journey and is able to work out where The Pin lives—control again. They arrive at a nondescript little house. The Pin—young, caped and with a gammy leg—operates from his mother's basement. Kind of scary, but also somehow creepy and pathetic, The Pin is intrigued by Brendan but in no mood for bullshit. He'll listen to Brendan's pitch but 'it better be really good.'

See how the stakes have been raised in this beat? The Pin isn't Dode, who can be slapped, or Kara, who is transparent. Brendan's next words will have a major influence on the future of his kneecaps, maybe even his life.

So Brendan offers his first proof; he knows The Pin's address. He gives this away as a freebie to demonstrate his words have the weight of proven street smarts behind them. Embarrassed at his own failure, Tug strangles him in anger, not listening when The Pin tells him to stop. This is an important lesson, because this is where we realize Tug is not a disciplined thug; he's kind of a nut job. Finally Laura comes in and Tug stops—take a note—when *she* tells him to. Anyway, it's all more punishment for poor old Brendan.

### Partnered with: 'Er . . . little help?'

This is a simple escalation parallel. It's about measuring the size of the holes in your road. In other words, it is all about *testing*. Specifically, it tests the designs of your patented hero/ine spanking and stake raising machines. It reminds us, as writers, that however hard things are for our hero/ines in the second angle, they need to get much harder in the third. **Meh** can still be overcome without major help or sacrifice. **Er … little help**, as its name suggests, is where hero/ines are searching both outwards and inwards for a way forward. They look deeper into themselves, to friends, to anyone they can, and maybe as a last resort to a newly emerging inner strength, in order to survive. Note that they may not actually ask for or get help from others. The point of the beat is to express how the stakes have been raised beyond easy fixes.

Brendan is taking bigger risks in **meh**, but this is nothing compared with the risk he takes in **er … little help**. *Importantly, these beats echo or mirror each other directly*. Both revolve around Brendan putting himself between Tug and The Pin. Only in the second beat the relationship dynamics are reversed. In **meh**, Brendan undermines Tug in public to get in with The Pin, whereas in **er …** he questions The Pin's trustworthiness to get in with Tug. The difference is one of degree, because in the former he just gets to come into The Pin's world while in the latter he becomes a political player in that world with the major stake raising that entails.

## 8. 'Leap? But it's dark'

This beat is all about understanding the move to the midpoint. Brendan is going to have to sell himself to The Pin and open himself up to major consequences if The Pin isn't buying what he is selling. The outsider is coming inside and, no matter what he tells himself about motives and moral rectitude, he's turning himself into a Louisiana wetland after the Deepwater Horizon disaster. In other words, no matter what he does, the scum will now be rising around him.

Remember that Brendan is all about *control*. His instincts are to be in tight control of himself emotionally and to manipulate other people through his intelligence as well as his strength both of will and fist. He tried to control (or possess) Emily, just as he is trying to control the investigation. To cede control at this point in the story is a very big deal for him. It signals a major pragmatic shift in his attitude to the theme. This beat sees him working hard to minimize any loss of control, but he can't avoid it completely.

So, despite the whole almost being killed by Tug thing, clearly Brendan has passed a first hurdle with The Pin. They go upstairs and The Pin's incongruously sweet mother faffs about getting them cereal and juice. Remember, the movie is telling us at this point, they may be playing for keeps, but we are still in the world of high schools and kids. Also, as the Porter in Macbeth has taught us, a little levity lets us breathe and prepares us for the next wave of badness.

Now Brendan offers his second proof: he'll only talk to The Pin alone. Tug threatens him—who'd have thought? Brendan remains unmoved. The Pin orders Tug out. This is bluster but important bluster. Whatever deal happens, it is between the two of them. It plays to the objective of 'respect' for the boss, and the fact that nobody else need know the terms gives The Pin a certain independence and security also. Brendan knows he has to jump, indeed in one sense he jumped when he let himself be put into the trunk of Tug's car. That's not the real jump; it can't be, because Brendan is still working hard to make sure the water is deep enough to land in safely.

It's important to see this work because, yes, going with Tug took some control away from him, but without meeting The Pin, understanding his setup and deciding how to play the encounter, Tug's trunk is a false midpoint. It is the pre-jump jump, so to speak. Brendan's decisions about undermining Tug (he knows the address) and working The Pin's decision before it is made, speak to the work that is still going on to prepare for the bigger leap—coming inside—but on something like his terms. Yes, The Pin controls the outcome, but the beat is about how Brendan sells his jump and in doing so sells himself to The Pin as a viable alternative to Tug.

This still applies, even if you time the jump from Tug's car. In that model you view this whole beat as Brendan jumping and frantically trying to soften his landing while he is in midair! For me, however, the leap and the midpoint come now because this is the true borderline between Brendan being outside and being inside The Pin's world.

Second angle = Brendan is outside, manipulating everyone to get in
Third angle = Brendan is inside, fighting for control as the current carries him along ever faster

### Partnered with: 'Bigger kids came'

Actions have *consequences*, leaps have landings. If you jump into a shark pool, sharks will react. This is a simple cause-and-effect parallel, but it contains the equally simple pleasure of seeing early story payoff for the hero/ine's decision to commit. Once again, structure is about setting up the expectation of pleasure and then paying that debt. Sometimes we have to wait a while for the bill to be paid, but this time it comes in fast.

For Brendan the risk is clear, but he jumps anyway. Will he be rubbed or hired? Also, after he jumps, his actions throughout the first up angle will start to have unforeseen consequences for him. One of those consequences will be carrying a knife.

### Did you spank your hero/ine today?

How many beatings is enough? Rian Johnson knows Brendan is too strong willed to show his vulnerability unless he takes terrible punishment. The emotional punishment is mostly yet to come, but in this angle Brendan gets the stuffing knocked out of him again and again, even when he wins the fight. This weakens him enough for the punishments to come to have their full effect.

### MIDPOINT—JUMP!

Brendan sells himself to The Pin. This is the act of ceding control he has been trying to avoid. He sells himself on his uniqueness, as an insider's outsider. He'll tip The Pin to moves by the authorities and also do 'whatever serves your interests.' The pitch is out there.

Brendan has jumped. Welcome to the **Midpoint**.

OK, I said Brendan just jumped, but how do we know this for sure? Well, The Pin tells him what it all means: 'I'll have my boys check your tale and, seeing how it stretches, we'll either rub or hire you. You'll know which by the end of the day tomorrow.'

Welcome to limbo, Brendan. Welcome to freefall.

Also he accepts a ride back to school from Laura. She's already helping. He's already letting her. She helped him before when Tug had him on the floor of The Pin's office, but he had no control over that. He had no chance either to accept it or reject it; the moment was about inscribing Laura's connection and power in what we can now start to see as a Pin–Tug–Laura 'triad.' I use the term with care. Now he does have a choice and he still goes along with it. Yes, it's only a ride, but small concessions lead to bigger ones. Something must have changed … oh yeah, he jumped. See how the axis of the story world just shifted a little? Things will never be the same again. Welcome to the second down angle.

### SECOND DOWN ANGLE—COMMITMENT

This angle is all about exposure. Brendan learns some hard truths about himself and about Emily on his way to learning the big truth about who killed her and who was truly responsible. Brendan is still taking punishment, but now it shifts from the physical—he is already badly hurt and his battered body starts to fail him more and more as the angle progresses—to the emotional. The emotional punches are much harder to absorb.

**Commitment:** It's pretty simple; Brendan has now entered the inner story world that killed Emily. He is swimming with the great big fishes and trying not to get swallowed. He can't stand outside and observe because the current is carrying him along and his actions have potentially dire consequences. He now has to swim fast to keep ahead but each step brings him closer to the truth but also closer to real danger.

### E. From leap to crisis

### 9. 'Bigger kids came'

In the movies as in life, they always do. This is a standard ramp-up-the-pressure beat, but also a beat which is about Brendan adjusting to new conditions after the **Midpoint**'s tectonic shift. 'New conditions' includes the **B Story**, which comes back to centre stage. After all, this is about midway between our two **B Story** parallel (5 and 12) beats, so it's about time to up the game on this. Laura looks like Brendan's only ally on the inside, but there's that whole femme fatale issue nagging at him still. At least she is offering him a narrative of Emily's path towards doom, but what door is she trying to open with that key? There are other, more direct threats in this beat, all framed by the big overarching tension of waiting for the biggest kid to come: Brendan is waiting for the outcome of The Pin's big decision.

So Laura drops Brendan at school. She asks him if he trusts her now. He walks away. She cuts him off. 'Less now than when I didn't before.' Maybe he could trust her if she tells him her 'angle in all this.' Laura starts in on her version of Emily post-Brendan. She left Laura's crowd with a drug habit she couldn't control and a connection to The Pin who could feed it. Next, The Pin is furious about one of his bricks of heroin going missing. Brendan doesn't believe Emily would have stolen the drugs. Laura tells him: 'You weren't there. She wasn't herself.'

Then Laura turns the conversation from history to his story off this hint of an opening. 'You think nobody sees you eating lunch behind the portables ... I always see you ... Maybe I see what you're trying to do for her. Trying to help her. And I don't know anybody who would do that for me.' Brendan: 'Now you are dangerous.' Oh yes. She played that brilliantly. Femme fatale camp really paid off for her because she knows that the best lies are also the truth. Yes, I believe she really does 'see him.' Yes, I believe she really does wish somebody would be there for her like he still is for Emily. That doesn't change who she is and what she has done—more of which anon—but it coats her portion of grilled manipulation in a sauce which just might be made from real organic feelings, and that's hard to resist.

Brendan does resist. He still knows she is dangerous and he is still strong enough to keep her out, but his walls are starting to crack. After all, in **you may not realize this yet, but ...** he wouldn't even have countenanced having this conversation.

Also remember that a good antagonist must be a match for your protagonist. This means you should also match your hero/ine's theme in the talents of other characters. Laura is a master manipulator in her own right, and this is the beat where she begins to show her true mettle. This is not only important in terms of setting up the resolution of the Emily story to come, but also because the possibility of Brendan being interested in Laura gives us yet one more rug to pull out from under him at the end.

Brendan stops off at drama world and lets Kara know he is now connected with The Pin. She won't tell him where Dode is, even though Brendan offers safety for information now rather than unknown and possibly dire consequences later.

Next morning Brendan gets another locker note—different handwriting, same public phone deal. Right then, a young guy with a knife attacks Brendan in school. He won't say if The Pin sent him. Brendan runs, knife boy follows. Brendan trips him and knife boy whangs his head on a post but Brendan has picked up a knife slash on his arm to add to his other injuries. Brendan checks the guy's ID with Brain, who tells him knife boy is known but doesn't run with a crew. This is not The Pin's answer; in fact, we find out later he was hired for some revenge by Brad Bramish.

Just then The Pin pulls up. Brendan is hired. He's told where to be at 6pm for his first Pinworld event.

### 10. 'Er . . . little help?'

Help can come from the strangest places. This beat has Brendan make dangerous new alliances inside Pinworld as the plot thickens. He learns more about Emily's descent and he feels the pull of its gravity more strongly as very uncomfortable truths begin to be revealed.

So Brendan just makes the phone call rendezvous. It's Dode, and he says: 'I saw you hide her.' So it was Dode in the tunnel. Dode threatens Brendan, telling him he will turn Brendan in but he won't know to whom.

Brendan makes The Pin's appointment by the pier on the beach at 6pm. The Pin is in contemplative mood. He explains Brendan's dealing job, tells him he is just finishing up a big deal. There were problems but it's over now. He also tells Brendan he was hired in part as cover because Tug is becoming increasingly unpredictable and dangerous. Cut to Tug watching them talk. He is not a happy bunny.

Now home and sleep. Brendan better make the most of it. Too late: Brain calls him and tells him not to come into class because the VPs are looking for him. He also tells him Frisco Farr, one of The Pin's guys, was recently found in a coma. No overdose, just bad chemicals cut into the heroin: *bad Brick*. Brain also says Laura came by, tried her charms and wants to meet. Brendan refuses: 'I'll be at The Pin's at 1.'

Now Brain's big news: the local newspaper has the story of Emily going missing. The clock is running faster now.

Brendan calls VP Trueman and realizes he has been cut loose. The clock is running faster now. He tells Brain leads have dried up. He needs to find Dode—he led Emily into things? 'I'll have to push things a bit.'

Brendan is at The Pin's place. It's empty. He searches The Pin's desk, finds stacks of cash. He checks out another basement room and finds a big brick of heroin. Tug finds him with the drugs and attacks him, assuming Brendan is skimming it. Brendan reasons with him through the whole being throttled thing. He tells Tug—thinking on his feet here and playing to Tug's own insecurities, the insecurities of the mistrusted deputy—The Pin isn't telling him the whole story and he doesn't like being in the dark. He just wants information so he can protect himself. 'The Pin's not giving me the straight. That makes me nervous. Makes me angry.' This pushes the right Tug button and the throttling stops. Tug and Brendan go upstairs and have a heart to heart about The Pin and the bricks. This launches a new phase in which both The Pin and Tug look to Brendan as an ally against the other. It turns out everybody needs **er … little help?** This puts Brendan right at the heart of things. He couldn't be further inside if he tried, in fact the triad of Laura, Pin and Tug just got a fourth member, although the others may not realize it yet. This puts Brendan simultaneously in the best and most dangerous position possible. Potentially he can run the table again, but if he makes one mistake in his reads he's gone.

So back to the plot: there were ten bricks of heroin. Eight were sold on and two kept. One went missing and then miraculously turned up again, only it had been cut with bad stuff. One of The Pin's guys, Frisco, 'dosed off it and is in hospital. They are still searching for the thief.

Brendan asks about Emily's involvement, but Tug says he never heard of her. He's obviously lying but tells Brendan to ask The Pin. As if by movie magic The Pin shows up and, unbidden, tells them somebody called, claimed he has information about Emily. The Pin tells Brendan Emily was Tug's girl. So Emily was spreading her affections around at least Tug and Dode after she left Brendan. They agree to meet up at the drain at 4pm.

## F. Through crisis to revelation

### 11. 'It sucks to be me'

This beat is where things get deeply awful. Very bad things happen and Brendan learns something that shakes his world to its foundations. Meanwhile his body is falling apart on him. Laura is now fully involved and it isn't even discussed because Brendan is in no kind of shape to refuse help from any source at this point.

So Laura picks up Brendan from The Pin's. He is in bad shape and finds it hard to walk. He tries to call Brain but can't get through. He collapses. **It sucks to be me.** He wakes up on Laura's lap in her car. It's almost time for the meet and he freaks out. He heads out, stumbling, after asking her to warn him if Dode comes.

Brendan and Dode cross on the football field. They argue and Dode cannot get past his assumption that Brendan killed Emily. He says: 'We figured it out … Me and Kara, we're going to bury you and we're gonna get paid.' Who thinks Kara is playing Dode straight, show of hands? I thought so. Remember, Dode is an idiot and an easy mark. If he wasn't, he would have put 2 and 2 together by now and at least come up with 5 rather than 337, which is where his brain is at this point.

At least this narrows the field for Brendan's investigation, but it also forces a rage- and grief-filled revelation from Dode: Emily was pregnant when she died. Dode assumes the baby was his. He also assumes this is why Brendan killed her—out of jealousy. 'She was going to keep it. It was mine and you couldn't stand that.' Brendan is appalled: **it** *sucks* **to be me**. Dode heads out. Brendan can't even stand up properly and we feel that isn't just because of the beatings.

Brendan struggles to the meet. Tug, The Pin and Dode are already there. Dode says he knows who killed Emily. He wants payment in advance for the information. The Pin is weighing things up but, before Dode can tell his tale, Tug shoots Dode in the head. It looks like it *really* sucks to be Dode. Aha! Tug thought Dode was going to accuse him, because, guess what? Tug killed Emily. Mystery solved. Pack up and go home, right? Yes, Tug killed Emily, but untying the knot of ultimate responsibility and the knot of Brendan's current gang involvement won't be that simple. Clue: both knots are on the same piece of string. But then you already figured that out.

Anyway, for Brendan the whole **it sucks to be me** thing is all too much. He's out cold again.

## 12. 'Oh, riiight ...'

It still sucks to be Brendan and, because it does, his walls have crumbled for a moment. While his defenses are down a distinctly Laura-shaped somebody sneaks inside. She never would have got past Brendan's laser nets and gauss guns if he wasn't a physical and emotional wreck. He is, so she does, and this leads to the moment of **oh riiight** ... that lets Brendan put the whole mess together.

This is why I keep reminding you to spank your hero/ine.

So Brendan wakes up in bed in Tug's parents' house with Tug sitting on the floor talking to himself about killing Emily in a moment of rage. He doesn't believe she was pregnant. At least, that's what he's telling himself. Tug sees Brendan is awake. 'Everyone's assuming it's war. You're with us.' Dode's killing has finally split Tug and The Pin. 'The hell I am,' says Brendan, but it takes a while for him to get it together enough to leave.

Brendan phones Brain and tells him to get ready for everything to kick off tonight. There are still pieces missing, but Brendan knows that whatever plan he has better start right now otherwise he will be in the middle of a gang war with a large target on his back. The clock is racing.

He rousts Kara, as you do, and puts Dode's death on her: 'You set that poor kid up.' Kara rubs salt. Maybe the kid was Tug's, maybe Dode's: 'It was kind of a crowded field there at the end.' Next Brendan heads over to The Pin's. Everyone is paranoid. Brendan says talk, don't fight. He offers to set up a meet with Tug for that night. The Pin agrees. Laura drives him to Tug's and helps Brendan persuade Tug to go for the meet that is set for 4am.

Brendan goes back to bed at Tug's. Guess who comes to join him? No, not Dode's zombie vampire ghost—what are you thinking? Laura is all cuddles and soft words and care. Brendan really needs a little of that right now, because for a good long while he has been thinking **it sucks to be me.** She kisses him and he doesn't resist.

Cut to the post-whatever smoke. 'Don't go tonight.' See, she really has his safety at heart. Brendan turns and notices the butt of Laura's cigarette. It matches the butt flicked from Tug's car right at the start of the movie. **Oh riiight ...** This confirms it was Laura manipulating everyone all along. Laura wants a gang war so that everyone comes out dead or in jail and she remains as the new Pin. 'Don't go tonight' means: don't stop the war. So much for all the soft words and care.

Brendan gets up. There are no more rugs to be pulled from under him. He knows what he needs to know. It's time to put a plan into action to resolve all this corruption. It's time for the final angle!

### Did you spank your hero/ine today?

I think we can safely say: yes. Brendan ends the angle with his body and his dreams in tatters. He is still determined to sort things out, more determined than ever, perhaps, but he has taken more punishment than ever. Indeed, it is kind of miraculous that he is still able or willing to carry on and see things through. I guess that's what makes him a hero.

### SECOND UP ANGLE—RESOLUTION

In *Brick* this angle is the shortest by far. All that has to happen is for Brendan to pull all the strings of the plot together while staying alive. This will be no mean feat because he is facing potentially lethal opposition, some of it provoked by forces external to the immediate situation and, thus, somewhat unpredictable.

**Resolution:** This is a particularly fun example of a third act, or second up angle, because Brendan's attempt to bring an end to things while trying to prevent the unnecessary violence of a full blown gang war runs directly up against a second and equally powerful set of motivations: Laura's need to get everyone out of the way so she can be the new Pin. Some of this plotting is revealed only in the almost obligatory 'telling the tale' scene at the end, beloved of detective stories since way back.

## G. The plan and the pushback

### 13. 'I have a cunning plan'

This beat does exactly what it says on the tin. Brendan sets up his pieces on the board and makes his first move. This is usually a clean beat in movies because we want to understand the cunningness of the **cunning plan** before pesky things like opposition **bandits**, chance and circumstance complicate things.

So Brendan heads downstairs from Laura and her incriminating cigarette without saying anything to her about it. He asks for Tug's car keys so he can leave first: 'The scenic route, draw off any tailers.' Tug agrees. A final check: Brendan asks Tug for a cigarette but Tug doesn't smoke. This confirms Laura in the car, and Brendan can be confident in his deductions so far.

Next he calls Brain from yet another public phone and lays out the plan: First, call the cops just after 4.15am and tell them there are drugs in the trunk of Tug's car. Second, go to Tug's and tail Laura if she leaves.

Brendan takes a large black trash bag out of the trunk of Tug's car. We see later that he will use it to collect Emily's body and stow it in the trunk of Tug's car to implicate him fully.

Cut: Brendan arrives at The Pin's place. The Pin and Tug are facing off in the basement. Violence is in the air and Tug is leaking testosterone by the bucket. Brendan better put the fix in fast. 'Talk,' he tells them. See how far Brendan has come in the power relationship that nobody bats an eye at this?

The Pin's demands: all the heat from Dode's and Emily's deaths is on Tug. Brendan says fair's fair and the Tug grudgingly agrees. That was easy. But wait, The Pin has one more demand: How does he know the last brick is still good? He wants Tug to take a dose from it. Tug refuses. Looks like this could be a deal breaker, and besides, it is now awfully close to 4.15 and cop time. To move things along, Brendan offers to dose from the brick. They agree, and mini goons are sent to prepare the drugs.

So far Brendan thinks he is pretty much running the show—**I have a cunning plan**—despite agreeing to take possibly poisoned drugs. He's taking risks, but anything is worth finishing and getting out of The Pin's place before the cops come. What he doesn't know is that his solution has been undermined by something Laura has already done. In other words the pushback was in place before the plan was even finalized.

### 14. 'Bandits, three o'clock high'

This beat is all about proving the talents of your antagonist. Do they rate their status or are they just going to fold like a five dollar hooker … sorry, got carried away by the hardboiledness of everything there for a second.

So what's the one thing Laura could have done that would simultaneously queer Brendan's pitch and confirm her as a scheming nightmare of a femme fatale? Well, you answer, I guess she could have already stolen the final brick, but surely she wouldn't do that when she knows it will cause a meltdown and people, including Brendan, will likely die. Say it ain't so?

It's so, although at this stage all we know for sure is that the brick has gone. Maybe she meant it, then, when she told Brendan not to go. Maybe she isn't quite such a heartless bitch. Yeah, but she didn't care enough to warn him now, did she?

So welcome to the basement of The Pin's when the theft is discovered. Welcome to the gang war that kicks off in the house above and between The Pin and Tug below. There are sounds of scuffles through the basement ceiling. Somebody says: 'The brick is gone.' Tug and The Pin yell at each other. Tug attacks The Pin. Brendan takes away Tug's gun but leaves The Pin to his fate. He leaves the room, deaf to The Pin's pleas for help.

This is about Brendan proving his hardboiled attitude once again. With no gun for Tug to make a quick kill, The Pin will go hard. He hears the cops arrive and then slides Tug's gun back to him before crawling out a basement window and running off. He knows exactly what Tug is likely to do with a gun when faced with a police cordon, but then again Tug killed Emily even though he was also just another of Laura's dupes.

Back at Tug's car we see Emily's arm sticking out of the open trunk.

### H. The resolution and its meaning

### 15. 'Eat judge boot, creep'

This beat is where the villain gets theirs while the hero/ine gets what they have been striving for all this time or fails gloriously. Usually, your hero/ine has finally proved their worth and has overcome the best, or worst, that can be thrown at them and has likely prevailed. In *Brick* this is Brendan's chance to lay out the facts as he sees them and for us to catch up in case (because) we missed a bunch of clues along the way. It's a classic detective story moment, and Rian Johnson gives Brendan and Laura all the time they need to breathe every last acidic breath at one another.

So it's morning again and Brendan calls Brain for the 912th and last time. Laura never left Tug's until going into school. Brendan asks Brain to arrange a meet with her on the football field.

And now they come together for the last time and we are looking forward to this. Laura walks straight up and hugs him close and long. Brendan lets her. He opens with a tactical lie and tells her he took her advice and never went to the meet. This lets him ask her what happened so he gets to hear her version up front. The butcher's bill is six dead including Emily, Tug and The Pin. Tug died trying to shoot it out with the cops. The police tied the deaths of Dode (same gun) and Emily (trunk of his car) to Tug: 'You did all of this because you loved her and now it's finished.' She tries to seal that closure with a kiss.

'No,' Brendan is not finished. 'I set out to know who put her on the spot, who put her in front of the gun. That was you, Angel.'

Laura can feel the walls closing in and she asks him to lay it all out for her. How much does he know and exactly how doomed am I? Well, most of the plot we know, but the key connections Brendan makes are: Laura stole the brick from The Pin and cut it bad—by mistake or to queer The Pin's pitch, Brendan doesn't know. When it was discovered, Laura framed poor naïve Emily. Emily was terrified of Laura, hence her freak-out on the phone when Laura drove past in Tug's car back at the start of the movie. The Pin tracked Laura down and told her he wanted a meet to sort things out. The Pin sent Tug, but Laura told him about the baby. Tug went over the edge when he heard about the pregnancy and killed her: 'She took the hit for you and you let her take it. That's the tale. Tell me it's not true.'

Laura says it's not true. Brendan replies: 'I want you to have been on my side all along, not just trying to get me under your thumb. I think you knew that party was going to blow up. I think that was your final play. I hope I'm wrong. I hope you didn't steal the brick last night ...' She denies it. 'That means you didn't let me walk into a slaughterhouse. And you didn't lead The Pin and Tug and their crews to the slaughter.'

Cut: the school authorities open Laura's locker and the last brick falls to the ground and breaks. Brendan has tipped VP Trueman and tells Laura so.

Laura gives him 9 out of 10. She reckons she has nothing to lose in filling in the details now. What remains is her final stab at his heart: 'I told Em to tell Tug it was his. Told her it would soften him up. She said she wished she could keep it, but she didn't love the father. I was gonna drive her down to the doctor the next day ... She was already starting to show. Three months. Do you know whose kid that makes it? Or have you known all along?' She whispers in his ear, 'Mother—,' before walking off to her fate.

### 16. 'Oh brave new world ...'

This beat lets us dwell on the resolution and its consequences in parallel with the world of the first story beat. We may take time to absorb the nature of the changed, fixed world of our hero/ine's creation. Allowing your ending to resonate is a nice calculation, however, and one of the tricks of writing a good script is to know when it is over.

So in *Brick* this beat is very short, but it is still present. Brendan is left with the whole truth—this is the whole point of the story, after all. Rather than take time to process and accommodate it, the story fills in a couple of minor holes and then leaves us sharing the bitterness of Brendan's hollow victory. Laura certainly has cause to call Brendan names, but we are left with the literal interpretation of the insult: Brendan was the father of Emily's unborn child.

Brendan watches her go. Not much of a victory to celebrate, all things considered. Brain has turned up and fills Brendan in on a couple of loose ends, like Brad hiring the knife guy. Brendan tells Brain he did good. Finally Brain asks: 'What did she whisper to you?' 'She called me a dirty word.' All the while Brendan is looking away in the direction Laura left. What might have been? THE END—deal with it.

### Did you spank your hero/ine today?

It's official, Rian Johnson is off Brendan's Xmas card list.

# 7

## It's All About the Characters: This Time I Really Mean It

> IMPLIED YOU
> Finally!

> FRIENDLY ME
> Hmm?

> IMPLIED YOU
> Well, we are nearly at the end of the
> book and only now you have a chapter
> on characters?

> FRIENDLY ME
> Have you been skipping forward? Bad
> reader, no biscuit.

> IMPLIED YOU
> Oh, like you never do that.

> FRIENDLY ME
> Surely you realize we've been talking
> about character all the way through?

> IMPLIED YOU
> Yeah, but you've been saying how
> important characters are.

> FRIENDLY ME
> Remember we are working in film
> student order. That's why I have been
> sneaking character into all the stuff
> students are often more at home with.
> Most of my job has already been done
> for me.

> IMPLIED YOU
> Characters are hard, it's true. I
> mean, look how badly you've been
> sucking trying to develop me. But
> you have been kind of hard on film
> students.

```
            FRIENDLY ME
Nah. I have had the pleasure and
privilege of teaching many very
talented students. I have just been
caricaturing them gently because
they often start their journeys
towards a good story from
unconventional places. This book is
trying to make their journey easier
and more fun. Besides, if they
can't take a very gentle ribbing
from me, what hope do they have in
the real world?

            IMPLIED YOU
OK, but if we have been talking
about characters all along, what is
this chapter all about?

            FRIENDLY ME
It's mostly about how all your
characters should work together and
how the whole bunch of them need to
serve your theme and your story.
Firstly, however, I want to offer a
little note about character
development.
```

## Character development, or why writing a character bio is often a waste of ink

Students often ask me whether they should be working out the details of a character's background or 'backstory' while they are planning their screenplay. Well, the easy answer is yes, you should. Of course a screenwriter should know about their hero/ine. They should have evidence to help them imagine how a character will react in a given situation.

The problem, however, is that until writers have come to terms with the **wardrobe**, until they have established the relationship between character and the **theme** that will drive their story, most of this effort will likely be a waste of time.

I mean, does it help you to know that your heroine is 5′ 2″ tall, has red hair but no freckles, hates the shape of her earlobes, secretly reads trashy romance fiction, loved her mother more than her father, can't cook anything apart from toast, hates rice pudding, called her childhood pet bunny 'Mr. Melty,' had a crush on Amy Sedaris when she was twelve, secretly visits her reclusive albino uncle Franc against her parents' wishes, lived in Venezuela for six months when she was nine years old, has brown as her favorite color, dumped her first boyfriend because he always sang My Chemical Romance songs off key in the shower, is scared of moths, liked *Firefly* more than *Buffy*, collects contemporary Latvian pottery, hasn't talked to her twin sister since the embarrassing incident with Tim O'Brien on the bus last week, and went to a strict Scottish boarding school where she was an ace at field hockey and rubbish at geography? I don't know. Does it?

>                    IMPLIED YOU
> Are you asking me?
>
>                    FRIENDLY ME
> Sure.
>
>                    IMPLIED YOU
> Well, how would I know?
>
>                    FRIENDLY ME
> Exactly.
>
>                    IMPLIED YOU
> Exactly what?
>
>                    FRIENDLY ME
> How would you know?
>
>                    IMPLIED YOU
> I don't.
>
>                    FRIENDLY ME
> How could you?
>
>                    IMPLIED YOU
> That's what I'm saying.
>
>                    FRIENDLY ME
> Exactly.
>
>                    IMPLIED YOU
> Do you have a weapon of some kind I
> could borrow? I feel the sudden need
> to beat you about the head.

My point is that students often approach character development ass-backwards. They will arrive at class with loads of detailed knowledge about a character but no real clue what to do with it. They have spent a lot of time inventing random facts, but little or none establishing a story context through which to deploy those facts. This is the character development equivalent of 'hose-piping' with a video camera; point it at everything and hope something will be useful.

*If you have a great idea for a character, your first job is to decide what story they are going to help you tell.*

*Then work back from that story to establish your theme.*

*Then answer the central question: Why do they have a problem with or find a particular challenge in that theme?*

*Now we can start to invent and deploy character detail throughout our story and our plot and not just as random backstory.*

## Return of the bunnies: story goals, plot goals and the need to share the pain

Let's recap from Chapter 3 and elsewhere:

*Story is how your hero/ine addresses their theme played out through the movie.*

*Plot is the sequence of incidents we see on screen which get our hero/ine to the finish line.*

*Plot is surface, story is depth.*

*Plot is exterior, story is interior.*

*Plot is about changes manifested in the story world, story is about change negotiated within the character.*

Having said that, plot can be both motivation and reaction. Events in the world force us into a reaction and we then have to adapt ourselves so as to overcome or accommodate to the changed reality. Flip: deep motivations make us (re)act in the world, thus changing both it and ourselves. However you conceive your movie, it will be much the better for your hero/ine having linked goals in both the plot and story arenas.

We went a little way down this path when talking about bunnies, but we need to go further, because there is more to character motivation that we have not yet explored. To start with, remember that if you are *scared of bunnies in a world where 'ooh look, bunnies,'* you have two problems. Firstly you have an external problem: somehow those hateful bunnies wtfpwn in the story world, denying you your place in the sun. Secondly you have a linked internal problem: your fear.

Now to understand how to use that example properly, we can work backwards from the simplistic trope of fear to find real character motivation. In story terms, if fear is going to be a central problem for your hero/ine it needs to come from something and lead somewhere. In other words it is indicative of complex psychology, and is not merely an isolated manifestation of that psychology. By understanding that psychological, motivational arc we can make *scared of bunnies* into an interesting story problem for the character who suffers from it. Again the point is not 'bunnies,' the point is to think about how a personal weakness gives your hero/ine complexity and creates ripples across your story.

Let's think about some possible origins for that fear in the goofy spirit of 'ooh look bunnies.' Maybe when your hero/ine was a toddler they were left alone in the garden. Suddenly 'bigger bunnies came' and bullied them, sitting on them, nibbling on their nose and pooping on their toes. Maybe your hero/ine left their favorite stuffed bunny toy in the barn by mistake and evul spiders laid eggs in it. When they finally found it again and hugged it in relief and joy, all the little baby evul spiders came out and scuttled straight for your hero/ine's face. Maybe your hero/ine was attacked by the Horrible Hobo of the Woods who dressed in clothes covered in bloody bunny pelts. Maybe there was a dangerous machine in daddy's factory with cutting blades that looked like giant bunny teeth to an imaginative and impressionable child. That image can translate and acquire other meanings through any kind of family trauma. Maybe your hero/ine is claustrophobic and associates bunnies with the dark underworld of burrows and tunnels and the fear of being buried alive. Alternatively (potential Eew Warning) maybe your hero/ine's parents are plushies (look it up) and that led to a deeply disturbing primal scene moment involving bunny costumes and even rabbits of the battery powered variety.

OK, I'm not scared of bunnies yet, but now I'm a tiny little bit scared of myself.

Now let's look forward. Our hero/ine may or may not remember the cause of their fear of bunnies at the start of the movie. Indeed, the issue of remembering and healing that memory might have a lot to do with how the story plays out, like it does in *Spellbound* (1945). Hello Hollywood Freudian shorthand! Either way it doesn't take a great imaginative leap to see how any of those silly examples might have messed our hero/ine up.

Off the top of my head I can imagine those bunny origins leading to deep neuroses of many kinds, from a general fear of intimacy to numberless sexual problems, perversions and fetishes, including total impotence. I can see our hero/ine being deeply suspicious of family life and cynical about the joys of childhood. I can see them being unable to have any kind of normal loving relationship. I can see specific phobic manifestations like a horror of spiders, toys, barns and farms in general, fur, forests, masks, costumes (climactic scenes in Mardi Gras perhaps?), carrots … the list goes on: 'Tell me, Clarice, have the lambs stopped screaming?'

Yes, I know: /sigh@bunnies … but what we are starting to glimpse during our little trip down the rabbit hole is the complexity that lies beneath a simple motivation. We can also see the difference between a character problem as an individual, psychological issue and one that affects the world around that individual. 'I am scared of bunnies' is a simple, personal problem, curable perhaps with a good dose of aversion therapy. 'My fear of bunnies has turned me into the commitment-phobic boyfriend from hell' implies a problem for the two people in that relationship and probably their families and social circle as well. This is especially true if, down at the heart of it all, bunnies = people.

This is a much stronger problem around which to build a story. Your hero/ine starts with a weakness not only in themselves but one that is actively causing problems, doing harm and generally threatening or actually breaking their social world. Immediately, other characters are invested in the progress and outcome of your hero/ine's story.

Think of *Greenberg*'s Greenberg, whose paranoia and cynicism led to his rock band blowing their chance at a music contract. This is part of the backstory which returns to haunt the friendships in the movie's present. At the start of the film, Greenberg hasn't changed a bit, and the film will bring him up against the fallout from that past event in the lives and feelings of his friends and former bandmates. Greenberg's psychological problems are not simply contained in his person; they resonate across the other characters in his story world.

The best thing about these shared problems is that they link story with plot, the internal with the external, the world and the self. Not all movies work their structure like this, but if your concept lets you—or if you can find a way of molding your concept so it does let you—it will be the stronger for it.

Here's a good plot problem of the kind we dealt with talking about the 'V': *my world is broken. I need to fix my world.* Here's stage two of the thinking—moving us from plot towards story, but still focused too much on the individual in isolation: *I am broken. I need to fix myself.* (Oh, by the way, somewhere else—in the plot—the world is broken. When I get my act together, I better see what I can do.) And finally, here's the story problem encompassing the wider social world of the story: *I am broken and that is hurting my friends. I need to fix myself and thus fix my world.* The screenwriting maxim might be something like this: *a problem shared is a second act solved.*

## Wants and needs

OK, so if linking story and plot goals is a good thing to try to do, how does it work in a world where 'ooh look *no* $*#!ing bunnies'?

Basically your hero/ine should have goals that are concrete and manifest in the world—something they *want*—and goals which are personal—something they *need*: I want a bigger home for my growing family, but can't afford one. I need to earn my family's respect and prove I am a good provider. See how this want and need might link up to drive a story forward? So ideally both come from and speak to the same issue. This use of linked yet distinct plot and story goals is a common trope in screenwriting manuals. As you read more widely you will find it dressed in a variety of different clothes. Jule Selbo, for example, writes about 'immediate goals' and 'overall wants.'

We get similar ideas explored in slightly different terms by John Truby, who has a very good section on motivation. Truby adds the notion of a 'moral need,' one that tests a character's ability to 'act properly towards others.' This may, in turn, remind you of the function of the **C Story** relationship in Dara Marks's account. Remember we were just talking about how good story ideas involve others besides your hero/ine? Well giving them a moral need is a good way to work that out. If your character's problem causes them to hurt others, they have a moral need to change.

In *Brick*, Brendan *needs* to get over Emily in the story. He *wants* to find out the truth about her death and punish those responsible in the plot. Both goals come from the same place, are motivated by his feelings for her, and impact directly upon the other characters in *Brick's* story world as Brendan's investigation progresses.

In *Let the Right One In*, Oscar is lonely and *needs* to earn the love of vampire Eli in the story. He *wants* to get revenge on Conny and the class bullies in the plot, because they are the ones who condemn him to that lonely outsider status. Not only are these goals connected by what Eli does for him, they also make him the perfect candidate to become 'her' new day walker. Oscar's wants and needs allow the story to keep walking the tightrope between romance and manipulation.

In *Sunshine Cleaning* (2009), Rose Lorkowski *needs* to get some stability in a life spent juggling her eccentric failed family. She needs a future rather than an endlessly cycling present. She *wants* to raise enough money with her new crime scene cleaning company to send her weird son to private school. The opportunity to do the former emerges through the traumas of the latter in a way she could never have anticipated at the start of the movie.

Unless they are hermits, individual characters don't exist in isolation. They live in a world of your design and interact with other characters— also of your design—who respond to one other just as real people do. We have talked about how your hero/ines are central to telling your stories. We have also thought about some of the more obvious relationships that many movie stories establish for reasons of conflict, romance or both. What we haven't done yet is think about the interactions and functions of your characters as individuals within a group.

## The 'C Team'

By 'group' or 'team' I don't mean a cohesive bunch of allies within the story. Rather, I mean you should think of the entire character population of your story as your allies as a writer. However much they hate and despise one another in the script, they are all working for you because you have designed them to achieve your story goals. In this way your character population, even the enemies within it, work as your team to bring your story to a conclusion in an entertaining, enlightening or otherwise appropriate manner. Their interactions make the story sing.

This interdependent population is your 'C Team', the 'C' standing for 'Character' and for 'Clearly I don't have an imagination.'

Of course, the most important member of the team is your hero/ine.

## Hero/ines

By now you should be up to speed on the central importance of your hero/ine as a story engine. They are the personification of your story's theme. They are the **wardrobe** made flesh and bone. They don't exist in a vacuum but, before we think about the other character types with whom your hero/ine will be interacting, let's think about the important storytelling principles those protagonists embody.

### Your hero/ine is change

We have been over this before and it is at least implied in most of the other cases below, but it is the biggie. Your hero/ine changes and, in so doing, changes the story world. The story world changes and, in so doing, requires change in your hero/ine to catch up, adapt, fix or otherwise deal with that change.

### Your hero/ine is unfinished

They may think they are finished at the start of your movie, but chip away at that fresh coat of paint and there is either rust or unplastered drywall hiding beneath. If hero/ines were all perfect and buffed and varnished there would be no story, because whatever they needed to do they could just ... do. Yawn. Imperfections are what draw us to your hero/ines because we too are imperfect creatures and we can identify— well, I say we; obviously I'm perfect, but the rest of you clearly need work.

### Your hero/ine is potential

This is the more dynamic expression of the previous case. Make us excited by that potential—for good or evil, for finding true love, heroism, or whatever—and we will want to follow them to see how they live up to it.

### Your hero/ine is action

This is a Robert McKee maxim and it's a goodie. 'Show, don't tell' reminds us that actions often speak louder than words. Change is earned and learned, and we earn and learn things through our actions. Actions here should not be defined solely as running towards or away from stuff that is exploding. Actions may include talking to people and getting advice ... and then acting on it. Even *actively* avoiding acting is an action. See how it goes?

### Your hero is active not reactive

Following on from the above, make sure your hero takes initiative and moves their story forward. Of course, sometimes you want your plot to spank them unexpectedly; that can be great fun, but at the level of story your hero/ine needs to take responsibility for their own development as much as possible. The active vs. reactive equation tends to change as your story develops and your hero/ine learns to get a clue. If they need a kick at the start and the occasional whack as they go, that's fine, just don't fall into the trap of making them the can the story world kicks down the road all the time.

### Your hero/ine earns their pay in Act 2

The angles of act two are where the real character work of your story happens. At the start of act two your hero/ine has decided on a course of action, and at the end they begin to enact whatever version of it has survived to this point, but the work of the act is to transform them into the person who can at least have a reasonable chance of doing so successfully. All the rest is just exposition and resolution, which are merely empty slices of bread without the tasty filling that comes between them.

### Your hero/ine is a piece of a puzzle

By which I mean that they do not work in isolation. (Yes, of course there are exceptions.) They are linked in a network of friends, lovers, family, colleagues, enemies and others, all of which have their own lives and goals. It is the complex interactions of all of these puzzle pieces that work the story to its resolution.

### Your hero/ine is a mystery

They have hidden strengths, weaknesses, depths, hurts, damage and untapped resources. Part of your job as a writer is to bring these out through the course of the movie when demanded by plot and story. Don't tell us everything about your hero/ine and their world up front. Just make certain that you tell us at least enough that we can understand and judge their future actions. Let character be an ongoing revelation as the story develops. Remember, exposition does not end with the first angle of your story. Of course, sometimes your hero will be a real mystery wrapped up in an enigma, and that's fun also, but there should always be some unanswered questions, things for us to wonder about and keep us interested.

### Your hero/ine is entertaining

Oh please, please let it be so. We don't have to love them (Greenberg in *Greenberg*) or admire them (Harry Caul in *The Conversation*, Frank Galvin in *The Verdict*), at least not at the beginning, but your hero/ines have to make us want to keep watching. Part of this job is undertaken by your story world, certainly, but your hero/ine needs to be the absolute best person in story terms with whom we could be sharing that world. Entertaining does not only mean funny, engaging or charming, it can also mean *entertainingly* frustrating, infuriating, despicable or tragic.

### Your hero/ine is constrained

Part of the challenge any good hero/ine faces is that somewhere they come up against their own moral code. This code may not be one we share, either collectively or as individuals, and sometimes (for which, read the 1970s) it may be hard to find. If they truly are a hero/ine, and not a villain in hero/ine's clothing, then they can't have total moral freedom or freedom of action. If they do, where is the challenge and what are you trying to say? In some kinds of stories, the more you box in your hero/ine by their worldview the greater and more fascinating their challenge.

Alternatively, putting a less constrained yet still moral character into an even more constrained social context that they are trying—or are obliged—to respect or carefully work around can have a similar effect (John Book in *Witness* 1985). You can still have anti-heroes and you can still have moral ambiguity, but at least marginal separation from total villainy and thus some form of constraint is always important.

### Your hero/ine is doing something important

I mean important in the terms of your story. This can be a small thing in the scope of the world—they don't have to be curing cancer or ending the conflict in Darfur—but we have to understand your theme's central significance to *their* future happiness or personal development and that of *their* social network. In a horror movie, 'important' can just equal survival, ideally with all your parts intact. In a romantic comedy, getting the guy or girl is most certainly 'important,' at least in your hero/ine's mind. Basically none of those $50 debts to the landlord plots.

### Your hero/ine is needy

We just talked about this. It means your hero must have clearly defined goals in your story, not that they have to be an annoying, clingy, self-absorbed and needy boyfriend or girlfriend from hell. Of course, they could very well start out like this, and the challenge of the story would be to spank it out of them: Hello, Ben Stiller! Hello, Katherine Heigl! Their needs are what define them; they are what your audience identifies with, what makes them seem real for us, and what articulates your story.

*Your hero/ine is not an everyman ... even when they are*
That's all the more reason not to fall into the trap of undervaluing their uniqueness ...

## Why 'my character is kind of an everyman' often translates as 'I'm a lazy-ass writer'

Students sometimes pitch story ideas in class which involve a character who is an 'everyman.' This kind of pitch usually rings warning bells with me. Everyman pitches often turn out to be shorthand for a plot-driven concept in which the hero/ine is completely reactive and has no reason for being involved other than 'it has to happen to somebody, right?' This is what leads us the wrong way down the path from a good movie to 'stuff happened and we got to watch.'

The mistake is to assume an 'ordinary guy' is somehow a blank template as a character. Do you know anyone like that? I certainly don't. I like heroes and heroines because they are *exceptional people* and I'm trying to teach you guys about why your screenplays should always be populated with exceptional people. As it happens, that includes your everymen.

Let's start from the beginning. *Everyman* is an allegorical medieval mystery play in which the character Everyman stands for the human race as a whole. Everyman loses his complacency as he faces the prospect of imminent death and has to rely on his Good Deeds alone to assure his redemption in the afterlife. Everyman is pretty much devoid of individual characteristics, as befits his allegorical function. From his name we get the commonsense idea of an unremarkable person who 'could be anyone,' around whom certain kinds of stories can be woven.

Movies are not medieval mystery plays, however, and everyman characters in movies do not work in so simplistic and abstracted a fashion.

Typically an everyman is the kind of character who doesn't start the movie with a hat and a whip and a lifetime's experience of tomb raid ... um, of applied archeology to help him avoid the dastardly spears and spikes and darts and huge boulders the story throws, springs, shoots and rolls at him. Put an everyman into the start of *Raiders of the Lost Ark* and he doesn't make it to the chamber with the golden idol, much less back to the plane. The Nazis get the Ark and kill Marion in the process. It's a sad world, but there you go.

Everyman stories ask their audience to identify with the protagonist in a different kind of way than heroic adventure stories. It's not so much that we wish we could be imba and have Indy's epics (although: 'gief whip'), more that we recognize ourselves in and are resigned to being a bit too much like Dave Lizewski at the start of *Kick-Ass* (scr. Jane Goldman & Matthew Vaughn; 2010) or Truman Burbank in *The Truman Show* (scr. Andrew Niccol; 1998). What happens then is our everyman gets into an extraordinary story and we play the 'what would I do in that situation?' game all the way through the movie. When told well, this kind of story can be a classic. Think of *North by Northwest* (scr. Ernest Lehman; 1959) or even *Blue Velvet* (scr. David Lynch; 1986). On TV think of Jim in the US version of *The Office*, or Homer Simpson in *Whale Wars*—just checking you are awake. When told well, these everymen transcend their ordinary guy status and prove a point. When told well, these everymen are people who are *exceptional and individual in their ordinariness* and are just waiting for circumstance to spank their untapped brilliance out of them.

You have to remember everymen are not all alike—Jim isn't a clone of Jeffrey Beaumont. We love Dave Lizewski, but he is no Roger Thornhill. For a start, Roger has the whole Cary Grant charm thing going on and Dave has ... comic books. For his part, Roger Thornhill is certainly no Dave Lizewski, although now I have an image of Cary wearing Dave's homemade superhero costume and that kind of made my day.

Just like every other kind of hero/ine, everymen start the movie with a specific set of talents. What differentiates them from your basic Indiana Jones or Cyclops is that their talents are the everyday kind of heroic talents that will help them struggle through to the end but which don't help the process along by shooting laser beams from their eyeballs. Instead, your everyman hero might start out equipped with talents like these: *+2 Innate Niceness*, *+4 Untested Resourcefulness*, an *Unremarkable Backpack of Schoolbook Carrying* and a *+3 Cantankerous Best Friend of Unerring Loyalty*. Also it usually takes longer for everyman heroes to recognize that they have actual hero talents, because it also takes longer for them to realize that they are actually heroes. For many everymen hero/ines the whole movie is all about earning the *hero* talent and adding it to their character sheet.

Dave Lizewski even outlines his everyman status in a voiceover covering pretty much the entire **in a world where 'ooh look, stuff'** beat of *Kick Ass*. Looking back on his 'origins' after the events of the movie have taken place, Dave tells us there was 'nothing special about me.' This is a classic everyman opening bid.

He goes on: 'I wasn't into sports. I wasn't a mathlete or a hardcore gamer. I didn't have a piercing or an eating disorder, or 3,000 friends on MySpace. My only superpower was being invisible to girls. And out of my friends, man, I wasn't even the funny one. Like most people my age, I just existed. Kick in my bedroom door and you'd probably find me watching TV, or talking to my friend Todd on Skype … or jerking off …' Dave defines his past self through negatives and mundanities. Even so, we learn enough about him and his little world to pull him one level up from faceless everyman. He's a knowing everyman, indeed an everyman who is going to resist and defy that status at the risk of his own life. He wants to change from the start, although he hasn't really come to terms with what that change will mean.

His narration continues, and his comparisons start to play against our expectations of superhero 'origins' stories: 'I was just a regular guy, no radioactive spiders, no refugee status from a doomed alien world … My mother was killed by an aneurism in the kitchen as opposed to a gunman in the alley so if you were hoping for any "I will avenge you mother," you're out of luck. In the 18 months since my mother died, the only epiphany I had was realizing that life just goes on.' OK then, what are you? We identify with his awkwardness, we enjoy his wry, self-deprecating narration, we empathize with his loss of a parent—see how he's becoming quite specific already? By now we want to see more. Expositional job number one: check.

Now we cut directly to the start of **if only**. Dave and his friends are sitting in their local comic shop and Dave says straight out: 'How come nobody's ever tried to be a superhero?' And we're off. An everyman, yes, but self-aware, yearning for transcendence—for all that his fantasy of superherodom will get him. That one remarkable, insane idea colors his life and his social world and takes him on a journey he will never forget. *Being a superhero will let me escape my suck.*

Dave's everyman status has been planned as carefully as a 'real' superhero's origins. He is designed to help us identify and play the 'what would I do' game, because of course we have all wondered what it would be like to be a superhero. All of us are at least 7% Dave (check my calculations by all means), and the story links us hard and fast to that shared daydream and goes on to offer us interesting, if problematic, comparisons between Dave/Kick Ass and the film's other 'superheroes': Chris/Red Mist, Damon/Big Daddy and especially Mindy/Hit Girl.

*The point is that a character's everyman status is designed specifically in relation to theme and story. Everymen are not blank templates without personality or individuality, so don't fall into the trap of writing them that way.*

Now that we have cleared that up, we can turn our focus onto the other members of our 'C Team'. The first thing that your hero/ine's wants and needs should tell you to create in their story world is opposition.

Specifically you need to create opposition directed at exposing and testing those wants and needs because your hero/ine has to work for their win. This comes in many forms, but one of the most obvious and essential is another member of your 'C Team', the antagonist.

## Antagonists

Well, any good hero/ine needs a challenge, and that challenge comes from your antagonist. I use the big boy word rather than simply 'villain' or 'bad guy' because not all antagonists are villainous. Save those words for when they are. Sometimes there are villains in a story, but the antagonist is kind of on the side of the good guys.

Think of it this way: your antagonist is the character who provides the greatest challenge to your hero/ine. If you can visualize your wardrobe, you know that your antagonist is the one trying to break off your hero/ine's clothes rail (arc) from the walls of the wardrobe (theme). Villains might just be a passing annoyance. They can be hanging off the clothes hangers watching your hero/ine's best friend or love interest working away at the wardrobe with their chisel while they wait for the chance to exploit the chaos.

Once again I defer to Christopher Nolan reflecting on the writing of *Inception*:

CN [Christopher Nolan]: … I never knew how to finish it until I realized that the antagonist of the film should be the guy's wife.
JN [Jonathan Nolan]: The antagonist had originally been his partner.
CN: Yes, it originally had been his partner. The heist movie conceit. His partner in crime, who had betrayed him and so forth. But that didn't lead anywhere emotionally. It didn't have any resonance. And as soon as it became his wife, that flipped the whole thing for me. That made it very, very relatable.

Here are some antagonist principles to be getting along with.

### *Your antagonist is at least the equal of your hero/ine*

This must *always* be the case. Never develop an antagonist who is a pushover. Remember, your antagonist is your primary Hero/ine Spanking Machine   and you know by now that you need to spank them hard, even in a comedy—maybe especially in a comedy. Did I mention this must always be the case?

### Your antagonist is fun

By which I don't just mean fun*ny*. She has many of the best lines and knows how to make them count. She has the license of opposition, maybe also the license to be evil and, at least in the terms of the story, is not constrained by all that heroic crap. If you are ever in doubt about this, take a deep breath and watch *Robin Hood Prince of Thieves* (1991) (don't do this). Put a loaded gun next to you on the couch before you start watching (don't do this). Whenever you are about to put the gun in your mouth and blow yourself into sweet Costner-free oblivion (don't do this), what happens? Yup, got it in one, Alan Rickman appears as the villainous Sheriff of Nottingham and brings with him an endless appetite for scenery. Chew on, Alan love, chew on.

### Your antagonist is a symbolic double or inverse of your hero/ine

You know how this one works; they are two sides of the same coin, like Batman and the Joker. Whenever we have a line in a movie that goes something like: 'We ain't so very different, you and I,' take a drink. This is an old cliché, but it comes from somewhere interesting, and that is the idea that both hero/ines and villains are excessive creatures and are often separated only by ends not means, or maybe means not ends … Well, either way, I'm pretty sure ends and means are both involved. As with all story clichés, what counts is how, not whether, you use them.

### Your antagonist is all easy answers and the seductive path

If a life of crime was sold as the hard way to riches, who'd be a criminal? All Luke Skywalker has to do to come over to the dark side is to give in to his anger. You don't need to do any of that wandering around in an endless swamp with an annoying force goblin on your back. I bet the dark side looks pretty cushy when you are trying to lift heavy crates and robots and spaceships out of ponds with your mind.

Another way of thinking about this principle is as the opposition between certainty and uncertainty. Certainty is easy, it cuts out the need for complex thought and results in easy decisions because a thing either fits the model or it doesn't. Uncertainty is fraught and complex and can lead to moral vacillation and indecision. Now this can work in reverse also (morally upright hero/ines versus a world of corrupt but tempting relativism), but many villains are absolutists in one way or another. They take reasonable ideas and philosophies to a Manichean or even Procrustean extreme and become monstrous because of it.

[*Manichean* = sees (or cynically presents) the world as black and white, good and evil, right and wrong, with no room for grey. George W. Bush frequently presented himself and his administration's policies as fundamentally Manichean; in opposition to an 'axis of evil' and so forth. Whether that makes him a hero, a villain or just a dangerous fool I'll leave to your individual judgments. The point, in strict *story* terms, is that it could be any of the above, depending on your intentions for your character and your stance and philosophy as a writer.]

[*Procrustean* in the terms of this discussion = an inability or unwillingness to understand and allow deviation from an arbitrary norm and the punishment of that which does deviate. Procrustes was a great villain, a bandit who tortured his captives by stretching them or cutting off their legs so they fit the length of an iron bed. Check him out on the Internet.]

### Your antagonist is sexy

The Devil has the best tunes. Sexy does not have to mean physically beautiful. Sexy means attractive in a primal kind of way. Sexy can be all about personality, sense of humor, voice, charm and intelligence. In other words sexy is the full Rickman; for some, the full Lecter. Evil can—perhaps should—be sexy. We want our sexy villains to be onscreen and we want them to be given a free hand to be themselves. Genuine people are sexy in their very genuineness, and villains often have the luxury of being genuine. Of course, in this context, genuine can also be really horrible and evil.

### Your antagonist is flawed

Well, obviously. But the point of their flaws is to offer your hero/ine a way to defeat them. For this reason most antagonists either don't broadcast their vulnerabilities or defend them with their best troops and it takes effort and commitment to expose and defeat them. Also make their flaws interact nicely with your hero/ine's so that, even when they are discovered, they still pose a major challenge. In *Brick*, Laura would probably have got away free and clear if her greed hadn't pushed her to steal the brick from The Pin's place before the meet.

### Your antagonist 'could have been me'

This is the antagonist as moral lesson, or the antagonist as fallen hero. This kind of villain exposes the fragility of heroism and the humanity of evil. Think of Harvey Dent/Two Face in *The Dark Knight* (2008). This is the villain who has given in to temptation or provocation in a way we can all recognize—in a way we can't be sure we wouldn't give in to ourselves. Think of the way the conflict emerges and very bad things happen after the guys find the 'free' money in *A Simple Plan* (scr. Scott B. Smith; 1998).

### Your antagonist is 'real'

This can be another version of the previous example. Let us identify with and have sympathy for your villain and you give them power. Make them truly human and we will connect with them, for all their evil designs.

### Your antagonist is terrifying

She may or may not be actually monstrous, but scaring our hero/ine is always a good thing, because fear = hard spanking. Remember, love can be terrifying, and so can being in the presence of beauty or the sublime. OK, silly example of scary love: remember Garth needing to 'hurl' whenever he saw his dream woman in *Wayne's World* (1992)? This also reminds us that fear can be funny when it is happening to other people. On the other side of the scary coin we have villains like Don Logan in *Sexy Beast* (2000), who cow everyone else on screen by the sheer force of their terrifyingly twisted personalities.

### Your antagonist is immoral or amoral

There's a difference and it is philosophical. Immorality is about doing things you believe to be wrong. Amorality is about rejecting or living outside of a moral code of any kind. They both offer a license to our antagonists to do bad things, but they speak of different personalities and worldviews which you can work into your stories.

A devoutly religious person who breaks the moral code of his faith is immoral in his own eyes but may or may not be immoral in the eyes of the audience, depending on the context. The same character who adheres to his own perverse version of such a code, but whose resulting actions are abhorrent, is also immoral in the eyes of the audience while potentially remaining moral in their own eyes. Harry Powell in *The Night of the Hunter* (1955) is such a man. The same character who has no personal faith but uses religion as a cynical weapon, such as Matthew Hopkins in *Witchfinder General* (1968), is likely to be amoral.

### Your antagonist is redeemable

They are Darth Vader, not the Emperor. Some of the best antagonists see the light at the end. Usually it is too late to save their own lives— Hollywood loves to punish the bad guy somehow. They may redeem themselves by making a moral choice, helping the hero/ine or understanding the true nature of their former misguided actions.

### Your antagonist is irredeemable

They are the Emperor, not Darth Vader. Some of the best villains are just gleefully awful, so let a true bad seed be a bad seed. Iago is the best character in *Othello*, as is Edmund in *King Lear*. The wonderfully Sadeian Count Zaroff in *The Most Dangerous Game* (1932) hunts humans for sport. He's not suddenly going to wake up one morning and open an orphanage, unless it is to raise better prey for the chase. Similarly Harry Powell is too wonderful a villain to constrain. I can hear him now, calling out into the darkness of the riverbank: 'Children! Children!'

I'm just taking a quiet moment to thank Robert Mitchum and Charles Laughton for that one.

### Your antagonist is your hero/ine

The standard versions of this trope are when your hero is actually villainous, as in *Macbeth*, or *Hannibal* (2001), or *Dexter* on TV, or when 'you are your own worst enemy.' Usually a film will also have another, external prick to kick against, but sometimes a film focuses so strongly on a character's inner struggles that we understand that turmoil to be the point of the story almost to the exclusion of external factors. Roman Polanski loves a bit of mental turmoil, and both *Repulsion* (1965) and *The Tenant* (1976) explore this. Or of course there are movies about twins (*Dead Ringers* 1988), split personalities (*Dr. Jekyll and Mr. Hyde* 1931) and other general Spock-with-a-goatee type shenanigans.

### Your antagonist can be your hero/ine's situation (CAREFUL—HERE BE DRAGONS)

Sometimes, especially in high concept movies, the role of the antagonist is taken by that very high concept. Judd Apatow's stories do this sometimes, notably *The 40 Year Old Virgin* (the problem is the virginity) and *Knocked Up* (the antagonist is the unborn baby). In an interview with *Creative Screenwriter* magazine he remarks: 'My head rarely goes to "who's the villain?" I just try to think of real situations and stories where people try to get through normal, everyday stuff. Hopefully the texture of the story and the comedic point of view make it more interesting.'

In *Brick*, the antagonist is the whole corrupt social world Brendan hates and resists, more than it is any one of the other characters. Laura, The Pin and Tug all play villainous roles, but even Laura is in her way merely a pawn of the poisonous environment. In archetypal terms one might think of them as corrupt mentor/lover; corrupt king and corrupt warrior respectively. None of them gets to be Brendan's true shadow, however. The stakes are raised for Brendan by the responses of a combination of differently motivated opponents, not one mastermind sending out minions to destroy him. This is why Brendan's task in finding out the truth is harder and why he has to dance fast to play them off against one another.

### Your antagonist is your hero/ine's lover or best friend

We already talked about how many romantic comedies and buddy movies make the central couple their own protagonist/antagonist pair. What would credulous Fox Mulder have been without skeptical Dana Scully to rein him in when his imagination got the better of him in *The X Files*? Indeed, what would blinkered Dana Scully have been without intuitive Fox Mulder to expand her horizons towards the 'truth'?

### Your antagonist almost wins

If she doesn't, your antagonist sucks and you are not spanking your hero/ine hard enough. The stakes need to be high and we need to *at least* half believe in the eventual defeat of all that is good or even all that is romantically hopeful, floppy haired and Hugh Granty.

### Your antagonist actually wins

Because that's the only way your hero/ine will learn. Because sometimes evil does triumph, just almost never in Hollywood. Wait, that doesn't sound right. Ah, got it: just almost never in Hollywood *movies*. The devil and/or the coven in *Rosemary's Baby* (1968), John Doe in *Se7en* (1995) and even sort-of protagonist/antagonist Judah Rosenthal in *Crimes and Misdemeanors* (1989) come to mind as notable exceptions to this rule.

### Your antagonist has earned his or her own theme tune

Sometimes they actually get one (Darth Vader). Other times they just feel like they could carry one off. What I mean is your antagonist carries major story weight; write them as if they do and you won't let them down.

## The rest of the C Team

Right, so we have already worked out that we will need to populate our story with a range of lesser, but still important characters. They are going to do important work for us, helping, hindering and reflecting upon our hero/ine's struggles and challenges. When you are planning your cast you need to ask yourself not only what a given character's *plot* function is—are they a friend or an enemy, a lover or a mentor—but where they fit into your *story*.

*The best way to integrate a character into your C Team is to link their plot function to your theme.*

Every important character in your story should have a specific attitude or position vis à vis the theme. That's how you get the deadliest enemies to pull together and work towards the same goal, even while they are trying to kill one another in the plot. It's a romantic comedy and your hero/ine's *best friend* (plot function) is *cynical* (attitude) about *love* (theme), for example. Here's another one: it's a coming-of-age story and your hero/ine's *nemesis* (plot function)is *scared* (attitude) of *growing up* (theme).

Both of those simple cases should give you loads of opportunities for drama, conflict and character interaction. In our first example, the best friend is basically Elizabeth Perkins back in the 1980s. They mean well, but they are likely to give our hero/ine glass-half-empty advice about relationships. They will start out very suspicious of our hero/ine's new love interest. They will assume the worst and interpret all those dangerous little ambiguities that crop up in lovers conversations according to their own apocalyptic code. They might even take it upon themselves to follow or investigate the lover, just to make sure they are on the up and up. This could be great fun—it could even lead to the best friend becoming the antagonist if you take their cynicism far enough.

The nemesis in the second example is the personification of everything our hero/ine needs to transcend on their path to maturity. They could actually be a friend, a nemesis in theme if not in affection. They could be jealous of our hero/ine's attempts to grow up and find companionship with members of the opposite—or same—sex, or to take on adult responsibilities. That could lead them to try to scupper our hero/ine, to make them look foolish and immature. Deep down, perhaps they are desperately afraid of being left behind, and so they act out.

Remember, your story explores different attitudes to your theme. Don't just give that task of exploration to your hero/ine alone. Give everyone in the story their own investment in your theme and build their individual arcs around your hero/ine's struggle to resolve that theme. If you do this, your theme will be a proper site of conflict and it will play strongly in your story world.

So now you also have interesting choices to make about how your supporting characters' final positions reflect on your hero/ine and their accomplishments. A very Hollywood arc would have the cynical friend also find love, or at least cure themselves of some of that pesky cynicism. Importantly, they do so *because of your hero/ine's story*. If they hadn't been trying so hard to break up the relationship they wouldn't have learned their lesson, or met the love of their life, or … The point is, it's the friend's arc, but it reflects well on your hero/ine's good action by extension.

A character may combine more than one plot function. They should not, however, combine more than one attitude to your theme—at least not at the same time. Of course, any character can and, indeed often should, change their attitude to the theme like anyone else as the story progresses. The cynical friend in our romcom finally succeeds in driving a wedge between Jennifer (yup, she's back) and her new beau. Only after she has helped to split them up does the friend realize she was wrong and now she has to try and put things right.

How about giving us a girlfriend-as-mentor-cum-antagonist, like Evelyn Thompson in *The Shape of Things* (2003)? Her motivation for transforming her boyfriend's lifestyle is shockingly revealed at the end of the story. That revelation also transforms our understanding of her story function. How about an enemy who is really a mentor and sort-of on your own team, such as Hannibal Lecter in *The Silence of the Lambs*? Or one of the many buddies-cum-betrayers that crop up in movies, like Jimmy Conway in *Goodfellas*? What links them is that their reason for being as they are, or changing into what they become, is always necessary for the story. Evelyn never loved Adam; his transformation is her MFA art thesis. Lecter has his own dark motivations, but would Starling have succeeded without his help? Jimmy's betrayal is a major catalyst for wise guy Henry to turn grass.

I mentioned this before, but it's worth repeating: *if you are not sure what a character's role is in your story, ask yourself whether they should be in your screenplay at all.* A classic example of the useless characters often found in student scripts is the friend who engages your hero/ine in random banter to establish that that he has a social world, but doesn't engage in any way with the problem at the heart of the story. They talk about girls, or drinking, or getting high, as the real story stagnates around them. 'Color' is for extras and spear-carriers; characters should have a deeper function than this. Once again, this is about **narrative economy.**

Of course, we learn the most from our characters when we see them interact with others. As long as these interactions have a clear story function, this is an important kind of action. We have already established the importance of your hero/ine being 'proactive' (hated term). Also remember that our behavior changes depending on the social situation in which we find ourselves. We learn a lot from observing those changes in our characters, so populate your story with such opportunities.

For example, a person can be confident and fun when they feel secure in a group of friends but very insecure and reticent out of their social comfort zone. They may be good company with their own gender, for example, and very shy with any other—or vice versa. They may impress adults with their confidence and maturity and yet seem out of place amongst kids their own age. Encountering these situations early in a story gives us a better sense of how our protagonist sees herself in the world. It may also indicate the nature of their social challenge in the story.

When you are designing the supporting characters for your story remember the following principles:

1 *Supporting characters are not static.* Apart from the most throwaway messengers and thugs, all your supporting characters are 'real people' and, thus, have goals and dreams and plans just like your hero/ine. Sometimes these are easy to work out because they directly reflect some aspect of your hero/ine's arc. Sometimes you have to work a little harder to give them a life of their own.

Major supporting characters should have some kind of arc that they follow in your film. Give them needs and wants that intersect with, impact on, assist and/or retard that of your hero/ine. In *Brick*, Dode blames Brendan for Emily's death, and his desire to get revenge and a payoff into the bargain costs him his life. He operates independently of Brendan in this, interacting when their individual arcs demand it.

2 *Supporting characters are not one-dimensional.* Interesting characters interact with and challenge your leads on a number of levels. Certainly this should be the case with a well-written romantic partner. Also think of your closest real-life friends; would they be your close friends if they didn't engage you and fascinate you and make you work in all sorts of different ways? Our close friends tend not to be boring, at least not to us. Even if yours are—and I'm very sorry to hear that— make sure your hero/ine's are not.

Even characters in a screenplay whose whole point is to be boring are boring in interesting ways. Remember, there is a big difference between that entertainingly awful bore Mr. Collins in *Pride and Prejudice* and a false everyman bore who's just dull.

Yes, minor characters may have only one significant characteristic. This is especially true in comedy where some characters are designed to embody an idea or trait in the extreme, like the wonderful Soup Nazi in *Seinfeld*. All of your important characters need to have more depth than this, because to arc you need the strength to bend without breaking.

## Ensembles do it (sigh) together

As we know, not all stories follow a single protagonist or a loving or buddy pair. Stories that center on a group pose particular structural challenges, but offer promising new ways of addressing your theme. Having said this, a character is still a character and their interaction with your **wardrobe** should not somehow be reinvented just because they like to socialize with their friends.

You still need a strong and consistent theme. The difference is that, rather than having a single hero/ine's clothes rail attached to the wardrobe's stout walls, we now have a number of rails. They are no less straight and no less firmly attached. The challenge is that you have to play them all out with proper arcs, otherwise the characters they represent are not true members of an ensemble.

Because of the sheer structural complexity this requires I usually don't encourage new writers to launch themselves into an ensemble as their first experience of screenwriting.

Some stories use multiple protagonists precisely in order to address theme in a more complex manner. One of the common purposes of an ensemble movie is to offer different perspectives, different approaches and reactions to a universal theme such as racism, adulthood, parenthood, mid-life crisis and so forth. *Parenthood* (scr. Lowell Ganz & Babaloo Mandel; 1989) has an ensemble taken from the generations of a single family to explore the meanings and challenges of family life. As the title suggests, it does so by asking what it means to be a parent. *Diner* (scr. Barry Levinson; 1982) focuses on how a group of young men deal with relationships and coming into adulthood in 1950s Baltimore. *The Big Chill* (scr. Lawrence Kasdan & Barbara Benedek; 1983) brings a group of friends back together for the funeral of the first of their group to die. They are all kind of at sea, dissatisfied with life, love or career and approaching early middle age. The unexpected reunion gives them the chance to work things out.

Ensemble stories have also been used to address complex social and political problems. Thus *Traffic* (scr. Stephen Gaghan; 2000) uses a series of vignettes to illustrate the interconnectedness of every aspect of the current war on drugs. *The Breakfast Club* (scr. John Hughes; 1985) and *Fast Times at Ridgemont High* (scr. Cameron Crowe; 1982) both use their ensemble casts to embody constituents in dramas concerned with the social fragmentation, pressures and opportunities of high school life.

War movies often tell their stories through ensembles so as to sell a particular vision of war as epic, spectacular and complex. We see this tactic used in films like *Is Paris Burning* (scr. Gore Vidal and Francis

Ford Coppola et al.; 1966) and *The Longest Day* (scr. Cornelius Ryan et al.; 1962). In this way they can attempt to cover events the sheer scale and concurrent nature of which would not be possible with a single protagonist. These films also tend to use their ensembles to introduce us to the effect of war or major historical events on people at all ends of the social, political and military spectrum.

'War caper movies' like *The Great Escape* (scr. James Clavell and W. R. Burnett; 1963), *Kelly's Heroes* (scr. Troy Kennedy Martin; 1970) and *The Guns of Navarone* (scr. Carl Foreman; 1961) also use ensemble casts. So do ordinary heist stories and other supergroup movies where everyone has their distinct part to play, from *Ocean's Eleven* (scr. Ted Griffin; 2001) to *X Men* (scr. David Hayter; 2000). Caper movies divide the story labor amongst a group of characters but usually have a defined lead—Squadron Leader Bartlett, Danny Ocean and Kelly for example.

*The Great Escape* even signals the collaborative, greater-than-the-sum-of-its-parts function of its main characters through their credits. Bartlett is 'Big X,' the leader of the escape organization, but we also have Danny the 'Tunnel King'; Hilts the 'Cooler King'; Ashley-Pitt 'Dispersal'; Hendley 'The Scrounger'; Blythe 'The Forger'; Sedgwick 'The Manufacturer'; Ives 'The Mole'; Cavendish 'The Surveyor' and MacDonald 'Intelligence,' just in case we weren't sure how it all worked.

When well told, each character in a 'caper group' not only gets their moment in the spotlight but also has at least the hint of an arc. In practice, however, the more plot-driven the movie and the larger the cast, the more uneven that development tends to become. In *Ocean's Eleven* and *The Great Escape* some characters get more development than others. We remember Blythe's attempts to prove he isn't going blind so he can join the escape, but I can't remember a single interesting fact about Ashley-Pitt other than his posh name.

Historical epics like *A Bridge Too Far* often use established stars to carry off a character vignette rather than a fully arced individual. I always think of Edward Fox doing his 'this is a story you will tell your grandchildren and mightily bored they'll be' turn as General Horrocks briefing XXX Corps. Your star comes on, gets to embody a character principle or act a heroic moment, and then bows out.

I remember Horrocks for Fox's performance, but that would be nothing without the sparky dialogue he gets to work with. Good dialogue can be hard to write, but we'll give you some tips in the next chapter.

# 8

## Dialogue is Not Just People Talking

Dialogue is one of the joys of a well-written script and one of the hardest things to write well. Good dialogue tells us more about a character than almost anything else. Good lines stay in the memory and turn a mere character into a legend: 'Here's looking at you, kid.' Dialogue can elevate an ordinary story into the status of a movie classic and condemn an otherwise engaging story to bland oblivion.

One of the challenges of teaching about dialogue is that it is so personal, so attuned to the specificity of individual characters. Because of that, making useful generalizations to help aspiring writers tackle their dialogue can be tricky.

There are some general principles we can start by laying out, however.

### Dialogue is unnatural naturalism

It is *naturalism* because dialogue is continually referencing, but not duplicating the way real people speak. It does this in order to convince us of the humanity of our fictional characters. Even our science fictional aliens reference normal human speech; only they often do so in the negative, inverting and altering accepted speech patterns and idiomatic language so as to highlight their otherness. Remember naturalism is natural + an *ism* (oh, you spotted that yourself?) and isms are *about* the thing, not the thing *itself*.

It is *unnatural* because each line is designed to encapsulate and condense a thought without being redundant. It is much more precise and directed than real conversation and it usually cuts out the 'ums' and 'ers' and repetitions and half thoughts and 'likes' and 'totallys' and all the other unconscious rubbish we all load our everyday speech with. Listen, good actors will play the reality of your lines, led by their understanding of character and story. Give them clean lines to work off and they will thank you.

Of course, sometimes writers do the exact opposite, just to confuse us.

Woody Allen, for example, fills his speeches with hesitations, repetitions, half thoughts and general stumbling. This is central to his performance style and shows the traces of his origins in stand-up comedy. It goes some way towards explaining the way he uses monologues and the one-liner, for example.

In movies, good dialogue doesn't waste time or page space. It serves your drama by getting to the point and moving on. (La la la **narrative economy** la la la.) This is not the same thing as saying that all scenes should be short and functional. On the contrary, only short and functional scenes should be short and functional. What it does mean is: don't waste our time on the stuff that isn't important.

## Mundanity is boring only when it is mundane

The trick, therefore, is to realize when 'stuff' is unimportant and when it is serving a real purpose. A common beginner's mistake is to think that, because in real life people talk about inconsequential day to day issues before getting to the point, having that happen in your screenplay will give it the gloss of 'authenticity.' What this assumption fails to take into account is that your audience just sat down in a cinema, or in front of the TV, or computer screen or iPhone or random wet-wired cyborg implant (hello future!) with the active intention of watching a movie.

When we watch movies we are all contractually bound into the principles of dramatic storytelling and have no investment in your replicating some abstract notion of 'reality' for its own sake. Italian neorealism isn't reality and we don't think it is. Neither are mumblecore movies, improvised dramas, cinéma vérité films, kitchen sink dramas, documentaries in general, reality TV shows or any other mimetic genre (mimetic = *imitating* reality). We can tell this by their very nature *as* mimesis.

Your job as a screenwriter is to construct a *fictive* reality, however mimetically or fantastically you define it:

dramatic > realistic
realism > reality

Of course, a key distinction in dialogue—as in drama in general—is between surface playing surface and surface playing depth. Actually, no, let me correct that, because you can have surface playing surface precisely to expose a lack of depth. On second thoughts, that's just another way of thinking surface playing depth; as you were, then. Sometimes two characters talking about the weather or why the stupid buses made them late might be the most pointless waste of screen time in the history of motion pictures. Other times it may be the most eloquent expression of their inability or reluctance to say what they actually want to say: weather = I love you; buses = I want to break up.

What you *never* want to do is simply fill or vamp, waiting for the real scene to come along. Even those awkward, don't know what to say so I'm saying random awkward stuff moments between characters who have just met or who are dealing with the aftermath of an unexpected or embarrassing situation (think of them as 'sooo ...' or 'did we ...?' moments) play as 'don't know what to say so I'm saying random awkward stuff moments.' They have a direct dramatic purpose and speak directly to character and situation. *This is not the same as having characters talk crap for no reason.*

What you can always work with is the fact that sometimes human beings talk around their feelings and work their way towards them from unusual angles. As long as the audience feels that we are going somewhere, feels the dramatic value of the dialogue, you are in good shape. *Mundanity is only boring when it is mundane.*

You need to be able to judge when to top and tail and bring us into and out of a scene at the right moment. Sometimes that is the moment when your characters get to the point. Bang, we are in and right away there's a line of dialogue that keys us into what's going on. We are moving forward immediately and everything is dynamic. Here's a little example from *Traffic*:

```
INT. HALLWAY — DAY
Robert and Seth stand in the dim, dingy hallway. A JUNKIE
leaves.

                    SETH
          You're gonna get me killed.

Robert shoves Seth toward the door.
```

And so it goes on. The scene starts on a dramatic beat and flows straight into action as the situation plays out. There will be guns and threats and arguments and we are never in any doubt about the scene's intent.

On the other hand, sometimes we need to let a dialogue scene breathe and develop at its own pace because that relaxed tempo is telling us something eloquent about the scene's dramatic purpose. Narrative economy is not about speed, just efficiency. Sometimes your script gets the best mileage when you drive it in first gear. Here's an example from *(500) Days of Summer*, the first time Tom and Summer go to IKEA. This is early in the relationship, day (31) no less, and one of their happiest times. They turn the shopping trip into a charming game of playing house. The scene starts with Tom asking Summer what she is looking for. They chat; he checks out some IKEA signs and wonders if she would like a 'fluehg'? Apparently she can resist the temptation. When they arrive at a display living room Tom sits and says: 'Ah. Home sweet home.' Summer joins the game and they play through into a kitchen. They talk and joke about dinner as if they actually live in the IKEA displays, to the bemusement of other shoppers. At this point in their relationship, Tom and Summer are very much in sync.

Now, strictly speaking, we could start this scene with Tom sitting and beginning the game: 'Our place is lovely.' All the stuff about the 'fluehg' could be cut and we would still get the scene's basic conceit and have fun watching these two young people do their thing. On the other hand, this is a happy time. We already know things will go bad for Tom, and it's important to spend some time with him and Summer to see how good they were together when it was easy.

The opening does a number of jobs. Firstly it speaks to the universal shared experience of a trip to IKEA. Last time I checked, it was illegal under international law to visit the place without making a weird made-up Swedish word joke. Give us 'fluehg' and we are 'there' with them, on board and sharing the essential IKEAness of the experience. Secondly, it allows us to witness Tom's imaginative shift from joking to play acting. It shows his creativity. Remember, he is a frustrated architect and the script will eventually get him back on track with that aspect of his life. Finally, we see how he turns the everyday shopping trip into a statement of intent for his relationship with Summer. Yes, he's making a game of it, but he's making *that* game. The opening lets us flow into the moment so that it doesn't seem forced, either to us or to Summer. The scene isn't just about the play-acting, it is about Tom initiating it—Tom controlling that beat. You need a lead-up for that moment to play.

## Sociolect, genderlect and idiolect, or 'vocabulary' for grad students

One of the other common traps aspiring screenwriters fall into is to try to make their characters 'sound like real people' in a generalized way. There is no default condition to the way real people sound. This comes from the same mindset that confuses reality with realism. There are many problems with this, the most obvious being that it results in all of your characters sounding bland and interchangeable or uncannily like you and your mates and your mum and dad, because they are the only 'real people' you know.

Look, we have just spent a couple of hundred pages talking about how your characters are carefully constructed to enact particular story functions and to embody ideas, problems, challenges, philosophical conundrums and so forth. They are part of your carefully and laboriously developed master plan of storytelling and you have written them to be original and meaningful in so many ways. If that's the case, why would you want them just to sound like Some Random Guy? Even everymen are unique everymen—we saw that in the last chapter. Even random guys should have their own personal speech patterns and vocabularies. You have to work on your characters' dialogue just as you would every other aspect of them.

Some of this work is simply a case of being specific and true to a character's intention. For minor characters, this may cover most of the task, but for your hero/ine, their antagonist and other major characters, you will need to add levels of personality and uniqueness to how they speak.

Linguists have come up with a number of useful bumper big boy words to talk about the various ways in which a person's vocabulary and language use speaks their origins, social situation and so forth. Three of the most useful to keep in mind are *sociolect*, *genderlect* and *idiolect*. I'm going to use them in a screenwriting rather than a strictly linguistic context, so all you linguists feel free to laugh and point.

## Sociolect

This refers to a social dialect spoken by a group. We are all influenced by our regional, economic, ethnic, social and educational upbringing, and it shows through in the way we talk. Sometimes this is obvious and manifest in strong accents, and other neon lit markers of specificity and difference, but sociolect can simply refer to a few shared words or phrases within a group of school friends. In this way you can use language to bring us into a group, or make us feel excluded. Here's a simple little example from the opening of *Diner* (scr. Barry Levinson; 1982):

```
                    BOOGIE
          What's up, Fen?


                    FENWICK
          Just breaking windows, Boog.
```

```
                  BOOGIE
What for?

                  FENWICK
It's a smile.
```

They call each other by nicknames and now we know those nicknames, so welcome to the group. Also, Fenwick uses the word 'smile' where we might say 'laugh' or 'it's fun.' They are comfortable with each other and we are being introduced to that comfort, to that group, through shared vocabulary and inside language.

Anyone who has seen even a few minutes of *The Sopranos* knows what a sociolect is. 'Not for nothing,' but those guys talk a certain way, have a certain accent and use a specific vocabulary which is part local (New Jersey), part class (working class), part ethnic (Italian-American) and part occupational (criminal). The women have their own version and one of the distinguishing marks of Tony Soprano's boss status is that he is able to transcend much of his gangster sociolect, especially when he is speaking to people outside that world.

## Genderlect

This is sociolect associated with a character's gender. Men and women sometimes speak different 'languages,' whether or not they are currently inhabiting Mars or Venus. Academics differ on whether female speech rules are imposed by patriarchy or develop through socialization—personally I imagine it is a bit of both—but nobody is disputing the reality of gendered difference in dialogue.

Men and women also tend to speak differently in mixed company than they do amongst their gender peers. Indeed, they may sometimes find it hard to accommodate to these changes in expected discourse. It reminds me of the old comedy standards (ok, clichés) of a straight man in all-female company struggling to keep up with an in-depth conversation about shoes, or the woman who is all at sea in a sports bar amongst jocks or stat nerds.

In both these examples the discomfort emerges not merely from the subject matter of the conversations, but from the way they work as language games for the initiated and, thus, as language puzzles for the uninitiated. The epic sports quiz that Eddie makes Elyse take before he will marry her in *Diner* is an extreme, if imaginative, exploration of the problem of navigating these gendered worlds in a relationship.

The LGBT community also has distinct and historically inscribed vocabularies and ways of talking. These differ by period and location, just as other marker factors do. A gay British actor in Soho in the early 1960s might sprinkle his conversation with terms from polare, for example. A gay American activist from San Francisco in the early 1970s most likely would not.

Here are a few common observations about gender difference in conversation noted by prominent linguists, including Georgetown University Professor Deborah Tannen:

1 Men tend to change subject more frequently than women.
2 Women tend to 'take turns' in conversation whereas men tend to focus on their topic or simply don't respond to overtures to change topic.
3 Men advise more but don't reveal much about themselves in trying to *solve* a problem; women reveal more about themselves in *sharing* a problem.
4 Men tend to be more verbally aggressive.
5 Men seek status from conversation; women seek connection.
6 Women listen more; men interrupt more (see 5 above).
7 Women talk more in private conversations; men talk more in public conversations.

Assuming these are all true as generalities, it would be naïve to propose that all women and all men act in this way. Indeed, you could make subtle statements about gender and personality by following, varying or reversing these assumptions in structuring your characters' conversations.

Here's an example of a female character breaking the rules. We learn a great deal about the marital health of prospective adoptive parents Mark and Vanessa Loring in the scene in *Juno* where they discuss painting their adopted child's bedroom. In this scene Vanessa takes control of the discussion and plays against the female gendered markers outlined above.

Vanessa asserts herself using 'masculine' conversational tactics. She dominates the conversation and will not countenance Mark's attempts to defuse, distract and deflect her agenda. He clearly doesn't want to paint the room before they actually get the baby. Mark's tactics are 'feminized.' He doesn't confront her directly, just tries to question the timing and make little jokes to defuse the situation. Vanessa completely shuts down his opinions: 'And I disagree.' There is no comeback to that line, because she beats him on strength of character and holds all the family management and budget cards.

Vanessa has a tendency to feminize and infantilize Mark throughout the movie. In fairness, he kind of deserves it because he is a bit of a child. After this scene, we are not surprised that their relationship doesn't survive. The strength of the writing, and indeed of Jennifer Garner's performance, is that Vanessa goes on to transcend her masculinized behavior with Mark. She shows Juno that she has the desire and capability to be a great mother. Juno is happy to give the baby up to her at the end, even though she has split with Mark. What's more, we endorse that decision.

## Idiolect

Basically this means that individuals have their own personal speech patterns, common vocabulary and favorite idioms, grammatical usage and pronunciation. While the origins of any character's idiolect overlap with their social and gender status, the term is really referring to the expression of their personality in their dialogue. Think about it this way: people fall into patterns of speech in part because they find them the most comfortable and best suited to how they typically interact with others. They also do so when they are flustered or put on the spot, or if they are basically Annie Hall:

```
                    ANNIE
        Oh yeah? So do you. Oh, God, whatta
        … whatta dumb thing to say, right?
        I mean, you say it, 'You play well,'
        and right away … I have to say well.
        oh … God, Annie … Well … oh well …
        la-de- da, la-de-da, la-la.
```

Here's a longer example, once again from *Diner*, in which we find Modell annoying Eddie. Modell has an eccentric manner, he is always 'beating about the bush,' and it rubs Eddie up the wrong way. This is not a vocabulary note, it manifests in habitual conversational tactics and patterns of speech, not individual word use:

```
                    MODELL
        Gonna finish that?


                    EDDIE
        Yeah, I'm gonna finish it. I paid
        for it. I'm not going to give it to
        you.

                    MODELL
        Because if you're not gonna finish
        it, I would eat it, … but if you're
        gonna eat it—
```

```
              EDDIE
What do you want?! Say the words.

              MODELL
No, … if you're gonna eat it, you eat;
that's all right.

              EDDIE
Say the words: 'I want the
roast-beef sandwich.' Say the words,
and I'll give you a piece.
```

To extend the example from *The Sopranos*, one of the idiolectal markers of Silvio Dante's dialogue is how he sprinkles it with quotes from the movies. Sometimes it's all about referencing famous screen gangsters ('Just when I thought I was out, they keep pulling me back in'), but he has been known to dip into other genres when the mood takes him ('With great power comes great responsibility'). Sil has his party pieces, but he uses movie quotes in his everyday speech as well.

A character might have different versions of speech patterns depending on a social situation, stress level and so forth. We already talked about how Tony Soprano is able to shift his registers depending on who he is talking to. Indeed, breaking out of a familiar pattern of speech might in itself offer important dramatic information as to their state of mind. A loquacious character suddenly shuts up. A usually laconic or taciturn character suddenly starts talking ten to the dozen. A foul-mouthed character tries to be polite. An uptight character starts cursing, or any variant you like.

Here's something of an extreme example of idiolect. The very extremity shows all the variance in speech patterns and vocabulary you could possibly get away with as you write character. Remember scary gangster Don Logan from *Sexy Beast* (scr. Louis Mellis and David Scinto; 2000)? He's not a stable guy, and his idiolect shows it.

Basically Don is nuts, and this gives him the license to break language and dialogue rules. He speechifies, he swears all the time, he punches with words like the instinctive bully he is, and he talks in strange half thoughts and staccato beats. At times his thought process connects ideas into insults almost like improvisation or blank verse: skin/leather/suitcase/crocodile …

Here's one of Don's speeches (very NSFW I'm afraid):

```
              DON
Shut up, cunt. You louse. You got
some fuckin' neck ain't you.
Retired? Fuck off, you're
```

```
revolting. Look at your suntan,
it's leather, it's like leather
man, your skin. We could make a
fucking suitcase out of you. Like
a crocodile, fat crocodile, fat
bastard. You look like fucking Idi
Amin, you know what I mean? Stay
here? You should be ashamed of
yourself. Who do you think you are?
King of the castle? Cock of the
walk?
```

## Articulacy is not a default human skill

Just because you are smart and verbally dexterous doesn't mean all your characters are or should be. Pointless witty repartee gets old fast, especially when you put it in the mouths of intellectual laggards. Just because they are in a movie doesn't mean all your characters should speak like Walter Burns or Hildy Johnson in *His Girl Friday* (1940). Let dumbasses be dumb, but let them inhabit their dumbness as individuals.

This should be pretty straightforward without me having to open a can of Forrest Gump on your ass. Whatever you think of that character or the movie as a whole, Forrest teaches us that dialogue is like a box of chocolates. Some of your characters speak like caramels and some speak like pralines, but always they speak like individuals.

On the flip side, remember that many very smart people are also socially awkward, repressed or just strange. The sitcom *The Big Bang Theory* plays into this as its central conceit. Sometimes this is because their great big thoughts occupy so much of their mental landscape that it is hard for them to find room for conversations with mere mortals. Other times it is the legacy of too many wedgies in high school. Sometimes it is both.

Also, don't forget that there is no necessary connection between intelligence and social status or education. Daddy's connections might have got your character into Harvard. She may look the look, dress the dress and speak the speak of the Boston Brahmin. She may also be as dumb as a rock.

An even more important distinction is that between intellectual and emotional intelligence. A character demonstrating a moment of genuine emotional eloquence does not always require a sonnet with which to do so (Bob and Jenny). Conversely, a character with all the poetic, romantic lines is as likely to be a doucheo as he is a Romeo. Think of Lloyd, the cute but emotionally neutered English coed in *Undeclared* (2001–2) if you need an easy example.

I'm reminded of the brilliant scene in the coffee shop between Travis and Betsy in *Taxi Driver* (scr. Paul Schrader; 1976). Travis is not that bright and certainly socially inept, but he is sincere. He really likes Betsy, and his dialogue shows it, although poetry it ain't. Of course the relationship is doomed, but at least he tries. Remember that everyone has real feelings and the bigger those feelings the harder most people find it is to encompass them adequately in words. Don't be afraid of letting even your smartest and most articulate characters use simple expressions when necessary, and don't be afraid of the transcending eloquence of silence.

## Movie dialogue is dynamic—except when it isn't

The basic piece of advice here is to spread your dialogue between your characters, not to let them speechify. In most movies, a longer speech should be something of an event, not the default. A character should earn the right to mouth off—Brendan gets to lay it all out for Laura at the end of *Brick*, and you have to say he has paid for the privilege.

```
              IMPLIED YOU
So the way we have been talking is
not the way dialogue should happen in
movies?

              FRIENDLY ME
We have been speechifying.

              IMPLIED YOU
Because our conversations have been
about explaining things.

              FRIENDLY ME
It's been more about teaching than
chatting, yes.

              IMPLIED YOU
We don't exactly socialize.

              FRIENDLY ME
Professional boundaries.

              IMPLIED YOU
Also you are totally old.
```

```
              FRIENDLY ME
     And you are kind of annoying.

              IMPLIED YOU
     There go those boundaries.

              FRIENDLY ME
     Now we are talking more like movie
     characters.

              IMPLIED YOU
     Shotgun—antagonist.

              FRIENDLY ME
     Trust me, you don't have to call it.
```

Here's an example of a short comedy scene from Judd Apatow's screenplay for *Knocked Up* (2007). Note that everyone present participates in the conversation.

```
     INT. DEBBIE AND PETE'S HOUSE — KITCHEN
     Debbie, Pete, Charlotte, Sadie, Alison and Ben eat
     breakfast together.

                    CHARLOTTE
          Who's he?

                    BEN
          I'm Ben Stone.

                    ALISON
          He's my boyfriend.

                    PETE
          That's nice.

                    SADIE
          I never met him before.

                    ALISON
          He's a new boyfriend.

                    BEN
          But a boyfriend.

                    SADIE
          So he came over for breakfast
          because he's your new boyfriend?

                    DEBBIE
          He came from his house, drove over to
          our house because he thought it would
          be fun to have breakfast with us, so
```

he drove his car from his house to
our house to have breakfast.

                    PETE
          Because he likes breakfast so much.

                    CHARLOTTE
          I love breakfast.

                    BEN
          You guys wanna hear something neat?
          We're gonna have a baby together.

                    SADIE
          What?

                    BEN
          Yeah, a baby.

                    SADIE
          Well, you're not married. Aren't you
          supposed to be married to have a
          baby?

                    PETE
          You don't have to be.

                    DEBBIE
          But that should be because they
          love each other and people who love
          each other get married and have
          babies.

                    SADIE
          Where do babies come from?

                    DEBBIE
          Where do you think babies come from?

                    SADIE
          Well, I think a stork, he drops it
          down, and then, a hole goes in your
          body and there's blood everywhere,
          coming out of your head, and then
          you push your belly-button, and
          then your butt falls off and then
          you hold your butt and you have to
          dig and you find your baby.

                    DEBBIE
          That's exactly right.

In dialogue writing we find significance in establishing patterns and breaking patterns. Apart from anything else, these changes often signal scene beats. When a pattern of dialogue breaks it usually means someone is saying something important or reacting to the unexpected or the uncomfortable.

For example, the scene above opens with snappy lines as Sadie questions Ben and Alison about their relationship. The first longer speech occurs when Debbie reacts to the uncomfortable direction the conversation is taking. She doesn't want her daughters to understand that Alison and Ben sleep together, so she intervenes with an incoherent ramble about how Ben got to the house. It's funny in part because of the silly nature of the cover story and in part just because it breaks the established pattern.

The short mid-section of the scene gives us somewhat longer speeches of a couple of lines or more after the revelation beat at: 'We're gonna have a baby together.' People are a little flustered, and explanations and veiled comments leak into the atmosphere. If you made a graph of the scene (or if you just looked at it) you'd see a gradual increase in speech length as social control fluxes, until we reach the comic climax when Debbie manages to turn the conversation back on Sadie and asks her where she thinks babies come from. Sadie's explanation piles one weird assumption on top of the next. The humor again emerges from the content and the hyperbole. The payoff is Debbie's short rejoinder at the end, taking us back from chaos to false order and briefly re-establishing the pattern we had at the start.

The principle is that dialogue is about conversations between thinking and feeling people, so the drama emerges both from what is said and how others *react* to what is said. Think about Bob and Jenny on their big dinner date again: what does Bob care most about? Yup, the look in Jenny's eyes when he tells her he loves her—in other words, her reaction. That look will tell him how to read the next words out of her mouth. Writing dialogue scenes in which two or more characters go back and forth with short, directed lines is the most efficient way for us to understand where they all 'are' in a given moment and to make sure that we play off reactions as well as lines.

Also, if your characters are worth their salt—are worth our attention as members of your audience—they are going to have something to say for themselves in a given situation. Remember that drama is conflict and conflict is not really conflict unless it is expressed from at least two directions. Make sure your screenplay is placed to catch them. One of the early lessons one teaches students in a film production class is to make sure their shot coverage plan for each scene picks up reactions as well as dialogue. Your writing should also facilitate that.

Remember also that you don't need to write in long speeches to tell us a lot about your characters. Short, snappy lines and short speeches not only keep up the pace of the scene but let us see how people *interact*. We learn as much, if not more, from that than if they were going on at length about their thoughts and feelings.

Take the scene where Ben meets Alison for the first time in *Knocked Up*. It's a high-pressure scene for Judd Apatow because this movie is based on the unlikely premise that Seth Rogan is really going to fall for Katherine Heigl when he's clearly waaay out of her league. I mean, in her dreams, right? It's a big ask because the audience is going into the movie with one basic requirement of the screenplay: 'Let's see you pull that one off Mr. Clever-Clever Screenwriter.' Well, let's see how he does it. Let's see how he structures the scene and teaches Alison some important lessons about Ben that will set up the rest of the movie, and all with short lines and no speechifying.

They meet at a bar in a club. Ben can't get the barman's attention and bitches to Alison that he's had no luck, when she also tries and fails. Ben offers a jokey compliment: 'And if you can't get service, what am *I* gonna do, you know?' They share a moment of annoyance that Ben breaks by leaning over the bar and grabbing two bottles. He gives her one. She is delighted and he tells her he once got punched for trying the same thing at the Comedy Store. Oh no—she forgot she needs a beer for her sister. Ben gives her his other bottle. She tries to refuse but he won't hear it: 'Please, I very rarely look cool. This is a big moment for me. Just take it.' Alison introduces herself. Ben responds. There is a little pause … Ben doesn't fill it, so Alison takes off, but she's smiley-friendly. We hold on Ben: 'I'll see ya later. No I won't 'cause I'm a pussy.'

So this is a smart reworking of the classic 'offer to buy the cute girl a drink' pick-up scene, only designed to make the impossible possible. Nobody believes Ben would have the guts to make a move on Alison normally, and nobody believes she would go for it if he played it random-guy-in-a-bar-straight. Apatow's solution works it so that, before any potential connection is even hinted at, the situation of being ignored connects them both in frustration and breaks the ice neutrally and non-sexually. It even opens the way for Ben to throw a nice compliment her way (the 'you're hot and you still can't get served' line) without seeming to be coming on to her creepily.

This isn't a bare your soul through verbal eloquence or poetry kind of scene, so Ben has to impress in other ways. What he does feels spontaneous and organic to the moment, and not premeditated or set up, another point in his favor. He even uses it to tell a story against himself—how he got punched last time he tried it. Welcome back to

**show, don't tell**: he grabs the beers, *showing* he has some audacity and then gives up his own beer for her sister when she remembers she promised to get her one. He then backs off, happy to be cool for once and not pushing his case (in fact he's a total coward, but she doesn't know that).

That's four points in his favor (nice compliment; gets the beers; gives his up; doesn't push it) in the space of a couple of pages. How could you not be well disposed toward him? The scene is led by the situation and by Ben's action. *Dialogue reinforces the action but does not draw attention to itself.* Indeed one could argue that point five in Ben's favor is the fact that he doesn't try any corny lines or fancy talk at any point in the scene.

This is an example of the effectiveness of simple dialogue when paired with a clever turn on a classic situation and a clear scene goal. Alison learns enough about Ben to *offer* him her name at the end before he has to ask. That simple moment speaks volumes for how well he has done in turning round a chance encounter with a most unlikely romantic prospect. He doesn't take the opening—and she closes it down fairly fast—but there was one and they both know it.

On the other hand, we love a good, clever, revealing and emotional speech when the situation warrants it. When Miles and Maya finally speak from the heart in *Sideways* (scr. Alexander Payne & Jim Taylor; 2004) they do it through the language and culture of the wine they love. Here Miles is talking about Pinot Noir, but really about himself:

```
                 MILES
   I don't know. It's a hard grape to
   grow. As you know. It's thin
   skinned, temperamental, ripens
   early. It's not a survivor like
   Cabernet that can grow anywhere and
   thrive even when neglected. Pinot
   needs constant care and attention
   and in fact can only grow in specific
   little tucked-away corners of the
   world. And only the most patient and
   nurturing growers can do it really,
   can tap into Pinot's most fragile,
   delicate qualities. Only when
   someone has taken the time to truly
   understand its potential can Pinot be
   coaxed into its fullest expression.
   And when that happens, its flavors
   are the most haunting and brilliant
   and subtle and thrilling and ancient
   on the planet.
```

This speech also reminds us that, in movies at least, people often avoid saying what they mean in plain language. They speak in metaphor and analogy and test out the waters, rather than giving it the full Bob and Jenny right away. Besides, if Miles spoke like that all the time he'd be way too much of an annoying pretentious wanker. Oh, and yeah, the poignancy of the moment would be buried and we wouldn't feel he had earned his connection with Maya. Of course, he blows it right afterwards, but that's Miles for you. Bless.

## Why clarity always spanks dialect

Now there will be times when you are writing a character whose background will suggest that they have a strong accent or a specific dialect. The beginning screenwriter—I've done it myself—will tend to try and encapsulate that specificity in the way they write the character's lines. So far so good. Unfortunately that encapsulation is mos' lik'ly ta'en up makin' 'em artikylate the'selves sump'n liken ta this ... y'all.

```
Th' FRIENDLY ME KID spits a wet gob of chawin' tobaccy
into th' dang spittoon.

                    SPITTOON
               (ironically)
          Ting.
```

Imagine page after page of that stuff and you should immediately understand why it is not your friend. More importantly it is not the friend of the script reader who has to plow through all of it and try and work out what (th' hootin' heck) your character is saying. Anything that gets in the way of clarity, anything that slows up the read and makes us struggle, is not authenticity; it's just a pain in the ass.

I lived in the lovely city of Norwich in the even lovelier county of Norfolk in England for a number of years. In that time I absorbed enough of the local Norfolk accent and way of speaking to be able to write a minor character as a local villager. Now, even though a typical Norfolk greeting sounds something like 'Aah yoar ryt booy?' I would still write it as: 'Are you all right, boy?' That's because I know that authenticity for the writer is in the personality of the individual expressed through their words whereas authenticity for the audience combines that with such surface gloss as accents.

Authenticity in that expanded sense is what the actor/director/voice coach combination will bring to the final performance. Authenticity is the 'research' the film star will blather on about on Letterman.

Authenticity is what authentic Alabamans or Norfolk villagers are for. It's not the way you write dialogue. What you do when faced with a dialect question is *indicate and enable*. When the character is introduced, mention their accent or dialect in your character description. If you want to indicate it in their dialogue, focus on how they inhabit their region or class as an individual. In other words, don't go adding a bunch of y'alls for the sake of it, but play with speech patterns and vocabulary as you might for any character.

Here's an example that goes about as far as you can in this direction without being completely over the top. This is an extract from Johnny Caspar's long opening speech in *Miller's Crossing* (scr. Joel Coen & Ethan Coen; 1990):

```
                CASPAR
        The sheeny knows I like sure
        things. He's selling the
        information I fixed the fight. Out
        -of-town money comes pourin' in.
        The odds go straight to hell. I
        don't know who he's sellin' it to,
        maybe the Los Angeles combine, I
        don't know. The point is, Bernie
        ain't satisfied with the business I
        do on his book. He's sellin' tips
        on how I bet, and that means part
        of the payoff that should be ridin'
        on my hip is ridin' on someone
        else's. So back we go to these
        questions—friendship, character,
        ethics.
```

Caspar's speech is stylized, reflecting the culture, period and source material behind the Coens' script. They played with material from Dashiell Hammett's *Red Harvest* and *The Glass Key*, although *Miller's Crossing* is a direct adaptation of neither novel. It also uses contractions here and there, but the read flows easily enough. The contractions sell the speaker, but they don't overwhelm the speech. It is appropriate to give someone awkward or idiosyncratic syntax if they need it, just don't go re-spelling everything an' choppin' th' en's off'n ever' word.

When you have a whole group of characters speaking the same dialect, one of the ways you can save yourself from the hell of overdialec-tifying is to embody most of the dialect*ness* in one of the characters and let the others get away with the occasional turn of phrase. Within every group there will be variation; work that to your advantage, just don't let anyone drive too far down the apostrophe highway.

Kevin Bicknell, a friend of mine and a talented musician and writer, reinforced this point, with his usual dry wit, when he kindly read a draft of this section:

> Your point about 'overdialectifying' being a hindrance to fluidity for a script reader is especially true. When I am doing coverage on a script which suffers from this type of writing it is inevitable that after a few pages I begin unconsciously replacing the stuttering text with something that sounds more like 'mumble, mumble, mumble' than the dialect intended by the screenwriter. In the end, when writing out my coverage I will often comment that the dialogue is unrealistic simply because I remember it as 'mumble, mumble, mumble' and unless your character is a Muppet or Cousin It, that is a far cry from impressive authenticity.

You have been warned.

The same principle holds for the use of 'bad language' in screenplays.

### Having all your characters constantly swear like troopers is basically you holding up a big sign reading: 'Don't buy my script!'

In the real world, people—like me—swear and curse, and sometimes your characters and stories may want to reflect this. Sometimes people use what we might call robust language because it's just part of their everyday manner of speaking. Sometimes it's about being under stress. Drama = conflict = stress = it's likely you may sometimes want your characters to swear and curse. Craig Ferguson nailed it when he said: 'Sometimes only a curse word will do.'

There's nothing necessarily wrong with this, as long as you are not trying to write a children's magical adventure story for Disney. One of my students who could not settle on a title once submitted a work in progress to me under the glorious header: *Motherfucking Wizards and Shit*. I giggled, because I'm twelve, but Disney executives probably wouldn't, because they are grownups. At least not out loud.

As with dialects and accents, the problem comes when the robust language takes over everything and we can't (effing) see the (effing) wood for the (effing) trees, although Don Logan is the exception that proves the rule here. When aspiring screenwriters overdo their swear words it tends to be for one of the following reasons:

1 You think it's big and clever to use big boy bad language *in and of itself*. Only little boys think so.
2 You think it's realistic. (We've been here before.)

3 You are scared you can't write dialogue so you are covering by writing lots of words that begin with f and end in yawn. Don't fret, just be simple and have your characters say what needs to be said. That's good enough for a first draft; subtlety can come later.

4 You think tough guys signal their toughness by talking tough. Some might, but the tougher you are the less you have to prove it by being all shouty or with bad language. Think of Meryl Streep in *The Devil Wears Prada*. I'm also guessing that, for dramatic purposes at least, a mook swears more than a made guy.

Having everybody swear the whole time is boring. Remember, familiarity breeds contempt. At its worst, bad language is the surface veneer of adulthood with none of the depth. It is one of the biggest giveaways to experienced readers that your script has been written by a novice.

The great crime of overdoing bad language is that it loses its impact when you *should* be using it. Swear words are wonderful, percussive, evocative and powerful. Look at how Don Logan uses them as weapons in *Sexy Beast*. Remember the funny opening sequence of *Four Weddings and a Funeral* (1994) when they wake up late for the first wedding and run around swearing? If you are going to use swear words, let them have the weight their rudeness deserves. So use them sparingly and for a purpose. Be indicative and creative and find ways for your characters to play 'tough' or 'working class' or 'masculine' or whatever it is you are trying to say, without making every second word a swear word.

As with accents, try assigning one character in a group the job of swearing for the bunch. Here's another 'Julian used to play ice hockey badly before he got old and fell apart' story to illustrate the way this works. As anyone who has been in a locker room will testify, hockey players are not known for their restraint when it comes to calling a hoser a hoser. The air in those places is bright blue and that's not just from the cold. What I'm saying is that it takes a lot of swearing to impress a room full of ice hockey players.

One team I played for had a defenseman who swore more than anyone else I've ever met. In fact he may have sworn as much as everyone else I've ever met combined. Every second word out of his mouth was scandalous and, when you combined it with a deep and almost impenetrable Brummie (Birmingham) accent, the only words you could readily identify tended to be bumper big boy bad words.

The way he spoke acted like something of a curse word black hole, drawing the need for that kind of language from others and into himself. When he was in the room, everyone else noticeably swore less. We just kind of tacitly admitted our own lack of hard-core commitment to scatology and blasphemy and left it up to him. We were mere amateurs in the awesome presence of a true professional.

## Dialogue comes to life in the re-writes

If you follow those examples and discussions you should at least be in good enough shape to avoid the biggest pitfalls of dialogue writing. In my experience, dialogue is almost always the last part of your screenplay to be locked. Indeed it is often substantially re-written when casting is set and is tweaked right through production.

Writers will often be asked to rework their dialogue by adjusting it to the personas of stars or because an actor discovers something in performance which they and the director want to follow up. In fact, sometimes a new writer will be brought in at that point just to polish dialogue or because the star trusts them—and isn't neurotic … at all—and wants their help in finding the right voice.

A few years ago I was brought in to do re-writes on an indie feature and stayed through production. I remember being asked to write additional dialogue scenes overnight because a well known comic actor had just agreed to come in for a day to play a small part and the producers wanted to make the most of him. The scenes didn't get shot in the end due to scheduling issues, but that kind of dialogue change is very common at all levels of production.

Sometimes these changes are merely technical. How things sound in your head is one thing, how they sound out loud in the mouths of real actors can be quite another. You always have to fiddle around, removing the occasional tongue twister and helping smooth out a few lines that are otherwise hard for an actor to speak. You can take steps to pre-empt some of that, however. When it is in good enough shape to consider submitting, try and organize a reading of your script. Get actors in, or at least friends of yours who can speak clearly and understand the intention of their lines. You will be surprised what you pick up.

Whenever possible, we do this in class with work-in-progress pages. Yes, I know a random bunch of writers may not be the most dynamic table read cast—although sometimes you would be surprised—but we pick up all the easy changes that way. One thing I would avoid, however, other than for comedy value, is the automated reading applications you get with screenwriting software like Final Draft. They try, bless them, but, unless you plan to have all the parts played by Stephen Hawking, it won't be of much help.

Speaking of re-writes …

# 9

## OK, What Now?

So you have in your hands a neat stack of paper, three-hole punched and secured with shiny brass brads in the top and bottom holes—but not the middle, never the middle. You look down and read the title of your screenplay and your name, proudly displayed beneath it. It's quite a moment, no? You finally did it. You worked through your concept. You played it to theme, to character, to change expressed through story and to plot, and hung it up in the wardrobe of your imagination. You planned the story out across three acts, four angles, eight half angles and sixteen beats, or whatever method you found to get you from your version of 'in a world where ...' to 'oh brave new world.'

You wrote all your scenes, never forgetting to turn them dramatically and to work your scene beats along the way. You even remembered to go back and correct your grammar and cut down the most egregious examples of overwritten action description before you finally allowed yourself to declare: 'Woot! I have a first draft!' (OK, the 'woot' is optional.)

Well done. That's what alcohol and ice cream were invented for.

Now here you are, sitting in your favorite chair, a slight alcoholic buzz or ice cream coma playing with your senses, and wondering what comes next.

### Well, now we start rewrites

Show of hands—who hates me now?

OK, put 'em down and let's get back to work. One of the 712 sacred clichés of screenwriting is: *the real writing starts with your rewrites.* Of course, this is a gross calumny, disregarding the hard, hard work it took to get you this far—especially if it's the first time you wrote a screenplay. Sadly, it is also true because, let's face it, your first draft sucks.

                    IMPLIED YOU
    But you haven't read my first draft.

                    FRIENDLY ME
    I don't need to.

                    IMPLIED YOU
    That's so harsh. How do you know it
    sucks?

                    FRIENDLY ME
    Because, no matter how well you
    have planned your story, you always
    wander off the path into 'stuff
    happens and we get to watch'
    territory. Your first pass at
    dialogue will be too on the nose
    and bland …

                    IMPLIED YOU
    Says you.

                    FRIENDLY ME
    Says me and pretty much every
    other screenwriter. Don't believe
    me? Go check. I'll wait right
    here. Go on.

Implied You leaves in a huff. Friendly Me amuses himself
by emptying CAGES full of fluffy RABBITS onto the lawn.

Implied You returns, downcast.

                    IMPLIED YOU
    OK, I asked all the screenwriters.

                    FRIENDLY ME
    Even Charlie Kaufman?

                    IMPLIED YOU
    He wasn't in, but I talked to all the
    actors playing him. They were very
    helpful.

                    FRIENDLY ME
    Yeah, they're good guys. So?

                    IMPLIED YOU
    So, I guess you're right. I have a
    long way to go. It's just so
    depressing. Ooh look, bunnies!

                    FRIENDLY ME
    I thought that would cheer you up.
    Now you can write with your mind full
    of thoughts of happy bunnies.

```
                    IMPLIED YOU
        That was really sweet of you. I still
        call antagonist though.

                    FRIENDLY ME
        I wouldn't have it any other way. Now
        go write.

    Implied You skips off happily into the house. Friendly
    Me looks out over the sunny garden.

                    FRIENDLY ME
        Oh brave new world that has such
        bunnies in it.
                                            FADE OUT.
```

Happily, writing is not an exact science. As you write you discover a whole mountain of possibilities you hadn't considered or fully understood when you were planning out your story. Of course, this is one more example of the joys of **writing what you don't know**. You want this ongoing process of discovery to happen, if for no other reason than because it keeps you interested.

For example, I didn't know I was going to write another Implied You/Friendly Me exchange here, let alone one with 'ooh look, bunnies,' until I actually wrote the words '... your first draft sucks.' I knew the purpose of this section when I started, but when I wrote those words, Implied You suddenly perked up in my mind and demanded a moment to protest. On reflection I should have thought in advance about giving those scenes a little closure, but I had my mind on other things.

So it is with inspiration when you write. The more inspiration, the more likely it is that you are going to veer off your original path. Sometimes this is a good and productive thing; the new path leads to undreamed of vistas, clever character development and elegant story solutions. Sometimes it means you are being self-indulgent and ignoring the needs of your characters and story. Sometimes you can't tell which it is until you have followed the new path far enough to get a different outlook on that story.

*Even productive deviations change your structure. This is normal, but it also means your first draft isn't going to be perfect.*

There is also the problem of writing your way into your characters. We have seen a tiny example of this with my throwaway jokes about learning how to write Implied You as a character in this book. It doesn't matter how well you think you understand a character, they always speak up and surprise you as you get to know them through the writing. Usually the characters you are writing at the end of your draft don't quite sound or feel the same as the ones you began with. OK, part of that can be understood in terms of character change: your hero/ine is now more confident (or whatever) and so their dialogue reflects that. But still, in my experience it is very rare to find your long-term relationship with a key character hasn't caused you to reflect on your opening assumptions about them.

Hopefully you are starting to get the idea here. First drafts suck for many reasons, but they are not necessarily anything to do with whether you are a good writer. Here's a quick checklist of things to look for as you dive into your rewrites.

### Remember to kill your darlings

Start by working outwards from first principles, using the model of the **wardrobe**:

1 Open your **wardrobe** and check your **theme**. Is your hero/ine's arc still locked to it or has the rail fallen to the floor? What was your character searching for or lacking at the start? What have they found, achieved or tried but gloriously failed to achieve by the end? Are they the same things? If so, then you did a good job. If not, you went astray somewhere. Go back and check where it happened—hint: look at the **if only ..., oh, all right then, leap? But it's dark** and **oh riiight ...** beats for a start and don't forget the **midpoint** either.

   When you know where the break occurred, repair it one way or the other. I say that because you may have found a better theme in the process of writing. It may be this theme should replace your original idea, or it may be you just lost focus on that idea and need to refocus now you can see the whole story laid out.

2 Are the clothes hangers of your **story** still on the rail of your character arc? Work back through your draft and check that all of the major story beats are doing their job. Remember, their job is *only* to advance the progress of your hero/ine along the path of change in relation to your theme. Are you treading water at any point? If so, pick your strongest swim stroke and get it moving again.

3 The way to tell you are treading water is when you find a pile of clothes with no hanger. In other words, if you simply advance the

script in the **plot** and don't reflect those events back into the story (character/change/theme) you need to make changes.

4   Ask yourself, does everything feel dramatic and well paced: **are the stakes high enough?** If not, get your paddle out because it's hero/ine spanking time. Ask yourself: is the conflict between my hero/ine and my antagonist vital to the story? Conflict is at the heart of a good movie story, so you better make sure yours has it in spades. If a section lags as you read it, or if an event happens way out of its logical place in an act or beat, you have some corrections to make.

5   Check your **B Story**. This is probably a romance, a crucial friendship or a kind of mentoring relationship and it needs to have a direct impact on the hero/ine's transformation in Act Two. Ask yourself: could my A story resolve satisfactorily without help from my **B Story**? If not, you probably have some work to do there.

6   Does your **C Team** consist of original characters with individual voices and do they each have a clear dramatic purpose? Are any of your significant supporting characters all color and no depth? If so, ask yourself: Why are they in the script?

7   Take a pass through the script once things are in reasonable shape just to cut down description even further and **top and tail** your scenes. For each scene, ask yourself: Do I need all this dialogue? Where should my scene start and end for pacing and dramatic clarity?

8   Take a pass through your **dialogue** and check it for your characters' distinctive voices. Watch out for instances of being on the nose when it isn't called for—remember Bob and Jenny?

9   Take a pass just looking for instances of **narrative economy** and **show, don't tell** fails.

And finally...

10  Make a point of going right to all your favorite scenes and ask yourself honestly: **Do I need to kill my darlings?** One of the hardest things for any writer to do is to sacrifice well written moments which don't actually advance the storytelling. Just because something is cool or you really like it in isolation doesn't mean it needs to be in your script. To scandalously misquote Mr. Spock: 'Logic clearly dictates that scenes for the many outweigh scenes for ... you.'

Put your unwanted darlings in your outtakes document—did I mention you should have an outtakes document for every writing project? Who knows, you might be able to put something back in a later draft or even use it in another form in your next script. If not, you can just visit it late at night and bring it milk and cookies and talk about the good old days.

All screenwriters have had to kill their darlings at one point or another in their careers. Sometimes we do it without prompting as our projects develop through the drafts. Sometimes we lose an argument with a writing partner, producer or director during writing or development, and sometimes our darlings are killed in production or post-production for creative or simply pragmatic reasons—the film is running too long, or pacing isn't working, or production is behind schedule. All these lead to scenes being cut, or combined, or otherwise smushed around.

This sounds like a terrible thing to have to deal with. At times it can certainly feel that way. I've been through it, all my writer friends have been through it, and I have heard similar stories from all stages of development and production. Sometimes we look back and grudgingly accept that the cuts were made for the greater good. Sometimes we cringe when we think of the material that was cut from a project that would, in our humble opinion, have been transformed or at least improved by it. At the end of the day that's the price writers pay for working in a collaborative medium.

In a useful little article by John Buchanan in *Script* magazine, William Wisher Jr. (*The Terminator*) gives us the glass-half-full version: 'What I would tell a young writer is that even the stuff you love the most, even the stuff you think is so incredibly clever, in the end it won't kill a movie if it has to go. You just have to figure out a different way to get the same thought out. And that's life.' In response I would only add: Let's hope we always get the chance to do the reworking.

In the same article, Melissa Rosenberg (*The Twilight Saga: Eclipse*) sums up the situation succinctly:

> New writers have to really understand that film is a collaborative medium and that they can't get attached to things … The other lesson is to pick and choose your battles and to be open to alternatives, because if you dig in about things, you're not necessarily helping the process. So fight for the important stuff, but allow that things will change and that they have to change sometimes for very pragmatic reasons. And you should try to be a part of that as much as possible so you can help make sure that things are changing in the right direction.

## Kind of a kick in the butt: keep at it

There's a whole lot more one could say about rewriting, but I think those tasks will keep you busy for your first couple of screenplays. Now comes the really hard part, because you need to accept the probability that those first screenplays will not warrant much attention in the rewrite process. That's because they are your highest learning-curve projects. That's also a polite way of saying they aren't going to be very good.

Sorry, but there it is. Hey, if it's any consolation, mine weren't very good either. Nor were the first scripts of most of the writers I have worked with and talked to. Don't get me wrong, they weren't all terrible—although in all honesty a couple of mine were pretty bad. At least most of us had worked in movies or taken screenwriting classes, so we knew what we were *meant* to be doing. A reader could see we were kind of on the right track.

Apart from a few geniuses—show of hands if you hate them—writers improve by doing a lot of writing. That takes time, effort and commitment. Forgive me for repeating myself, but there really isn't a shortcut around that one. You may have found some help in this book, but you'll still do most of your learning by doing.

Think of your first screenplay projects just like you would your first movies in film school. They serve a valuable purpose, and that is to get you familiar and more comfortable with your creative process. They help you begin to find a 'voice' and to develop your technical skills. When I was in film school I remember some students endlessly reshooting and re-cutting their first films—sometimes over a period of years—in the hope that somehow they would be magically transformed into works of transcendent genius with the addition of this new scene or that reworked ending.

Invariably, what those students needed to do was learn what they could from the process of making their film and move on to their next project. A new project explores new story types, develops new skills and is liberating because of it. It's yet another reason to **write what you don't know**, because it refreshes your creativity and keeps you moving forward rather than stagnating in over-familiar territory.

What makes it so hard, especially at the start, is thinking back to all the effort and struggle that it took to get you through your first script. I have to do that again, you ask? And it still may not be good enough? Oy and/or gevalt! That's what kept those film students coming back to a movie they should have shelved and moved beyond. Sorry, but if all you have in hand is a sow's ear, you would do better searching for new material from which to make that silk purse.

My friend and colleague Pat Jackson (supervising sound editor on *Jarhead* 2005, *The English Patient* 1996, and too many more wonderful films to mention in one breath) comes in to my undergraduate thesis production class every year to brief our students on the intricacies of digital workflows and pull downs and other things my screenwriter's brain can't get hold of properly. She also takes the opportunity to give them an invaluable piece of advice. Every year, Pat warns them not to get too precious about their film. 'No matter how good you think it is, it is not, we hope, your best one. The next one will be better,' she says; and she's right. Learn and move on.

The same applies to screenplays. Well, the good news is that some parts of the writing process do get easier. The learning curve evens out fairly soon. You still need to put the mental effort into making your story work, but all the other stuff becomes more like second nature.

That brings me to another manifestation of this problem, an experience I share with many of my colleagues who teach screenwriting. What do you say to the student to whom you gave an 'A' or even a 'B' grade who thinks that means their script is ready to be sent out to agents and producers and hawt movie stars? Friends, if you got an 'A' for the first draft of your first screenplay and your professor isn't *also* telling you in no uncertain terms that your script is the best thing since sliced cliché and is ready to be sold … it isn't. You got the 'A' because the work you did was very impressive or showed great dedication and improvement. For a first draft. Of a first screenplay. In an introductory class. You are not William Goldman. Yet.

Yes, patience sucks, but do please have some. You are now an aspiring screenwriter and that means patience is one of your most important professional skills. Don't blow whatever contacts you may have in movie land by sending them a dodgy screenplay. Your name will be associated with that work and it may hinder your chances of getting reads when you do, finally, have something worth showing. Develop your skills by writing, and learn from that experience. Use that 'A' grade as the jet fuel for your ego to get you through the lengthy and often frustrating process that lies ahead.

That brings us to a final pep talk. You might be forgiven for thinking I'm not very good at them, given the lead-up I just gave and how the last one went. Maybe that's true, but maybe some of you understand my core intention with the style, tone and content of this little book. I believe in being realistic as well as encouraging, and I'm still trying to warn you about those pesky snakes on your path—remember them? The secret of this section is that, as a writer, you put some of the snakes on the path yourself, and those can be the most dangerous and poisonous snakes in the jungle.

The most important advice I can give you is that the way to become the best writer you can is to see the path as a long hike, not a short sprint. That means you need to equip and pace yourselves for the long haul and find the discipline that all successful writers have, if you are going to succeed. If this is 'kind of a kick in the butt,' the lesson is that from now on you are the ones that have to do the kicking. Only you can find the inner resolve and determination to make it to the end of the hike, although I hope this book might be a helpful and friendly companion on your travels.

Finally, I wrote this book because I don't want you to forget to have fun learning to write movies. It beats the hell out of sitting at home in your farting pants watching the third hour of the *When Bulgarians Exfoliate* marathon on TV, right? I have found screenwriting to be an endlessly enjoyable and fascinating craft' and my simple hope is that you can share in that pleasure.

So keep pushing yourselves, experiment, learn new things and expand your horizons as you continue to **write what you don't know.**